STORYTELLING

Theatre and Performance Practices

General Editors: Graham Lay and Jane Milling

Published

Christopher Baugh	*Theatre, Performance and Technology*
Greg Giesekam	*Staging the Screen*
Deirdre Heddon and Jane Milling	*Devising Performance*
Helen Nicholson	*Applied Drama*
Michael Wilson	*Storytelling and Theatre*
Cathy Turner and Synne K. Behrndt	*Dramaturgy and Performance*

Forthcoming

Deirdre Heddon	*Autobiography in Performance*
Philip B. Zarrilli, Jerri Daboo and Rebecca Loukes	*From Stanislavski to Physical Theatre*

Theatre and Performance Practices Series
Series Standing Order
ISBN 1–4039–8735–1 hardcover
ISBN 1–4039–8736–X paperback
(outside North America only)

You can receive future titles in this series as they are published by placing a standing order. Please contact your bookseller or, in case of difficulty, write to us at the address
below with your name and address, the title of the series and the ISBN quoted above.

Customer Services Department, Macmillan Distribution Ltd
Houndmills, Basingstoke, Hampshire RG21 6XS, England

Storytelling and Theatre

Contemporary Storytellers and their Art

MICHAEL WILSON

Foreword by Jack Zipes

First published 2006 by
PALGRAVE MACMILLAN
Houndmills, Basingstoke, Hampshire RG21 6XS and
175 Fifth Avenue, New York, N.Y. 10010
Companies and representatives throughout the world

PALGRAVE MACMILLAN is the global academic imprint of the Palgrave
Macmillan division of St. Martin's Press LLC and of Palgrave Macmillan Ltd.
Macmillan® is a registered trademark in the United States, United Kingdom
and other countries. Palgrave is a registered trademark in the European
Union and other countries.

ISBN–13: 978 1–4039–0664–9   hardback
ISBN–10: 1–4039–0664–5   hardback
ISBN–13: 978 1–4039–0665–6   paperback
ISBN–10: 1–4039–0665–3   paperback

This book is printed on paper suitable for recycling and made from fully
managed and sustained forest sources. Logging, pulping and manufacturing
processes are expected to conform to the environmental regulations of the
country of origin.

A catalogue record for this book is available from the British Library.

A catalog record for this book is available from the Library of Congress.

10   9   8   7   6   5   4   3
15   14   13   12   11   10   09

Printed and bound in Great Britain by CPI Antony Rowe, Chippenham, Wiltshire

To Wrey, a great storyteller, and Murphy, a remarkable woman –
both the very best of people

Contents

General Editors' Preface

This series sets out to explore key performance practices encountered in modern and contemporary theatre. Talking to students and scholars in seminar rooms and studios, and to practitioners in rehearsal, it became clear that there were widely used modes of practice that had received very little critical and analytical attention. In response, we offer these critical, research-based studies that draw on international fieldwork to produce fresh insight into a range of performance processes. Authors who are specialists in their fields have set each mode of practice in its social, political and aesthetic context. The series charts both a history of the development of modes of performance process and an assessment of their significance in contemporary culture.

Each volume is accessibly written and gives a clear and pithy analysis of the historical and cultural development of a mode of practice. As well as offering readers a sense of the breadth of the field, the authors have also given key examples and performance illustrations. In different ways each book in the series asks readers to look again at processes and practices of theatre-making that seem obvious and self-evident, and to examine why and how they have developed as they have, and what their ideological content is. Ultimately the series aims to ask: What are the choices and responsibilities facing performance-makers today?

Graham Ley and Jane Milling

Preface

It is not usually considered good practice to begin a book with an apology, yet whilst what follows does not really amount to such a thing, I think it is important to add some context to this present study. Scholarship on the contemporary storytelling scene is still at an early stage, both in the United States and in Europe, but this is particularly the case in Britain and Ireland. That is not to say that the cupboard is bare, but it is certainly a long way from full. With this in mind, it could be argued that what is really required now is the kind of history and critical survey of the British storytelling scene that is represented in the United States by Joseph Sobol's excellent *The Storytellers' Journey* (1999). I have to say that this book is not it. Besides, a brief history of the British storytelling movement does exist, at least up to 1998, in Simon Heywood's *The New Storytelling* (1998) and his subsequent doctoral thesis, 'Storytelling Revivalism in England and Wales: History, Performance and Interpretation' (2000). Likewise Patrick Ryan's survey of the Irish storytelling scene, *Storytelling in Ireland: A Re-Awakening* (1995), commissioned by the Verbal Arts Centre, offers a solid overview of storytelling in both the north and south of Ireland.

This book has emerged from a commitment to contribute towards the mass of critical writing on storytelling, from two separate impulses. The first comes out of the experience of teaching storytelling to undergraduate drama students at the University of Glamorgan. When I arrived at the university, I was asked to write a new module for the BA Honours degree in what was then called Theatre and Media Drama, and a course on storytelling seemed an obvious choice. I quickly became aware, however, that if there was a paucity of critical writing on contemporary storytelling, there was even less that was aimed at an undergraduate readership, and specifically at students of performing arts, in whose field storytelling is most commonly taught at British universities.

The second impulse was to engage with the debate around the relationship between acting and storytelling, which would be of particular interest to Performing Arts students. To some degree this also reflects a personal journey and has always interested me for that reason. I worked as a full-time professional storyteller for over ten years, from the middle of the 1980s to the late 1990s, involving myself closely with the burgeoning storytelling movement in Britain at that time. However, prior to that my training had been in theatre and my professional experience had been as an actor, director and writer in small-scale community theatre. As a student and an actor, I had been particularly interested in narrative and theatre and in the work of Bertolt Brecht. It was my attempt to answer a problem about acting that first led me towards storytelling, but as I became increasingly involved in storytelling, I felt myself moving further away from my roots in theatre. Had I been asked at the time, I would undoubtedly have drawn a clear line between acting and storytelling. Now, I'm not so sure.

This book is unashamedly centred around storytelling in Britain and Ireland. Again this primarily reflects my own experiences within storytelling. The most substantial storytelling revival (inevitably, perhaps) has taken place in the United States (and more about that later), but there have also been significant independent movements throughout the world, from Australia and New Zealand to Canada, from France to, more recently, other European countries. The English storyteller Ben Haggarty is exaggerating only slightly when he talks of storytelling as a 'world-wide movement' (Haggarty, 2004, p. 6). Each revival is distinctive and whilst it has not been possible to discuss each of these, perhaps storytellers from other countries will compare my observations of the British and Irish scenes with their experiences in their own countries.

Even within the British and Irish storytelling scene, there are distinctions to be made, largely involving the way the movement has decided to organize itself. While storytelling remains primarily an activity carried out by freelance professionals and semi-professionals, since the early 1990s the development of storytelling in England and Wales has centred around the Society for Storytelling (although it also recruits members from Scotland and Ireland); in Scotland the Scottish Storytelling Forum, based at the Netherbow Arts Centre in Edinburgh, has fulfilled a similar (though distinctive) function. In Ireland, on the other hand, it is only recently that a similar organization has emerged, in recognition of the growth of the art form in both north and south of the island. Whilst the geography of the islands – that is, the travelling distances between parts of England, Wales and Scotland, as well as the stretch of water that divides Ireland from the rest – has no doubt allowed each to develop with some degree of independence and to develop its own identity, there is still justification for talking about the British and Irish storytelling movement as essentially a single entity, in the sense that it fundamentally operates as a single market with storytellers working freely over all parts of the British Isles. In recent years this has been made easier by the advent of cheap flights between the major UK and Irish cities. Undoubtedly too, devolution in the constituent parts of the United Kingdom in the late 1990s, and the ongoing development of the European Union, have led to a greater self-confidence and a weakening of self-imposed cultural boundaries. Furthermore, storytelling in Britain and Ireland shares similar characteristics in that it is usually performatively informal (some may say conversational or even non-theatrical), small-scale and predominantly concerned with the telling of traditional stories.

In the United States things are very different and it is particularly interesting that those aspects of storytelling that British and Irish storytellers often quote, in support of their art form, as embodying its fundamental distinctiveness and values are habitually absent in America. The economy of scale has led to a situation where storytellers in the States will often perform to hundreds of children in a school at one time (often for an appropriately elevated fee), whereas British and Irish storytellers will more usually limit their school audiences to about fifty at a time, with a preference for even smaller numbers, often agreeing to do extra performances to accommodate this. The sense of intimacy engendered by small group storytelling is generally viewed by British and Irish storytellers as a fundamental and non-negotiable part of the storytelling experience. While British and Irish storytellers will usually build their repertoires around traditional material – so much so that a storytelling audience will naturally *assume* any storytelling performance to be based to a large degree upon traditional stories – discussions around the appropriation of stories from other cultures (in particular from Native American cultures) has led to acrimonious disagreements and even threats of litigation in the United States (see Sobol, 1999, pp. 207–12). It is, therefore, more usual in the States (with one or two notable exceptions, of course), for storytellers to draw primarily upon autobiographical material as the basis for their repertoires. In addition, one will generally find a more 'theatrical' performance style in the States than in Britain and Ireland. As Liz Weir from Northern Ireland says:

> in Ireland there's much more natural quality to the performer, whereas in America the storyteller is built up to be a star. ... Standing ovations are commonplace in the States in storytelling performances. In Ireland if you get a good round of applause, you're doing really well.   (Interview)

The reasons for this may be complex and it may in part be due to a stronger need for British and Irish storytellers, for aesthetic and economical reasons, to make themselves distinct from their colleagues within the post-1968 alternative theatre movement. It is also worth pointing out that the United States has a strong tradition of dramatic rhetoric and what is called Readers' Theatre, which is still in evidence within the education curriculum but hardly exists at all in Britain and only slightly more so in Ireland. Instead the British and Irish traditions of recitation and joke-telling, often centred around the social institution of the pub, require less dramatic intervention on the part of the performer.

In spite of these fundamental differences between storytelling on the east and west of the Atlantic, one clearly cannot fully consider storytelling in Britain and Ireland without being aware of the American context. The larger concerns of both sets of storytellers, concerning the direction and future development of storytelling, are the same. Whilst some storytellers, such as Patrick Ryan, have always worked regularly in the United States and in Britain and Ireland, the continuing establishment of storytelling festivals has led to greater opportunities for American storytellers to visit Britain and Ireland, and vice versa. Some American storytellers, such as Dovie Thomason for example, are regular visitors to Europe.

It is for these reasons that in writing about storytelling and theatre, I have tried to keep one eye on the United States, while concentrating fundamentally on my home ground. For a more detailed perspective on the American storytelling scene I would advise the reader to consult Joseph Sobol's book on the subject, but I have also included in this volume an interview with an American teller, Michael Parent.

With all this in mind, this book begins with a chapter that aims to locate contemporary storytelling within its historical context, before embarking upon a discussion of the relationship between storytelling and acting. From that follow chapters on different kinds of storytelling practice, including the work of theatre practitioners and companies for whom storytelling is fundamental to their work. It is hoped that from these chapters the readers will garner a sense of the vast range of practices, performative and non-performative, that are carried out under the auspices of storytelling. It is intended that each of the chapters within this book could be read as an individual essay, yet readers will also notice a number of recurring themes (such as tradition versus revivalism, naturalism versus narrative, the informal versus the formal, to name but a few) and these arguments can be followed throughout the course of the book.

There are many more people who must be properly thanked for their help on this project. I would like to thank all the storytellers who talked to me, however informally, or agreed to be interviewed. They are Niall de Burca, Ben Haggarty, Michael Harvey, Nuala Hayes, Jack Lynch, Jim May, Mary Medlicott, Daniel Morden, Claire Mulholland, Michael Parent, Patrick Ryan, Donald Smith, Billy Teare, Taffy Thomas, Liz Weir and many others whom I have met over the years.

I would also like to extend my gratitude to all my colleagues at the University of Glamorgan who generously tolerated my absence during a period of research leave, and to the University's Future People's Scheme, which funded the replacement teaching costs. I am also grateful to the Arts and Humanities Research Board who provided funding that allowed me to travel to various storytelling festivals and events and conduct the interviews for this book, which were painstakingly transcribed by Emma Robinson.

I would also like to thank Tom Pow from the University of Glasgow, who during my annual visits to Dumfries to act as external examiner for his storytelling course, provided me with both hospitality and beer-fuelled intellectual nourishment. In addition, thanks must go to all those storytelling students at both Glamorgan and Dumfries, whose sense of enquiry has often led me to revisit previously held assumptions. Special thanks should also go to Jack Zipes and Carol Dines, whose continuing friendship, support and hospitality have been nothing short of inspirational.

Finally, I would like to extend my deepest gratitude to my wife Jayne Tucker, and the rest of my family, for their incredible support and for putting up with me.

M.W.

Foreword

The Possibility of Storytelling and Theater in Impossible Times

Jack Zipes

We live in impossible times when lying passes for good storytelling, and when spectacle is expected from theater, rather than artistic and serious performance. The swindlers, the con men, the phony celebrities, the hypocritical politicians, the double-speak newscasters, the medicine men and women of television hawking their wares, the commercial designers of misleading advertisements, the untrustworthy journalists, and so on – they have become our cultural heroes of storytelling and theater. We admire or disdain them because they flout the law and every conceivable norm as they use story to communicate untruths that we have come to buy with relish, a shrug of the shoulders, or a helpless smile.

It has become impossible to tell a story because the truth content of storytelling and theater has been emptied of its significance. Lies, deceit and imposture reign through the power of the culture industry that dominates our lives. Even though we continue to tell genuine and truthful stories of all kinds and even act them out with considerable artistic skill, storytelling in the public sphere is propelled and determined by the culture industry. It is within the public sphere that culture is formed and manufactured, where we pass on models and modes of storytelling and acting to our young without discrimination. This troublesome legacy is why I want to address the impossibility of storytelling and acting within the public sphere, for it is the impossibility of storytelling and theater that cries out for its possibility. And this book can be considered an important step toward helping us to see the possible within the impossible and to distinguish between the different forms of storytelling and acting so that we can make our own choices. It suggests ways to make *contemporary* storytelling and acting into more vital art forms so that they bespeak the truth.

I realize that, when I link storytelling and theater to immoral deception, I am perhaps overstating my case and implying that there are authentic and ideal modes of performing that can no longer be attained. In fact, one could argue that storytelling and theater in the UK and the US are more alive, numerous, diverse, and resilient than ever before. One could even speak about a renascence of storytelling and theater. But all these positive signs are deceptive, if we do not view them in their social and political context and analyze how the commodification of the arts and education are driving forces behind storytelling and theater and how they create a tendency to pander to market expectations rather than to aesthetic and ethical standards.

To his credit, Wilson sets his analysis of acting and storytelling squarely within a social and historical context to demonstrate that there is hope for storytelling and theater and there are many different ways to classify storytellers today: traditional storytellers, teachers and librarians, performers, and amateur enthusiasts. Of course, almost all of them must contend with the fact that storytelling is becoming more and more institutionalized and commodified, something that has already happened to theater for the most part. In regard to storytelling, Wilson demonstrates there are clear parallels to theater when he examines the different conditions and demands of platform story-telling, applied storytelling, and theater, concluding that storytelling and acting are intricately linked. All his distinctions and observations are convincing and grounded in history and his own experience, as are the fascinating interviews that he conducted with diverse storytellers from the UK, Ireland, and the US. Anyone who reads this book will come away with a comprehensive grasp of the diversity of storytelling and theater, how they are connected, and what problems they face. Though there are no clear solutions to the problems that confront storytellers in contemporary society, I want to analyze a few of them with the hope that such analysis will lead to possible resolution.

Storytelling has always had and still has two basic functions: first and foremost, to communicate the relevant values, norms, and cus-tomary practices of a group of people – to conserve them and pass them on to future generations so that they will be better able to survive. The second function is to question, change, and overthrow the dominant value system – to transform what has been preserved so that the values, norms and customs enable a group of people not only to survive but to improve their lives and make the distribution of power and wealth more just. The dominant form of storytelling in any society must be conservative in positive and negative ways: positive because it brings about group adhesion and security, negative because it excludes contrary thinking and speaking, reinforces the power of hegemonic classes of people, and bars outsiders from participating in public discourse. The two functions, conservation and transformation, have been and still are contending forces in all people's lives and are based on the notion of free speech within the public and private spheres. The tension that arises between the forces of conservation and transformation emanates from rules and laws that have been established to codify speech of all kinds and to sanctify power. Since all people are storytellers of one kind or another, and since story can be used to undermine the hegemony of dominant groups that codify speech, limitations have always been set on free speech. There has never really been totally free speech in any society, and yet, people speak freely – a factor that has always troubled ruling classes and given rise to revolutions and progressive changes in all forms of government.

The gradual development of democratic societies in the nineteenth and twentieth centuries was based on the notion that free speech must be guaranteed, and laws were created to protect free speech. Yet, the more speech became standardized, legalized, and protected, the more it became limited and taken away from the majority of people, even when they were led to think that they could openly voice their opinion. Historians of literacy such as Carlo Cipolla (*Literacy and Development in the West*, 1969), Harvey Graff (*Legacies of Literacy*, 1987) and R. A. Houston (*Literacy in Early Modern Europe*, 2002) have pointed out that, with the invention of printing in the fifteenth century and the gradual institutionalization of education, people have been dispossessed of their words. In his essay 'Literacy and Industrialization – the Dispossession of Speech', E. Verne writes in 1981,

> We should bear in mind that workers are being taught to read and write and are generally being subjected to increasingly long training periods in order to condition them to receive an ever greater flow of uncontrollable information; so that they will grow used to exchanging conditioned objects rather than devoting their time to speech – their own and others. Whereas today, only industrialized objects and signs are regarded as legitimate means of communication. In place of speech as the measure of all things industrial, society substitutes the myth of knowledge seen as the criterion

for language, and legitimates the power of those whose authority is founded upon the exclusive possession of uncommunicable knowledge.[1]

But it is not just industrialization that has led to the dispossession of speech. Rather it is the proliferation of professional and exclusive 'speech discourses' accompanied by special modes of behavior connected to the acquisition of power. Let us be clear about this: the more literacies have come into effect, the more people have been deprived of their speech – their dialects, their invectives, their particular and peculiar customs of communication, their accents, and so on. All words in standard English, spoken and written, are words that we are to learn so that we can train and censor ourselves to produce for a specific social economy, and at the same time, we endeavor to play with words to resist the censorship and training, and, through resistance, forge our own identities.

But what happens when resistance becomes artificial negativity? As we know, resistance and negation can become co-opted and be used to demonstrate that a repressive political system allows for dissent and can call itself democratic. Words of protest that are genuine can be transformed into artificial words that legitimize the violence of a government that pretends to be threatened by free speech. What happens when resistance is propped up to make it seem that there is free speech when governments and the mass media manipulate speech so that they can hinder the articulation of truth? What happens when it is easy for so-called oppositional ruling groups to divide power among themselves and use spectacle and story to tell stories that cannot change anything because our social and cultural institutions delude audiences and distract them from their vital interests?

Since it is virtually impossible to know all the myriad ways that power is used by hegemonic groups for manipulation and how censorship functions subtly in democratic societies, it is difficult to know how to use story to learn about oneself and what is true and false. The more distinctions and mediations become blurred, the more speech becomes useless, and story has no other purpose but to entertain and to condition people to accept the current socialization process. The more the variety and modes of storytelling conceal the true conditions of our lives, the more we are distracted from the profound value of communication that can enable us to contend with what appears to be deadly fate or divine design. We are to offer ourselves for sale on the open market and hope for the best. Words are to be consumed today like commodities – whether they are spoken, printed, or represented through images on screens. They do not register the truth but contend for power over people's lives.

The renascence of storytelling in the UK and US, as Wilson suggests, began in the 1970s when performers, teachers, librarians and non-professionals emerged from the civil rights and anti-Vietnam War movements to struggle for the truth and to expose the hypocrisy of the so-called industrial–military complex. The initial impetus was to recoup free speech from those who pretended to protect it. The stories of the "new" storytellers did not corroborate the master narratives of their governments and the mass media. This non-corroboration and non-conformity constituted the appeal of counter-culture storytellers as well as the growth of non-commercial and experimental theater. Numerous storytellers and performers in the UK and US optimistically turned their backs on the social and political institutions to find authentic voices of the past and their own authentic voices through story. And they have persisted in their quest up through the present. Yet, with success, they have also endangered storytelling by professionalizing it and turning it into just another commodity that can be marketed for specific occasions.

The endangerment of anti-establishment storytelling – or potentially genuine storytelling – cannot be attributed to the storytellers so much as it is a result of the systematization of speech in the network of education and the culture industry. Storytellers must be skeptical and learn not to trust their own words and the words they hear in their daily lives. This book provides a clear depiction of the situation of storytelling and theater in the present precarious day and of why storytellers must become even more artful than ever before if they are somehow to capture and maintain the truth content of storytelling, even as professionals. We shall continue to use story in all walks of life, and the more conscious we become of how we use story and why we do this to narrate our lives, the more we shall be able to cultivate honest speech in impossible times.

1 History and Context

The last of the beer glasses are being refilled and as the next performer is introduced, a paid guest who has travelled the length of the country to be there, the applause is blended with the sounds of the cash register and the audience hurriedly finishing interval conversations, passing around drinks, and settling back into their seats. Cigarettes are distributed and lit. A few people attempt to hush those on nearby tables and finally the performer, introduced as a storyteller, rises from the table where he has been chatting to friends and takes the floor. Taffy Thomas is known to many in the audience, but more probably as a street performer than as a storyteller. He is dressed in his ordinary clothes and has no stage props around him. He begins the story with a lengthy introduction, telling the audience of how he came to hear the story, providing any necessary information in advance of the telling (for example, Thomas sets the story in rural Suffolk where he once lived and so a quick geography lesson for this Devon audience is necessary) and introducing the musician who has agreed to help with the telling.

The story is called 'The Devil's Music', a variant of a traditional, jocular tale that tells of a musician who plays dance music in his local pub in exchange for free beer. The musician's only shortcoming is that he is unable to play a hornpipe, on account of which he becomes the butt of many jokes within his local community. One evening, the musician encounters the Devil and makes a pact that enables him to play the fastest hornpipes. After an evening of frenetic dancing in the pub and much praise being heaped upon the musician, the following morning the musician has disappeared, his place having been taken by a shiny new jukebox that will play all manner of rock music, but has never been known to play a hornpipe.

Thomas's performance is steady and measured. His performance relies primarily on the vocal dynamic, but is punctuated by hand

1

movements, gestures and facial expressions. It is also interspersed with jokes and local or topical references, often at the expense of those people he knows in the audience, and on many occasions he will address the audience directly, often responding to a comment that has come from the floor. This is not the heckling that one might experience during a stand-up comedy performance, but is more the quick-paced banter between friends, offered in support and apprecia- tion of the performer, not issued as an aggressive challenge. The whole performance is a good-humoured affair and laughter is in abundance, from both performer and audience. Certainly the whole audience feels involved in the performance, as if they have con- tributed, as opposed to having been performed *at*. As the story ends, members of the audience turn to those sitting at their table to voice their appreciation and pass comment upon the story and the story- teller. The performance lasts about fifteen minutes and is followed before long by another short break to allow the audience to replenish their glasses.

The performance I have just described took place in a small folk club in rural Devon in 1987 and was one of the first times I saw somebody perform who was self-consciously promoting themselves as 'a storyteller'. As this book will show, storytelling has come to exist in many different forms and applications over recent decades, but Taffy Thomas's performance is both typical and a useful starting point in that it illustrates many of the features that have come to be associated with contemporary storytelling – the solo performer, the lack of props and costume, the dominance of the vocal dynamic and the informal, democratic relationship between performer and audience. It is a performance that is deeply rooted within the traditions of popular theatre.

First of all, though, let me tell you another story, a story of how I got involved in storytelling. At the time (in the mid- to late eighties) I was working as an actor in small-scale community theatre. I had got involved in community theatre because of an interest in popular and political theatres and, especially, theatres with a strong sense of narrative. At the heart of the work I had been doing had been a desire to take theatre to places and spaces that would not normally have hosted theatre, and so we took shows to hospitals, day centres, old people's homes, residential care homes, and so on. There was nothing particularly radical in any of this, but it was driven by a desire to allow the theatre-making process (from conception to performance) to be determined by a consideration of audience and its needs.

So when I began working with Marilyn Tucker and Paul Wilson, folk musicians and community arts workers from Wren (formerly the Wren Trust), in 1987, I was very impressed by how they could be responsive to an audience in a way that I couldn't. Where they could take out their instruments and perform in any situation almost spontaneously (often in the pub at the end of a day's work), I wasn't able to do that. As 'rough' as the kind of theatre was that I was used to producing, I still needed to have some props and costumes around me, perhaps a script, some modest scenery, at least one other actor and certainly a couple of weeks' rehearsal.

I began to think of how an actor might be as responsive as a folk musician in a performance situation and I identified two things that the musicians were doing that I, as an actor, needed to do. The first was to be minimalist to the point that I worked on my own without props, scenery, costume whatsoever, and merely occupied the space that my body took up. If necessary I needed to be able to perform sitting around a table. I felt much the same as Welsh storyteller Daniel Morden, when he says that there's 'something about the economy of being a storyteller, something about just standing or sitting and speaking, that appeals to me' (interview). Billy Teare sees such minimalism not as a restriction, but as a freedom, since 'as a storyteller, I can be an actor and I can be everything. I can be all the parts and all the props. I can be the king, the old man and the hen wife' (interview).

The second was to work from a repertoire of material, a repertoire that was continually growing, changing and developing so that the right kind of item could be chosen for the right situation. I was vaguely aware through my contacts in education and my colleagues' contacts in the folk scene that storytelling was emerging as a new force in Britain (I know it was already developing a good ten or fifteen years before that in the UK and longer in the US, but it really started to make significant inroads into the wider public consciousness in Britain in the mid- to late 1980s) and I thought that this might be worth looking at more closely. I was then introduced to Taffy Thomas, a former street theatre performer who had worked with Welfare State International (amongst other companies), a company whose work I had greatly admired. Thomas had turned to full-time storytelling following a sudden illness and before long I had seen not only Taffy, but also Duncan Williamson in performance and had met Patrick Ryan and a host of other tellers who were to influence my understanding of storytelling.

The purpose of that story is to show that for me this all began with using storytelling to try and answer a question about acting. Having come full circle, this book is an attempt to use acting to try and answer a question about storytelling.

Theatre and Storytelling

The idea of the actor as a storyteller is, of course, not a new one. It does not seem unreasonable to suppose that the earliest theatre was a narrative theatre based upon personal experience, in the same way that some of the early cave art to be found in northern Spain and southern France depicts stories of hunting. Of course, different theatrical forms throughout history and across cultures show different attitudes and relationships to narrative and the act of storytelling. The theatre of the Ancients Greeks, for example, or that of the Elizabethans might be singled out as early forms with particularly strong relationships to narrative, along with medieval religious drama or the Italian *commedia dell'arte*. In the twentieth century the Epic theatre of the German playwright, director and theoretician Bertolt Brecht (1898–1956) is an obvious example of a return to storytelling after the more anti-narrative stance of Naturalism. More recently, one might consider the one-man shows of Dario Fo in Italy, Spalding Gray in the United States and Ken Campbell in Britain, as well as the complex relationship to narrative of contemporary performance groups such as Forced Entertainment and the Wooster Group.

In this book, however, I do not simply want to consider the notion of the actor as storyteller, but will also look at the idea of the storyteller as actor. Since the beginning of the 1970s a new kind of professional performer has emerged, the professional storyteller, usually a solo, repertoire-based performer working with traditional and non-traditional narrative material in a range of venues from schools and libraries to theatres and arts centres. An international storytelling scene has emerged which exists alongside theatre, occasionally rubbing shoulders and even at times co-habiting with it, but it has gained recognition as an art form in its own right and has developed largely separately from theatre. Indeed within storytelling there is significant resistance to any attempt to equate storytelling with acting and there is a common attitude amongst storytellers (especially those who have not entered the profession via theatre) that actors make the very worst storytellers. In a recent interview, English storyteller Hugh Lupton voiced a commonly held view:

> Actors don't make good storytellers because they learn word for word and give essentially the same performance each time. Storytellers make each performance their own and different. Theatre is a formal experience – the audience and the performer are separated from one another by the proscenium arch. The successful storyteller breaks down the fourth wall. In fact, when things go well, the storyteller disappears, is lost to the listeners, and the material becomes greater than either.
>
> (www.spiked-magazine.co.uk/spiked8/lupton.htm, accessed 12 July 2004)

Asking himself the same question, but coming at it from a theatrical starting point, the theatre director Peter Brook, who has generally voiced interest in and support for the storytelling 'revival' in Europe,[1] comes to the opposite conclusion:

> the actors – ever since we started at the Center with all our journeys – have always stressed the fact that they are very, very close to storytelling. When a storyteller relates to an audience, he tries with everything at his command to lift the audience to an imaginary world – without disappearing himself. ... At the Center, the actor doesn't need to disappear. One of the things that keeps the story alive is that the audience sees the man who is telling the story as himself, and the audience is having a nice warm relationship with that person.   (Croyden, 2003, p. 214)

My intention, however, is not to deny the differences between storytelling and acting, but to draw attention to the similarities. What often separates storytelling from acting is not a misunderstanding about the nature of storytelling (many storytellers talk both articulately and with great authority on the matter), but rather a misunderstanding about the nature of acting.

What Do We Mean by 'Storytelling'?

So what exactly do we mean by storytelling? On one level, of course, storytelling can be defined very simply as that which is done by storytellers. The problem is that 'storytelling' and 'storyteller' are used to mean many different things. On railway station hoardings, the latest best-selling authors are proclaimed as 'master storytellers'. In a recent review of G. P. Taylor's children's book *Wormwood* (2004), Philip Ardagh states:

> Recently on the same author panel as G.P. Taylor in New York, I heard him
> describe himself as being 'a storyteller, not a writer'. Jeffrey Archer has also
> described himself in those terms, and both authors are brilliant self-
> publicists.   (*Observer*, 11 July 2004)

This is storytelling as a marketing device.

Film directors and TV scriptwriters are also storytellers as, of course, are politicians, lawyers and religious leaders. Ironically enough, actors are usually not considered to be storytellers (although playwrights can be), except when they are employed to reminisce on television chat shows, when they are called *raconteurs*. All these people are 'storytellers' by profession.

On the other hand, there is also a tendency to think of storytelling as a strictly non-professional activity, such as carried out by a renowned joke-teller in the local pub or a particular family member who has a recognized skill in recounting the anecdotes that make up the family's shared folklore. In other words, different communities or social groupings (however you might care to define them) will often bestow the status of 'storyteller' on certain individuals who are known for their skill in telling entertaining anecdotes or 'yarns'.

Sometimes, storytelling is thought of as something belonging to a pre-industrial or mythical past, an activity carried out by old men and women around cottage firesides in the days before television or industrialization, or by the great bards and soothsayers of the Middle Ages or classical antiquity. Either way it is something that belongs to the distant past and can be viewed both dismissively and romantically because of this.

In fact, what we mean by storytelling, in the context of this book, has connections with all these things, but is also none of them. We are talking about an art form that began to emerge in the 1970s in Britain and a few years earlier in the United States and has been enjoying increasing popularity ever since. It is a movement that largely grew out of the radical cultural politics of the 1960s, but has roots stretching back at least to the beginning of the twentieth century, and many of the current-day participants would see it as having a history and pedigree that stretched back much further than that, through generations and centuries. Welsh storyteller Michael Harvey's description of his excitement upon encountering storytelling for the first time is not untypical.

> I just thought it was the best thing I'd ever seen on stage. And then, half-way
> through, I thought, 'Yes, that's what I want to do, cos look, he's just standing

there on a stage, he doesn't have any gear, he doesn't have any kit, he's not doing his back in. I could do that sitting down, if I needed to.' ... I could see that Abbi had developed versions of the skills I already possessed. I was interested in the material, I was interested in the style, I was interested in the delivery, of that particular way of working. ... There was rapport with the audience, complete familiarity with the *material*, because obviously he wasn't working from a script, he was telling you the story. Also he was using *informal* presentation, he was just a guy on a stage. There was no costume, just him and his drum.   (Interview)

But storytelling is a broad church and is constantly developing and reinventing itself. It manifests itself in many ways and one of the purposes of this book is to explore some of those manifestations. It might be performance- or workshop-based; it might be site-specific; it might be centred around oral history; it might form part of a therapy programme or be used as a teaching tool. It is almost impossible to define and when we think we have it pinned down, something else happens that forces us to rethink our definition. So when we are talking about storytelling it is often better to talk about tendencies, rather than absolutes.

One might, for example, propose that storytellers work as solo performers. Whilst this is largely true, there are plenty of examples of collaborative storytelling: tandem telling between two storytellers, collaborative performances between storytellers and other artists, such as musicians, visual artists or craftspeople, and ensemble performances by companies of storytellers and actors.

It may be true that most storytellers work without set, props or costume, yet a closer study of a range of storytellers will reveal that they often do work with these things, albeit perhaps with a degree of subtlety. Some storytellers will 'dress' the space with wall-hangings or other decorative items. I remember some years ago watching Will Coleman, a storyteller from Cornwall and actor with Kneehigh Theatre, preparing for a show. He placed a rug on the floor in order to clearly define his performance space and to provide spatial focus for himself as a performer. A number of tellers will also make some concessions to costuming. This may simply be 'dressing for the occasion', or it may send out more specific cultural messages. Pat Speight from Cork always wears his trademark waistcoat and hat when storytelling. Costuming can also be far more elaborate and often theatrical. Some tellers will dress so as to emphasize their own, or even an assumed, ethnicity and others will dress in clothes which suggest a confusing mixture of ethnicities, presumably in an attempt to present a kind of global, non-Western, pre-industrial, spiritual, low-tech image. I remember seeing one storyteller who, Nosferatu-like, always performed in a top-hat and black cloak! Again, while the absence of props from storytelling performances is certainly common-place, many storytellers will make judicious use of them, especially when telling stories to young children.

Neither can working from repertoire be taken as a defining feature of storytelling performance. In the United Kingdom, most story-tellers will work from a repertoire of traditional stories, whereas in the United States the tendency is to perform longer, personal stories and it is not uncommon for one whole performance to be taken up by the performance of a single story. Indeed, even in Britain there is a growing fashion for 'self-contained shows' consisting of a pre-determined programme of linked stories or even a single extensive narrative. For some years now Ben Haggarty has toured a programme offering a single telling of *Gilgamesh*, and more recently Hugh Lupton and Daniel Morden have collaborated on retellings of Homer's *Iliad*, *The Odyssey* and Ovid's *Metamorphoses* to much critical acclaim.

It is often claimed that another defining feature of storytelling is that a storyteller always presents himself or herself and the story. The storyteller, it is claimed, never hides behind a character, but always remains visible to the audience. Storytelling is, accord-ing to Taffy Thomas, 'a reported art' (interview), and we are never under the illusion that, as in theatre, we are actually watching events as they unfold before us. There is no need for the suspension of disbelief. This is indeed a crucial point and one that will be discussed in detail later on in this book, but it is not quite as simple as it first appears.

Some storytellers will in fact create a 'storyteller-personality', which they will adopt for the telling of the story. This is clearly not the same as adopting a character from within the story, but it is still adopting a character, a different self, none the less. Other storytellers, such as the French-American Michael Parent, in a technique less popular amongst British tellers, readily step in and out of the narrator role to adopt characters from within the narrative for the purpose of introducing direct speech.

This is all to say that storytelling resists definition by absolutes. With this in mind, I might tentatively offer the following *indicative* characteristics of storytelling:

- It has emerged as a new kind of art form since the 1960s/70s.
- In spite of its 'youth', it often lays claim to a much longer pedigree and traditionality.
- It is ultimately a performative form.
- It is centred around a solo performer or group of solo performers.
- Storytellers usually work from a repertoire, in the same way that a singer or musician may.
- Storytelling is usually low-tech in terms of light, sound, set, props and costume.
- Storytellers rarely work with a director or choreographer, but they do often choreograph themselves or prepare carefully for an event as actors do.
- The central performance dynamic is usually the vocal.

Introducing 'the Performance Continuum'

In a previous book I wrote on storytelling (Wilson, 1997a, pp. 25–30), I developed a model called the Performance Continuum to illustrate how all the different types of storytelling were performatively linked. It looked something like this:

```
conversation ———————————————— cultural performance
low intensity ———————————————— high intensity
informal ———————————————————— formal
subconscious ————————————————— conscious
low risk —————————————————————— high risk
low rewards ——————————————————— high rewards
```

The model is based upon the assumption that all acts of storytelling are also acts of performance in the sense that 'performance' is understood as a mode of communication to which are attached certain rules and conventions that determine the behaviour of teller and listener. When this mode of communication is invoked, usually by some kind of (metacommunicative) verbal signal (such as 'Once upon a time ...' or 'Did I ever tell you about the time ...'), then teller and listener will act according to those conventions and rules until such time as the performative mode is ended by another metacommunicative signal (such as 'And they all lived happily ever after' or a punchline to a joke), which in turn gives all concerned licence to revert to their previous behaviour. These conventions of performance affect both performer and audience and are easily observed. They include an expectation that the audience will listen without interrupting, evaluate the performance and respond appropriately, usually by applauding or with an outburst of laughter. Likewise the performer will assume a responsibility to tell a story that is worth listening to (that is, it will entertain or enlighten or both), and will tell it appropriately and with skill.

The Performance Continuum assumes that these performance conventions apply to every act of storytelling, whether it is an anecdote, casually told in conversation in the pub or on the bus (represented on the extreme left of the Continuum), or whether it is a story told by a professional teller on stage at a high-profile festival to an audience of hundreds (represented on the extreme right of the Continuum). The difference between the two is ultimately the level of intensity at which the performance mode is operating. The higher the intensity, the more likely the rules and conventions will be strictly applied. That is to say that you are more likely to get an audience interruption on the bus than you are at the National Storytelling Festival.

There are, in addition, other differences that are associated with a difference in intensity. Some are more obvious than others, such as the fact that conversational storytelling tends to be less formal with less of a sense of 'event'. Likewise, much conversational storytelling can be unwitting, with the teller hardly aware that they are telling a story and the listener unaware that they are listening to one, whereas at the other end of the Continuum the performer is fully conscious of what they are doing, and manipulating their performance according to the context.

The two ends of the Continuum are also associated with different levels of risk and reward. At the low end of the range, there is little risk for the performer. If they fail to fulfil their part of the bargain, by performing badly or even forgetting the story, then there is nothing at risk beyond some limited social embarrassment. For a poor performance, the professional teller operating at the top end of the scale may literally be risking their livelihood. But with big risks come big rewards, whether those are financial rewards such as payment for the performance (few people have received more than a free drink for telling a joke to their friends in the pub) or simply a few cheers and a resounding round of applause.

Professional storytellers, as a rule, will operate in the top half of this Continuum and platform storytelling largely takes place in the top quarter. Of course, individual storytellers will operate at different points on the scale according to the context in which they are working and will even at times vary their position within a single story. This ability to move up and down the Continuum is part of the skill and artistry of the professional teller and is closely linked to the idea of managing one's identity according to the demands of the event, the space and the audience.

The Performance Continuum can also be a useful tool in the debate surrounding storytelling and acting. At the low-intensity end of the scale, where storytelling takes place within everyday conversation, we might have some difficulty in recognizing this as acting. There is nothing about the anecdote-swapping at the bus stop which could justify our defining this as acting. However, as we move up the scale and the performance becomes of a higher intensity and more formal, then we begin to recognize elements of what we might more readily call acting – formalized use of gesture, representation of character, performing to a sizeable audience in a recognized performance venue, until we reach the end of the scale with festival performances on stage with full technical support.

The key to this lies in the continuum line that runs between subconscious and conscious activity. This line assumes that at some point (and it's not the same point every time), the performer becomes conscious of performing. It also assumes that the act of storytelling can be a subconscious or a conscious activity. Acting, on the other hand, is always a self-conscious act of performance; the actor is always conscious that s/he is acting and deliberately and consciously manages and shapes the performance. We might, therefore, reasonably suggest that storytelling becomes a form of acting at the point when the performer becomes conscious of what s/he is doing and manipulates the telling accordingly.

A Brief History of the Storytelling 'Revival'

Whilst some people may still harbour the romantic, pre-industrial image of the village elder sitting by a roaring fire, the fact is that most young people now emerging from formal education will have had some experience of seeing a storytelling performance and that many arts centres will include one or more storytelling events in their annual programmes. Today there are dedicated storytelling 'clubs', currently fifty-eight in England and Wales alone (www.sfs.org.uk), often organized on the folk club model, and recent years have seen a huge growth in storytelling festivals in the United Kingdom. There is a Society for Storytelling in England and Wales, the Scottish Storytelling Forum and the long-established National Storytelling Network in the United States. There exist similar organizations throughout the world and, at the time of writing, a pan-Irish organization for story-telling, Storytellers of Ireland, has been formed recently. National Storytelling Centres have been established in the United States and in Scotland and plans are well advanced for similar institutions in England and Wales. *In other words, storytelling has arrived.* People talk of a storytelling 'revival', although the terminology is a subject of some debate.

If there is one thing that is clear, it is that nobody really agrees when this so-called revival actually began. One of the key voices in the development of storytelling in Britain, Ben Haggarty, recently orga-nized an event celebrating the twentieth anniversary of the storytelling revival (Hilken, 2002). This suggests that recent developments in storytelling date from the beginning of the 1980s, exactly the time that Haggarty himself became involved in storytelling. For myself, I first became involved in storytelling in the mid- to late 1980s and likewise felt myself as something of a pioneer. Indeed the late 1980s saw a very sudden and rapid growth in storytelling in Britain, which culminated in the founding of the Society for Storytelling in 1993, but storytelling had been emerging as a new art form for many years before that. Well-established storytellers such as Mary Medlicott were aware of things happening throughout the 1970s and Grace Hallworth was using storytelling as part of her work as a librarian in the 1950s, inspired by Eileen Colwell, another librarian who had pioneered storytelling in children's libraries since the 1920s.

Rob Parkinson (1995) claims that at some time around the end of the 1970s and the beginning of the 1980s something began to happen and he is right in the sense that there was a slow realization that what had begun to emerge in quite modest ways during the 1970s was gathering momentum into something tangible and significant by the end of the decade. Mary Medlicott agrees, saying, 'I realized that there was something going on about storytelling which was wider than Lambeth, wider than me. There were seeds in the air, there was something happening' (interview).

Simon Heywood's account of the history of the storytelling 'revival' in England and Wales is to date the fullest and most convincing attempt to identify the origins of the contemporary storytelling movement (Heywood, 1998). To summarize his argument, he locates the first murmurings of contemporary storytelling (that is *professional* storytelling) in the pioneering work of Marie Shedlock at the end of the nineteenth century and the subsequent development of storytelling by professional librarians throughout the twentieth century (Heywood, 1998, pp. 17–21). Heywood also acknowledges the influence of teachers and education professionals, particularly from the 1960s onwards, as well as the performing arts movement from the same period. At the beginning of his paper, Heywood lists eight factors that he feels have influenced contemporary storytelling (Heywood, 1998, pp. 7–8). From these and his subsequent argument we can conclude that the storytelling movement has largely grown out of the professional interventions of those working within three key areas: libraries, education and the theatre, with lesser influence coming from other areas such as writers, therapists, New Age spiritualists, folklorists and, of course, tradition-bearers. To my mind Heywood somewhat underestimates the importance of the post-1968 theatre movement. Joseph Sobol claims that 'the storytelling movement (in America) emanated from the civil rights and antiwar movement of the late 1960s and the diverse cultural radicalism of the 1970s' (Zipes, 2001, p. 137), a time when many people sought 'spiritual and ecological solutions to social problems' (Zipes, 2001, p. 138). Heywood is quite right, though, when he claims that the 'storytelling movement in England and Wales has a surprisingly long and complex history' (Heywood, 1998, p. 48). The same applies to Ireland and Scotland, of course.

More than thirty years after the event, it is easy to underestimate the importance of 1968 in the history of world politics and even easier to underestimate the effect the events of that year had on Western culture. In Britain, nowhere was that effect more evident than in the theatre. Sandy Craig describes the catalogue of world events which were to have such a marked effect:

The 'most publicized' political events of '68 include the May revolt of students and workers in France; the police riot at the Democratic Convention in Chicago; the Prague Spring and the brutal Russian invasion of Czechoslovakia that followed. There were continuing race riots and student sit-ins in America and the massacre at the Mexico Olympic Games.

> There was the escalating war in Vietnam and, following the banning of a Civil Rights March in Derry, the beginning of the war in the North of Ireland. Across the world, large-scale revolutionary demands by students, workers and peasants were answered by massive and brutal repression ordered by governments of every political leaning – capitalist, communist or social-democratic. And every tear-gas grenade exploding, every policeman's boot kicking, every Buddhist priest burning was voyeuristically filmed, as it was happening, for television.   (Craig, 1980, pp. 14–15)

It was against the backdrop of these world events that the alternative theatre movement emerged, bolstered in the UK by the Theatres Act of September 1968, which abolished the role of the Lord Chamberlain as the public arbiter of taste and morals on the British stage. The ending of censorship in the theatre for the first time in history[2] was, however, not as significant as it might first appear. The effectiveness of the Lord Chamberlain's Office was already becoming problematic and whether 'the groups would have paid any attention to the restrictions had they been in force ... is open to doubt' (Craig, 1980, p. 17).

The alternative theatre movement of the late 1960s and early 1970s was by no means a homogeneous collective of companies and individuals, encompassing, as it did, a whole range of approaches, styles and principles from the madcap pub theatre of the Ken Campbell Roadshow and CAST to the experimental physical theatre of the Pip Simmons Group and the People Show, and also including community theatres, performance artists, political theatre collectives and theatre-in-education companies. What this diverse group of artists had in common was a universal rejection of bourgeois theatre and its structures and a desire to democratize the theatre, to rediscover the vitality of theatre and to place it at the disposal of all of society, but in particular those who did not make up the usual theatre audiences. As Dublin actress and storyteller Nuala Hayes says about her early days at the Abbey Theatre:

> There was, however – because of the mood of the sixties and the questioning of the assumptions behind most institutions – always for me a concern about the audience. I was always curious as to why this wonderful form of expression that I loved so much, theatre and drama, was not accessible to more people and seemed to be the preserve of an elite few. I felt a crusading mission to introduce theatre to everybody and thereby change the world. I mean, this was the end of the sixties, after all! (Interview)

Their methods of achieving those goals may have been very different, but the alternative theatre movement shared a unity of purpose and, moreover, a set of principles that could also be found amongst the early exponents of storytelling. The events of 1968 and its cultural aftermath provided the ideal conditions for a fledgling storytelling movement to thrive.

Storytellers were not the only people looking towards folk culture (viewed as the authentic cultural expression of both agrarian and urban working-class communities) as a means of democratization and a source for reconnecting theatre with the people whom the bourgeois theatre had abandoned. The performance art group Welfare State International were perhaps the most prominent group making extensive use of folklore, ritual and communal celebration as inspiration for much of their work, and 7:84 Theatre Company toured Scottish Highland villages in 1973 with John McGrath's *The Cheviot, the Stag and the Black, Black Oil*, which blended the format of a traditional ceilidh with the popular entertainment tradition of the Music Hall. Even many of the new experimental physical theatre companies were firmly grounding their work in an understanding of ritual and myth.

Moreover, many of those who are now leading practitioners within storytelling have backgrounds within the alternative theatre movement of this time and their work is informed by those experiences (and is arguably an extension of that same work). Taffy Thomas, for example, worked with Welfare State International (WSI) before becoming a founder member of Magic Lantern and Charivari. Ben Haggarty also had experience of working with WSI in 1978 as their first apprentice image-maker.

What underpinned the alternative theatre movement at this time was a rejection of conventional bourgeois society and an embracing of alternative solutions. Politically, not unlike the anti-nuclear movement of the time, it presented a mixture of socialist and 'Green' perspectives and solutions. It is not surprising that out of this fusion of democratic passions and environmental concerns emerged the modern storytelling community. As the alternative theatre rejected the bourgeois theatre establishment, it ultimately came to question, and even reject, the concept of the 'play' as the cornerstone of theatre production. Instead it looked towards other forms of theatrical expression and discovered an emerging storytelling movement. It is my contention that it was the alternative theatre that most significantly influenced the development of storytelling by providing the cultural, political and intellectual environment in which it could flourish, and also by direct intervention which turned it into a professional activity along the lines of what we have today. By rights, the storytelling movement is best understood as a branch of a vibrant alternative theatre.

In recent times the storytelling movement seems to have developed in ten-year cycles with a significant spurt of development in the two or three years surrounding the turn of the decade. At the end of the 1960s and the beginning of the 1970s storytelling began to emerge in London with the appointment of Robert Lagnado by the Inner London Education Authority as the first full-time professional storyteller (Heywood, 1998, p. 23). In the United States 1973 saw the first National Storytelling Festival in Jonesborough, Tennessee (now an annual event attracting tens of thousands of visitors) and the subsequent formation of the National Association for the Preservation and Perpetuation of Storytelling (NAPPS).

At the end of the 1970s and beginning of the 1980s the storytelling movement in Britain underwent another period of rapid development, especially in London with the appointment of professional story-tellers by Lambeth Libraries and the emergence of two professional storytelling companies, Common Lore and the West London Story-telling Unit. The non-professional, self-styled College of Storytellers[3] also emerged in Hampstead in 1980. The same period saw a growth in community arts and community theatre companies, many of which were increasingly giving prominence to 'story' within their work. The 1980s witnessed a steady growth in storytelling, underpinned by the three major international storytelling festivals held in London and organized by Ben Haggarty. The biggest period of growth, however, took place at the end of the 1980s and beginning of the 1990s as a consequence of the education reforms introduced by the Government, which gave new opportunities to storytellers wanting to work within schools. At this time most professional storytellers were earning most of their living, either by choice or from necessity, by working within education, so great was the demand for their work. This period of growth culminated in the formation of the Society for Storytelling in England and Wales and the Scottish Storytelling Forum in 1992.

The storytelling scene seems to have matured somewhat since those rather hectic days. Some storytellers have left the profession, others have joined and some have consolidated their work into areas of specialization. There has been a significant growth in storytelling for adult and family audiences in the years leading up to and following the Millennium with the establishment of dozens of storytelling festivals. Frustrated perhaps by a reluctance within arts centres to programme storytelling at significant levels, the storytelling world has created its own circuit and its own venues to meet the growing interest from adult audiences. Thirty years on from the appointment of Robert Lagnado, storytelling seems to be enjoying another period of development that will further consolidate its position within the cultural life of Britain and Ireland.

Who are Storytellers?

The new kind of performers that have emerged with the advent of contemporary storytelling come with as broad a range of backgrounds and ideologies as the different kinds of storytelling that exist. The success of the storytelling movement is in part down to the fact that it has attracted such an eclectic group of people into the profession.

There have been a number of attempts to classify the different types of storyteller. Ben Haggarty (1996) divides storytellers into two distinct categories – the professional tellers of the court and the marketplace, and the amateur or hearthside tellers. Joel Schechter (1985, p. 11), in his discussion of clowns (amongst whose ranks he includes storytellers through the link with the historical figure of the Fool, a clown-cum-storyteller who challenges and subverts conventional wisdom and attitudes through humour), also suggests two categories, which might best be termed 'official' and 'unofficial'. The first belongs to a courtly tradition, defined by patronage, whilst the second belongs to the popular tradition of the travelling performer. Here the distinction is not a matter of professionalism, but rather a case of whom the performer serves: those with power, or those without it.

American academic Kay Stone (1986) suggests three categories: the traditional storyteller, the modern urban storyteller (such as the classroom teacher or librarian) and the neo-traditional storyteller (such as many contemporary professional storytellers). Of course, the classification of storytellers can be done in any number of ways, but for our purposes here, let me suggest a three-dimensional model – background, modus operandi and purpose.

The first dimension, which we could call 'backgrounds', might consist of the following:

- traditional storytellers;
- storytellers who have emerged from non-performance professions where storytelling may take place (e.g. teachers, librarians, ex-teachers, ex-librarians);
- performers who have become storytellers;
- hobby storytellers (or amateur enthusiasts).

Here we might consider the background of the storyteller and how s/he became involved in storytelling. 'Traditional storytellers' are those who are recognized as such by those involved in the storytelling movement, by virtue of the fact that they were telling stories, non-professionally, within their separate communities and have since been 'adopted' by the storytelling movement, and now often operate professionally or semi-professionally. Examples would be Duncan Williamson, a Scottish traveller storyteller, John Campbell from County Armagh in Northern Ireland and Ray Hicks from the Appalachian Mountains.

In discussing storytellers who have emerged from non-performance professions, we are often talking about teachers and librarians, such as Eileen Colwell, Grace Hallworth, Liz Weir, Patrick Ryan, Betty Rosen, Jim May and Michael Parent, but this group may include journalists such as Mary Medlicott or nurses, therapists, lawyers, etc.

By storytellers who have emerged from performance professions, we mean those storytellers whose backgrounds are in the performing arts, usually theatre or music. Examples would be Taffy Thomas, Michael Harvey, Richard Berry, Nuala Hayes and Jack Lynch to name but a few.

Finally we have those storytellers whose background has been an interest in storytelling. They may have been enthused by a visit to a storytelling performance or a festival and may remain as hobby storytellers, contributing unpaid floor-spots, or they may have developed into semi- or fully professional storytellers, but they have become performers through an initial engagement with storytelling as an enthusiastic audience member.

In the second dimension, which we might call *modus operandi*, we might find the following:

- traditional activity;
- storytellers who tell stories within the context of another job;
- self-employed storytellers who make their living (or part of their living) from telling stories;

- storytellers who don't get paid for telling stories. These will tell stories at clubs or festivals without payment. In fact, many actually pay for the privilege of telling stories, in the sense that they will pay for a festival ticket or for entrance to a storytelling club and will perform a floor-spot for free.

Here we are dealing with the *manner* in which certain storytellers operate and, consequently, the kind of storytelling events they engage with.

Traditional activity refers to all non-professional storytelling within defined communities where a tradition of storytelling has been established. On the one hand, we are all included within this category, because it might include such kinds of storytelling as that which takes place when families or a group of friends reunite for specific occasions and anniversaries. More precisely, however, it refers to those storytellers who have been specifically identified as such within their communities. This can be the case in traditional (e.g. traveller) communities, but can be equally so in modern communities; children will often identify one particular person within their social circle as having particular skills as a storyteller and the same phenomenon is often seen in the local pub where an individual is recognized as being an effective raconteur. One might even include 'local' after-dinner speakers within this category, who acquire a kind of celebrity status within their communities. In a modest way these people often become cultural spokespeople for that community.

There are also a number of storytellers who tell stories within the context of another job. These people would most likely be teachers, librarians and members of the clergy, for example. In spite of their high level of skill in storytelling and the regularity with which they have to put that skill into practice, they would be unlikely to define themselves as storytellers for the simple reason that their storytelling occurs within the service of a wider and (for them) more important role.

Also here, we have the self-employed storytellers. These are the professional and semi-professional tellers who identify themselves as such and make all, or part, of their living from performing and leading workshops in schools, libraries, community centres, museums, festivals and arts centres.

Finally we have the storytellers who work consciously as storytellers, but do not take payment for their work. These storytellers are invariably what might be called the hobbyists and tell stories, usually at dedicated festivals and storytelling clubs, for the sheer enjoyment of it or in order to promote storytelling. Although their technical ability may be high (although it equally may not be), they may simply not wish to take on the responsibilities of the professional.

The third dimension, which we might call 'purposes', might contain the following:

- tradition;
- education (especially literacy);
- cultural identity;
- entertainment;
- therapy (in the broadest sense);
- spirituality/evangelism.

These six categories (although this is not an exhaustive list) deal with the motivation of storytellers. Each of these is relatively self-explanatory and can be dealt with quite briefly.

The first category, clearly, contains those storytellers for whom the purpose of storytelling is the continuation of a tradition. This may include the telling of stories within the community to which that tradition belongs, but may also encompass the telling of stories outside that community in order to promote awareness of that culture to the wider community. Duncan Williamson might be an example, who has told traditional traveller stories within his own community, but also promotes awareness of those traditions to non-traveller communities at festivals and through educational programmes.

The second category concerns those storytellers who tell stories for educational purposes. This would certainly include teachers and librarians and many other professional storytellers too, since most professionals rely on work in schools for at least part of their income. Other storytellers, however, such as Patrick Ryan, espouse a particular commitment to working within educational settings and particularly as part of literacy development initiatives.

There are a number of storytellers for whom the articulation of a particular cultural identity is an important motivation for their storytelling work. Very often this is the promotion of a particular ethnic identity and culture, and Kiowa Apache and Lakota Storyteller Dovie Thomason Sickles would be another good example of this, as would the British-Ghanian storyteller TUUP and the British-Indian teller Vayu Naidu.

Several storytellers see themselves as emerging primarily from a music hall/variety tradition of popular entertainment. Taffy Thomas unashamedly describes himself as 'an entertainer' and as occupying 'the space between storytelling and stand-up' (interview), and Billy Teare comments that 'I've been described as a storyteller with a lot of music hall elements and a mixture of traditional stories' (interview). Other storytellers such as Jack Lynch and Packie Manus Byrne from Co. Donegal would also fall into this category. Such storytelling finds its natural home in community halls, in pubs and at festivals.

Many health professionals (particularly those working within the field of geriatric care) employ storytelling on a regular basis as part of their work. Alida Gersie, for example, has written extensively on her use of storytelling within a range of therapies and Nicola Grove has also conducted ground-breaking work, using storytelling with adults with learning disabilities. Many professional storytellers also regularly engage in projects, especially reminiscence projects, alongside health professionals and, indeed, some storytellers seek to specialize in this kind of work.

And, finally, we come to those storytellers who are driven by religious or spiritual motivations, in particular Christian Evangelism and New Ageism. Christian, or 'Bible' storytellers have long been a significant part of the American storytelling scene, but it is only in the past five or so years that this has been the case in Britain. Instead, Britain has had a number of storytellers who use storytelling to articulate a New Age spirituality, finding in traditional (and, in particular, 'Celtic') stories an idealized pre-industrial society and a pre-Christian belief system that embodies their own spiritual beliefs. What connects both sets of storytellers here is the desire to use stories as a vehicle for expressing and promoting their own spiritual and religious convictions as well as a way of interpreting and understanding the 'spiritual world'.

Of course, most storytellers, and certainly those who are professional or semi-professional, move by necessity around this three-dimensional model, but it may be a useful model to bear in mind when considering the work of a range of tellers.

Can We Really Talk of a 'Revival'?

The current storytelling movement is often referred to as the 'storytelling revival', even by those who object to the term, and those that participate in it are often called 'revival' storytellers, very much in the same way that one might refer to the resurgence of interest in folk song and music in the 1950s, led in Britain by (among others) the socialist theatre-maker Ewan MacColl, as the 'folk revival'. The term, however, is a source of great controversy amongst those working within the movement, for a number of reasons.

First, it is said, the term 'revival' suggests 'the resuscitation of an ancient and defunct artform' (Heywood, 1998, p. 7). This approach to storytelling as a relic of pre-industrial society, which must be preserved before it becomes extinct, is redolent of the approach to folklore collecting adopted by the nineteenth-century Romantics, and one that has been discredited by contemporary scholars of folklore. It is also one that is common throughout the storytelling movement in Britain and the original name of the National Storytelling Network in the United States (National Association for the Preservation and Perpetuation of Storytelling) suggests a similar attitude is prevalent in America. Taffy Thomas, however, objects to the term 'revival' because 'it isn't actually the storytelling revival because it's never actually died' (interview). But it is precisely this belief that 'storytelling comes out of the distant rather than the immediate past' (Heywood, 1998, p. 17), as echoed in Ben Haggarty's view of storytelling as 'a radically re-conceived, re-emergent, ancient art form' (Haggarty, 2004, p. 13) and storytellers as preservers and perpetuators 'of intangible heritage' (Haggarty, 2004, p. 12), that leads Heywood ultimately to defend the use of the term.

On the other hand, theatre director Peter Brook, interviewed for the *International Storytelling Festival Souvenir Programme* in 1989, talks of 'the building of a new kind of art around traditional story' (Heywood, 1998, p. 7) and here Brook is making a convincing and significant distinction. Brook is rightly arguing that what has emerged is *not* traditional storytelling, as it was (or as it is imagined to have been), but a new art that often draws upon traditional stories and some traditional storytelling practices. The *manner* in which story-tellers are currently working, though, is new, creating new material and performances from a range of sources and working in non-traditional contexts.

Furthermore, the term 'revival' becomes redundant in the sense that it is also used to differentiate between 'revival storytellers' (usually young or middle-aged, educated, middle-class, metropolitan and having come to storytelling from a profession) and 'traditional storytellers' (usually old, working-class, rural and having claim to being part of an unbroken oral culture and being a 'tradition bearer' within that culture). If the contemporary context for storytelling and the manner of its production and dissemination are new, then all storytellers are in the same position regardless of their back-ground, having to reinvent themselves and their art for the present circumstances.

Another implication of the term 'revival' is that, whether one agrees or disagrees with the implications of Brook's statement, the current storytelling movement has its roots within traditional oral narrative practices. Whilst one might agree that storytelling in its contemporary manifestation is new, it is simply a re-emergence of a much older storytelling tradition and belongs firmly within that tradition. There is something to be said for this position, but it is also problematic in that it fails to take into account two factors. First, those tradi-tional practices, which are usually perceived as low-key, amateur and 'homely' (at least domestic, if not 'home-spun'), are not reflected in contemporary practice, which amongst all tellers is predominantly self-consciously performative, professional and non-domestic (that is to say, largely occurring in public venues to much larger audiences). Ultimately the case for placing the roots of storytelling in the pre-industrial past depends upon the primacy of text over practice, of *story* over *storytelling*, another example of the influence of nine-teenth-century approaches to the study of folklore and traditional arts. Perhaps most significantly, however, there is a danger in the 'revivalist' stance that the cultural context from which the current storytelling movement emerged is ignored.

The Thorny Issue of Tradition

If part of the project of the alternative theatre movement was to reinvent theatre within a popular, rather than a bourgeois, tradi-tion, then the storytelling movement has always tried to locate itself firmly within a specific branch of popular tradition, chiefly a folk nar-rative tradition. It has often been the particular way that individual storytellers understand the term 'folk narrative tradition' (and the word 'tradition' in particular) that determines the kind of storyteller they become. Yet the concept of tradition has always caused huge problems for storytellers and is one of the most common subjects of debate within the movement, not least because of the often dis-proportionate importance that is attached to it.

What needs to be understood, as Joseph Sobol rightly identifies, is the fact that the storytelling movement is a project that is based upon idealism, 'basing itself on artistic and communal ideals located in an imagined past to heal a present brokenness and awaken an ideal future' (Sobol, 1999, p. 29). As a rejection of bourgeois values and the capitalist commodification of culture, it has always been under-pinned by the desire to rediscover a sense of cultural democracy and *communitas* through storytelling by returning to pre-industrial forms. This has led to the very best and the very worst instances of contemporary storytelling practice. At its best, storytelling has been a means of effective cultural empowerment, as can be seen by some of the projects described in this book, a rediscovery of storytelling as a way of building community, challenging existing power structures and questioning the perceived inevitability of current injustices, very much along the lines of the model espoused by Walter Benjamin in his seminal essay 'The Storyteller' (1973). At its worst, however, it results in the all-too-common uncritical reverence for *tradition* (or at least an imagined sense of tradition), including the unquestioning worship of storytellers who are perceived to be traditional. It forgets that stories were used and misused in pre-industrial society by the powerless and the powerful, just as they are today. There is 'good' and 'bad' traditional storytelling, just as there is 'good' and 'bad' contemporary storytelling. Very often the storytelling movement, or elements within it, have been guilty of viewing the past through rose-tinted spectacles with a whimsical nostalgia about 'the good old days', while forgetting that they were also 'the bad old days' (see Zipes, 2001, p. 132). Ironically, perhaps, this is most commonly seen at some of the larger storytelling festivals, where traditional storytellers are placed along-side contemporary virtuosos (here the commonly used American term 'platform storyteller' is most appropriate) on pedestals to be admired by the audiences for their displays of tradition and/or artistic skill. It is a phenomenon that comes in for harsh criticism from Jack Zipes as resulting in the kind of commodification that the storytelling movement sought to reject:

> as soon as the storytellers began a vital movement, organized themselves, and became professional, they also began to undermine their movement because they had to subject themselves to market conditions that transformed them into entertainers and performers compelled to please audiences and their customers, certainly not to provoke or challenge them. (Zipes, 2001, pp. 139–40)

Here Zipes is predominantly talking about the American revival, but much of what he has to say has resonance for Britain and Ireland as well.

Irrespective of whether we accept that the impulse for the current storytelling revival has its roots in post-1968 political and cultural radicalism, it is true to say that many storytellers claim a sense of their own work being influenced by, or modelled upon, an oral narrative tradition. This is evident from much of the language that is employed by storytellers when talking about their work, effectively attaching traditional values to non-traditional society. A quick trawl of storytelling and storytellers' websites will show the extent to which information is conveyed in a lyrical language, which is itself a nineteenth-century literary affectation designed to suggest a link with tradition and, specifically, an idealized, pre-industrial and even pre-literate past. For example, the website for the Society for Storytelling (the organization for the promotion of storytelling in England and Wales) offers the following definition of storytelling:

> Storytelling predates the written word, people have been telling stories for as long as we have had speech. Even after the invention of writing only a minority had access to the written word. Stories passed from lips to ears, changing as each teller forgot things, or deliberately left them out, and replaced them with their own inventions. This is the 'oral tradition'. Even now we think in narrative and tell anecdotes, urban myths and personal stories almost without realising it. Stories are learned image by image, rather than word by word, and are retold from the heart in gatherings with friends or in public performance. Each telling will be different as the teller chooses their words to suit their audience. This is oral storytelling.
>
> (www.sfs.org.uk)

Some storytellers even perform under names which have a traditional 'feel' to them, though in truth these will probably owe more to Arthurian Romance and/or J. R. R. Tolkien than to anything else.

When dealing with contemporary storytelling it is impossible to escape the issue of tradition, as many practitioners choose to locate themselves (and market themselves) within a tradition or sense of tradition. The real issue here is how different storytellers understand the term.

For many, this understanding is based upon the nineteenth-century assumption that an oral tradition is a relic of a pre-industrial past that must be preserved before it finally dies out. The tradition is here an artefact in its own right, a fixed entity. It also assumes that oral tradition is in a constant process of decline and disintegration and that, therefore, the older a particular tradition or story, then the purer (and, consequently, better) it must be. By the same token, the older the storyteller (or the older the source or informant from whom the storyteller got the story), then the better the storyteller. This explains the often uncritical adulation for age and tradition that can be perceived in some sections of the storytelling community. It is also a position that assumes the existence of an original *Ur-text* with a fixed meaning, which implies a chronological/historical understanding of the folktale, and it is, therefore, not surprising that those who subscribe to this particular understanding of tradition, also often subscribe to the concepts of fixed meaning and archetypes prevalent in the writings of Jung, Bettelheim and Joseph Campbell. It is also worth mentioning that in Britain, this kind of understanding of tradition is often closely linked to a particular romanticized view of a 'Celtic tradition'. Again the number of websites and publicity leaflets decorated with Celtic scrolls is plentiful and they are often used quite out of context. The website of Scot AnSgeulaiche (www.ansgeulaiche.co.uk), a self-styled Gaelic storyteller, is perhaps an extreme example, but illustrates the point well. The homepage shows a picture of the pony-tailed storyteller, dressed in a kilt and perched romantically on a rocky outcrop against a Highland mountain setting. Above this photograph he describes himself as follows:

> Travelling Seanachaidh [storyteller], roaming the bye-ways of the Celtic Lands and elsewhere, bringing to campfires & gatherings the Oral Tradition of Tales & Songs, in an old way, with colour and life, with respect.

As Dick Leith rightly points out (2003), this interpretation of tradition is closely related to a particular understanding of the concept of authenticity. It is also related to the precepts of late nineteenth-century Cultural Darwinism, which assumed that all societies evolve culturally in a linear manner, with the so-called 'primitive' societies of Africa, Australasia and North America at one end of the scale and the 'civilized' societies of Europe and *white* North America at the other end. Somewhere in between lay the 'less civilized' cultures to be found on the eastern and western fringes of Europe.

The assumption was that the European cultural model with its developed traditions of classical art (including an autonomous and literary theatre) and political democracy (of a sort) was the model towards which all other societies were moving and that the further one moved away from those centres of civilization, then the more primitive and uncivilized (and, of course, less white) those societies became. A study of 'primitive' societies allowed civilized societies, therefore, to understand their own cultural development and consequently re-affirmed their own feeling of cultural supremacy.

The problems with such an approach, with its assumption of cultural and racial superiority, are, of course, self-evident and it is more illuminating in what it tells us about the post-Darwinian European mind during the age of nineteenth-century imperialism, than in what it reveals about primitive societies or even contemporary storytelling. Nevertheless, it is a stance that dominated the study of folklore well into the twentieth century and continues to have some currency today in some quarters. Those nineteenth-century anthropologists who were unable to afford the not inconsiderable expense of travelling to the African colonies to carry out their fieldwork, concentrated their efforts closer to home, particularly in the west of Ireland and the Scottish Highlands. While the assumption of these early folklorists and antiquarians – that they were collecting the remnants and relics of primitive societies before they were *necessarily* wiped out by the benevolent progress of European civilization – may well have been confined to the dustbin nowadays, the love affair of some in the contemporary storytelling movement with celticism and exoticism can be read as a product of Cultural Darwinism, however well-intentioned it may be. The common assumption now, of course, is that stories or other cultural artefacts from primitive (i.e. pre-industrial, non-Western) societies hold the key to enlightenment and wisdom in a world where we have become disconnected from the environment and our spiritual selves. The contemporary storytelling movement may view these stories as superior, rather than inferior, but it is still a view based on the assumption that the cultures that produce such stories are fundamentally less sophisticated. The nineteenth-century anthropologist may have used words like 'primitive', 'uncivilized' or 'savage'; the twenty-first century storyteller may use terms such as 'pure', 'in harmony with the environment' and, of course, 'traditional'. Both stances, while seemingly reaching different conclusions, emerge from the same set of assumptions concerning the way culture develops.

The main criticism of this kind of approach to storytelling is that it adopts a specific (mis)understanding of tradition as a yardstick by which to measure the quality and acceptability of a particular story or storyteller. It has an unquestioning faith in the value of storytelling and, having set up boundaries and definitions, will seek to police those boundaries. On the other hand, Jack Zipes argues that the 'genuine storyteller is a skeptic, a doubter, whose wisdom is conveyed by the realization that there may be no wisdom or ethic to be passed on' (Zipes, 2001, p. 135) and Karl Kroeber says, 'Genuine storytelling is inherently antiauthoritarian' (quoted in Zipes, 2001, p. 133). The problem is that an approach to storytelling that does not continually question its own validity, ultimately supports the system it purports to challenge, by providing 'zany sideshows for the rest of us – just another form of entertainment – while confirming that our norms are normal and good' (Zipes, 2001, p. 145). It is ultimately a conservative and reactionary approach to storytelling that is challenged by those storytellers, who have a very different understanding of the value and nature of tradition.

This more radical approach understands tradition not as something fixed, but as an ever-changing entity, an emancipatory force rather than an oppressive one. Tradition here is not defined by age, but as a process that circumvents and subverts official channels of transmission and culture. 'Older' does not necessarily mean 'better' and traditions themselves can be relatively modern developments. These storytellers eschew any hierarchy that places one kind of story above another (for example, epic myths above urban legends), but place value on the context in which a story is told. To place a particular tradition, story or storyteller upon a pedestal as an exemplar is to grant it an official status that runs counter to the very strength of oral tradition, namely its unofficial status, its ability to exist in opposition to official culture. For these storytellers their instincts are democratic and they see storytelling and oral tradition as ways of challenging official culture and its associated power structures. According to Taffy Thomas, for example, 'the politics is that you actually stand in front of people and entertain them just by telling them a story – that is a political statement in itself in an era which is completely dominated by commercial mass media' (interview). It is more in line with Mikhail Bakhtin's interpretation of folk culture as an oppositional force, rather than as a means of justifying the status quo (see Bakhtin, 1984). Of course, storytelling can be used to both effects, depending on the context of the telling.

In reference to this ongoing debate on tradition it is worth recognizing that there is a distinction to be made between story traditions and storytelling traditions. As might be expected, the former is text-centred and considers individual stories in relation to other individual stories. In this way one might define certain stories as being part of a tradition of other similar stories according to events, characters, purpose, etc. (for example, Jack Tales,[4] Creation Myths,

Trickster Tales, etc.). The latter looks more closely at the contexts within which stories are told. The stories themselves are less important than the storytelling situations, so that an autobiographical (non-traditional) story or a joke might be seen to be part of a tradition if it is told within a traditional context such as a family reunion or a pub joke-telling session.

The fierce debate around tradition has been largely played out amongst storytellers in England and Wales. The somewhat different experience in Scotland is due to a separate evolution of the art form, the most influential factor of which was the role of the School of Scottish Studies at Edinburgh University under the direction of Hamish Henderson,[5] dedicated to promoting the understanding and appreciation of indigenous, traditional Scottish culture. Whilst not being at all immune to the counter-cultural movement of the late 1960s, the influence of Henderson's work, itself a partly politically inspired project, has left an indelible mark on the Scottish storytelling scene today. The Scottish Storytelling Centre (SSC), based at the Netherbow Arts Centre in Edinburgh under the direction of Donald Smith, and the associated Scottish Storytelling Forum (SSF), remain closely allied to the School of Scottish Studies and bear the hallmarks of Henderson's legacy. In the first place the SSC and the SSF have been able to acquire an official legitimacy as the authoritative bodies on storytelling through their funding and recognition by the Scottish Arts Council and the devolved Scottish Parliament, which the Society for Storytelling in England and Wales has been unable to achieve. This is partly, at least, because storytelling has become an integral part of the debates around Scottish national identity. As Smith says:

> In the twentieth century, a revival of interest in storytelling was one part of a cultural renaissance and of the reassertion of political identity which led to the creation of a Scottish Parliament in 1999.   (Smith, 2001, p.3)

Both the SSC and the SSF understand storytelling in nationalist terms, in the sense of folk cultures being true expressions of national cultures, and in particular national cultures that have been subjected to the cultural influences of a politically dominant neighbour. This is not to say that the SSC only supports Scottish storytelling, since it regularly hosts and promotes visits from storytellers from all over the world, but membership of the SSF is restricted to storytellers who were born, or who are currently resident, in Scotland. Furthermore, prospective members must be proposed by two existing members and

be assessed by a panel for their level of competence and their understanding of 'tradition'. These may seem like restrictive and protec-
tionist structures that run counter to the open and democratic impulses
of the storytelling movement, but the counter-argument is that it has
helped to ensure standards within the storytelling profession and
to provide training opportunities to enable those wishing to enter the
profession to reach the recognized standards. Membership of, or
endorsement by, the SSF is seen as a prerequisite for gaining storytelling work in Scotland, as the organization has taken on the role of
being an accrediting agency, a function that has been strenuously
resisted by the Society for Storytelling across the border. It has
perhaps been a success in Scotland because the storytelling movement
there has been able to unite around the principles and philosophy
established by the School of Scottish Studies. It is certainly a smaller
and less diverse community than in England and Wales, where
attempts to impose a similar 'closed-shop' regime to control entry into
the ranks of professional storytelling have always met with fierce
opposition. Furthermore, the SSF is not an authoritarian organization
by any means, but is an inherently democratic one that is run by its
members with the genuine mission of supporting and developing
storytelling in Scotland. It also embraces an open and flexible understanding of tradition. It remains the case, though, that it is an
approach that defines storytellers and stories primarily in terms of
their ethnicity and their relationship to both story and storytelling
traditions that reflect a national culture.

Internationalism and Commodification

If the storytelling 'revival' in Scotland has played a key role in raising
awareness of a *national* culture, then at the forefront of the 'revival'
in England and Wales has been 'a deep commitment to internationalism' (Haggarty, 2004, p. 9). In part this can be traced back to the
early use of storytelling in the 1970s as a tool of engagement with the
multiple ethnicities living in the heart of London and the multicultural
agenda of the Inner London Education Authority (Heywood, 1998,
pp. 22–3). Later, as storytelling developed throughout the eighties and
nineties, storytellers were seen by schools as a way of addressing the
needs of a multicultural curriculum, and the internationalist vision of
the global family, united through a shared passion for storytelling and
each other's stories, was further promoted by Haggarty's storytelling

festivals in London in the 1980s, which featured a dazzling array of international performers. It is a spirit that is today kept alive by, amongst others, the Beyond the Border International Storytelling Festival at St Donat's in South Wales.

Perhaps ironically, this agenda has encouraged storytellers both to define themselves more distinctly in terms of their own ethnicity and paradoxically to develop material from cultures with which they have had no contact and of which they have little knowledge or understanding. Sometimes this has been because of a specific request from a school for a storyteller to 'tell African stories', or because a storyteller feels that having a repertoire of 'world tales' will make them more marketable. Either way it has sometimes led to accusations of unethical behaviour and contemporary folklorists (such as Barre Toelken, Linda Dègh and Richard Bauman) have been particularly critical of storytellers who have wantonly re-interpreted stories from cultures other than their own, without an understanding of those cultures.

However, before making judgements about the success or otherwise of the internationalist project, we should be clear that the professionalization of storytelling has also led to the commodification of stories, where 'tradition' is used as a marketing tool. We should perhaps make a distinction between 'platform' storytelling (that is, storytelling as a performance art) and other forms of applied storytelling. It is within platform storytelling that the internationalist agenda is most prominent and it is also here where the commodification of stories most obviously occurs, where storytellers effectively offer stories up for sale as merchandise.

It could be argued that contemporary storytellers with their repertoires of collected stories are the true descendants of the nineteenth-century antiquarian folklorists who travelled the Empire collecting stories, which were then published in ethnocentric anthologies. Both are guilty of using stories as commodities. A comparison might be drawn between storytelling and that other great Victorian invention, the zoological gardens. In its conception, the zoo stands accused of being little more than 'an endorsement of modern colonial power' and 'a symbolic representation of the conquest of all distant and exotic lands' (Berger, 1977, p. 12), yet in the twenty-first century it has reinvented itself as a powerful tool in the field of world conservation, both for the educational opportunities it offers and as a haven for endangered species. Stories too can be plundered, but contemporary storytellers would no doubt see themselves in the role of promoting intercultural understanding and awareness, and assisting in the fight to preserve minority and traditional cultures in the face of globalization. In addition, the argument exists that there is a world of difference between, say, a white English storyteller telling a Maori story (where the story is appropriated by an outside culture and reinterpreted by that culture for its own ends) and a Maori storyteller telling that same story in England (where the story and its interpretation remains under the ownership of the original culture). Alternatively, it could also be said that whilst the former blatantly commodifies the story for Western consumption, the latter more subtly commodifies both story and storyteller.

Such debates have been particularly fierce in the United States, where the issue of the cultural appropriation of Native American culture is especially sensitive and politically charged. This, coupled with issues of copyright and ownership (perhaps another inevitable consequence of the professionalization of storytelling), has led to a position where most American storytellers will now only tell stories from their own cultural traditions, which for many means autobiographical or family traditions. This perhaps accounts for the preponderance of such stories in the repertoire of many American storytellers. Jim May's account of those discussions gives a hint of some of the passion and, indeed, acrimony with which they were conducted:

> Well, as soon as you connect money and making a living, then you get ownership rights. I've seen storytellers on this issue. We had a conference ... in St Louis and the whole purpose of the whole week, like we got here was this issue, who owned the stories? And after a week or so of debate and plenary and breakout sessions, here's what we came up with. If I write a personal experience story, that's absolutely my own creation. I'd copyright it and you probably should ask me before you tell it. That's really all we could agree upon. I remember there was one woman who got up and said, 'I believe you put into the common pot what you can and you take out of the common pot what you need.' In other words, storytelling communism, which I thought was a great idea. Now that same person, I won't mention names, is right there saying you can only tell stories from your own culture. (Interview)

In Britain and Ireland the same debates have taken place but been more muted and many storytellers continue to tell stories from around the world – some doing so responsibly with a strong understanding of and sensitivity towards the cultures from where their material originates, others doing so more thoughtlessly. It is also a debate that lies at the heart of the controversy around Peter Brook's production of *The Mahabharata* in 1985, which is discussed later in this book.

One should, of course, be wary of drawing too close a comparison between the nineteenth-century folktale collectors and twenty-first-century storytellers. The British Empire is long ended and, though other empires have grown up to replace it and threaten democracy, justice and human rights in turn, the internationalist cause in the storytelling movement is one that emanates from a quite different political perspective. It seeks not to glorify the superiority of European civilization by displaying the 'unsophisticated' offerings of African and Asian cultures, but rather to challenge the world dominance of Anglo-American culture and promote respect and understanding between cultures, races and nations by showing the sophistication of other cultures. These are laudable aims and storytelling, as it continues to internationalize itself, has shown it has an important role to play in countering the progress of globalization as championed by the large corporations and their supporters. However, it is also right that these debates around commodification, cultural appropriation and exoticism continue. For some, like Jim May, who 'believes those stories belong to everybody' (interview), the entire treasury of the world's stories exists, without ownership, for the whole of humanity to enjoy, transcending cultural and national borders; for others, national cultures must be respected and protected from those who would claim them for their own, and people should only tell stories for which they can claim ownership – that is, stories from their own culture. The situation is undoubtedly further complicated by Britain's imperial past and the United States's imperial present and one might even argue that the storytelling movement's internationalism and adulation of all things 'ethnic' (i.e. non-European) and traditional (i.e. pre-industrial) is symptomatic of postcolonial guilt. In this context, it is important for storytellers to recognize that there is a fine line between the use and abuse of storytelling.

Storytelling and Other Media

To finish this chapter, it may be worthwhile briefly reflecting on the storytelling 'revival' in respect of other media. The storytelling movement has always had some problems with any attempts by other media (but television and film particularly) to harness the power of oral storytelling for their own ends. Some have seen it as a cynical ploy by media corporations to cash in on a resurgence of interest in storytelling; others have seen it as a way of undermining the value of storytelling by blinding the audience with technical wizardry, whilst leaving them ultimately with a pale imitation of the real storytelling experience. These may be valid points, but it is important not to see bogeymen at every turn and there is a need to discriminate between those media and storytelling initiatives that seek to promote the value of genuine storytelling and those that would undermine it by encouraging conformity. Furthermore, the revival of storytelling should not be seen in isolation, but in the context of the broader cultural response to the resurgence of interest in story and storytelling, especially in the broadcast media, where the audience's perception of storytelling is critically shaped.

As previously mentioned, authors are now regularly promoted on the basis of their skills as storytellers in a way that was not happening before the storytelling 'revival' and it is not difficult to detect an increased attraction to storytelling and traditional story, over the past twenty or so years, across a range of media. In literature one might point towards Angela Carter's successful reworkings of traditional fairy tales for adults in *The Bloody Chamber and Other Stories* (1979) and her subsequent collections, *The Virago Book of Fairy Tales* (1990) and *The Second Virago Book of Fairy Tales* (1992), as examples of a general increase in interest in the use of traditional stories either for their own sake or as source materials. More recently one might consider the phenomenal success of Philip Pulman's *His Dark Materials Trilogy* (1995, 1997, 2000) or J. K. Rowling's series of Harry Potter books (1997, 1998, 1999, 2000, 2003). Interestingly both sets of books were originally written for children, but have become equally popular with an adult readership. While Pulman's trilogy essentially belongs to the fantasy genre (and is liberally peppered with literary and biblical references) and the Harry Potter books arguably owe more to the British public school boys' adventure story than anything else, the worlds created by the authors are at times redolent of fairy tales, inhabited by witches, giants, mythological beasts and talking animals. The same could be said of the revival of interest in J. R. R. Tolkien's *The Lord of the Rings* on the back of Peter Jackson's hugely successful film adaptations. Tolkien's Middle Earth may well be a fantasy creation, but it is also an idealization of a folkloric medieval England, where culture is characterized by traditional singing and storytelling. While these examples may be fundamentally different from the performative act of oral storytelling, they share a common interest in the structures, symbols and motifs of traditional narrative.

Jackson's trilogy is, though, merely symptomatic of an increased interest shown by the film world in traditional stories since the storytelling 'revival' became a recognizable phenomenon. In 1984, Irish director Neil Jordan made the critically acclaimed *Company of Wolves*, an adaptation of Angela Carter's reworking of 'Little Red Riding Hood'. Twelve years later Matthew Bright returned to 'Little Red Riding Hood' in his cult film *Freeway*, in which a teenage girl, on her way to visit her grandmother (who lives in a trailer park), outwits a serial rapist. However, it is not just traditional folklore that has exerted an influence on filmmakers. Contemporary folklore (urban legends/myths) has also been a rich source of inspiration, particularly for makers of horror films. As the titles suggest, *Urban Legend* (Jamie Blanks, 1998) and *Urban Legend: The Final Cut* (John Ottman, 2000) draw heavily for their plot on the contemporary horror legends commonly told by adolescents.

Perhaps more interesting, but less well known, is *Campfire Tales* (Matt Cooper, Martin Kunert and David Semel, 1997). In this film a group of teenagers are involved in a car crash and pass the time telling each other urban legends while waiting for the arrival of the emergency services. On one level *Campfire Tales* is a homage to Robert Hamer's 1945 classic *Dead of Night*, where a group of people gather at a country house to tell ghost stories. Like *Dead of Night* (arguably the earliest film on storytelling, even pre-dating Jean Cocteau's *La Belle et la Bête* of 1946), *Campfire Tales* was made by a team of directors who took responsibility for the individual stories that make up the film. Even the final twist at the end of the film is similar.

Perhaps the most successful (but also most criticized) film versions of traditional fairy tales are the feature-length films produced by the Disney studios (although fairy tales were also used as the source for a number of Mickey Mouse shorts).[6] Beginning with *Snow White* in 1937 and followed by *Cinderella* in 1950 and *Sleeping Beauty* in 1955, Disney established a reputation for the reworking of traditional fairy tales and employing innovative and, at times, witty animation. It was not, however, until the late 1980s that Disney was at its most prolific in producing these kinds of films, including *The Little Mermaid* (1989), *Beauty and the Beast* (1991) and *Aladdin* (1992). The main criticism to be levelled at Disney in respect of these animations is that they change the original stories in order to present a sanitized and conservative view of the world, a world where heroines and heroes are beautiful and handsome, villains are ugly, animal helpers are endearing and cute, and where everything ends happily in a wedding (only after, of course, the hero has rescued the submissive heroine in the nick of time). As lead players in a culture industry that works in the interests of big business and global capitalism, this is hardly surprising, but it is a far cry from Dreamworks's *Shrek* (2001) and *Shrek 2* (2004), which reinvent the fairy tale animation as a subversive form, continually ridiculing capitalist consumer culture and satirizing the genre that Disney created. These are films that offer alternative views of the fairy tale, where the heroes are the ogres and the handsome prince and fairy godmother are the morally corrupt villains and share similar subversive and democratic impulses to those of the storytelling movement.

The interest of the film industry in storytelling from the early 1980s has also been reflected in the television industry, where a number of storytelling-influenced projects of varying quality and worth have been realized. By and large these have been pioneered within the field of children's television, but adult television has not been unaffected by the revival of interest in storytelling.

Storytelling has played an important role in children's television programming for some time, of course. In Britain the BBC first broadcast *Jackanory* in 1965 amid fears that it might discourage children from reading. The format was very simple – a well-known actor or celebrity (the most prolific perhaps being *Carry On* actor Kenneth Williams) reading a children's book over the course of one week. Contemporary storytellers might justifiably draw a distinction between this brand of story-*reading* and their own storytelling, but the programme was hugely popular and ran until 1996. In the United States, in a slightly different and arguably more innovative vein, Jim Henson's *Sesame Street* has also been broadcasting since 1969, using stories as educational tools.

It was, however, in the 1980s, in the teeth of the storytelling 'revival', that a number of projects emerged that challenged the dominance of the 'Disneyfied' fairy tale. Between 1975 ('Hansel and Gretel') and 1996 ('Snow White'), filmmaker Tom Davenport produced eleven short films based upon retellings and reworkings of stories from *Grimms' Fairy Tales*. Shelley Duval's *Faerie Tale Theatre* was broadcast between 1982 and 1987 in the United States and also in Britain for a shorter period. Perhaps the most interesting and successful attempts to bring storytelling onto the small screen again came from Jim Henson. *The Storyteller*, written by Anthony Minghella with Henson as executive producer, was first broadcast in 1987 and a year later in the UK. Each programme took a single European folktale, which was retold through a mixture of simple animation and acting, but principally through the retelling of the story by a storyteller figure, played by the British actor John Hurt, accompanied by a talking dog, voiced by Henson's son Brian. The dog acted both as an audience for Hurt and as a means of asking pertinent questions about the narrative, as it unfolded. Indeed, the dog-character was crucial to the principles of the show, as it encouraged its audience to accept, in a very un-Disney-like fashion, that stories only reveal their truth when they are questioned and that any audience must be an active participant in the process by challenging previously held assumptions. So successful was the series, that a follow-up was produced three years later, this time tackling six of the Greek myths with Michael Gambon now in the storyteller's role, but still accompanied by the faithful dog.

Radio, as a sound-based medium, has perhaps always been seen as a more natural home for storytelling. Certainly as early as the 1950s, storytelling, in the form of oral testimony, was being used by the BBC within Ewan MacColl and Charles Parker's *Radio Ballads*. More recently storytellers find themselves increasingly asked to contribute short stories for radio, particularly for local radio. BBC Radio Cornwall, for example, was a key partner in the 'Clay Stories Project', discussed in the chapter on 'Applied Storytelling', and in the 1990s BBC Radio Ulster broadcast two series of storytelling shows, *The Gift of the Gab*, hosted by Liz Weir and featuring a range of amateur and professional, local and international storytellers. In the last couple of years BBC Wales has launched a substantial digital storytelling project via its website,[7] whereby people are encouraged to submit personal stories, which may be accessed via the internet or broadcast on radio or television (see www.bbc.co.uk/tellinglives/). In the United States, storyteller Ruth Stotter has hosted a storytelling programme for six years. Clearly, these are only a handful of examples among hundreds of the use of storytelling on the radio. Its prolific nature is perhaps, at least in part, indicative of it being the medium with which storytellers are generally most at ease, as they feel it is most sympathetic to their art.

It would, of course, be wrong to suggest that the storytelling movements on both sides of the Atlantic were in some way responsible for the revival of interest in traditional stories in different parts of the media. Nevertheless, this does perhaps indicate that the storytelling 'revival' has not occurred in some hermetically sealed vacuum. One might rather suggest that whilst the renaissance of storytelling may be most forcefully epitomized in the storytelling movement, it is part of a wider cultural shift that is also reflected in literature, film, television and radio.

We can see, therefore, that the phenomenon of contemporary storytelling manifests itself in a number of ways. A new breed of professional performer has emerged from the aftermath of the countercultural movement of the late 1960s, influenced by a range of traditional narrative materials and practices. It is a revival that encapsulates many debates and contradictions, but one that has organized itself and become an established part of the cultural life of the Western world. The following chapters in this book will seek to explore some of those debates and contradictions, alongside the phenomenon of contemporary storytelling, in greater detail. This will include explorations of the relationship between storytelling and acting, the formal performance work of storytellers, and the work of storytellers who choose to engage with their audiences in largely non-performative ways, applying their skills to projects which promote individual and community empowerment and social regeneration. Finally the storytelling work of selected actors and theatre companies will be considered as a study of the varied ways in which the world of theatre has engaged with, and drawn inspiration from, the emergence of the contemporary storytelling movement.

2 Acting and Storytelling

At face value, we might legitimately feel a little puzzled over the debate between storytelling and acting: that is, the extent to which storytelling is acting (and indeed the extent to which acting is storytelling). At least from a theatrical perspective, it can seem like a pretty clear-cut case. Theatre – even theatre that appears to deny or undermine narrative – can be considered as a kind of storytelling, and storytelling skills are an accepted part of the actor's repertoire. Usually, actors would not have a problem with being called storytellers, simply because telling stories is part of what actors do. 'Narrative', claimed Brecht, 'is the soul of the drama' (Brecht, 1978, p. 183). In addition, we may observe many, if not all, storytellers and recognize that they are applying many of the skills, techniques and devices that actors use. In other words, we can observe actors and recognize that we are being told a story, and we can observe storytellers and recognize the employment of practices that we would readily associate with acting.

Nevertheless, this is a debate that continues to rage within storytelling with many storytellers extremely resistant to the notion of storytelling as a form of acting. There are many reasons for it and this chapter seeks to explore those reasons, as well as to interrogate the relationship between storytelling and acting.

The Economics of Storytelling

In the United Kingdom, at least, one of the key reasons for this resistance is economic. One area where storytelling has always had the advantage over theatre is in the fact that it costs a lot less for one storyteller to perform than it does for an entire theatre company. It is not simply a matter of paying the wages, but also a matter of the associated costs. It is expensive to transport a theatre company around the country, not to mention the cost of building/making and transporting even modest sets, costumes, props and lights, and possibly even the expense of employing technical and administrative support. The business of theatre production is infinitely more complex, time-consuming and, consequently, expensive than storytelling. Unlike theatre companies, who will typically rehearse for a number of weeks, tour for a number of weeks and then discard the show before moving on to another period of rehearsal for a new show, storytellers hold stories in repertoire for years, constantly recycling material. Rarely do storytellers rehearse for long periods in the way that theatre companies do; more commonly they are constantly developing new items of repertoire alongside performing. As a result, storytellers can be performing (and therefore earning) for fifty-two weeks a year if need be. Actors have to earn a year's worth of money in half the time.

The fact that storytelling is economically so efficient has had two main consequences. First, it has meant that storytellers can charge a fee that far outstrips anything most actors would earn for a single show, and still undercut even a small-scale touring theatre company. Although storytellers would rarely be working for five days a week over a sustained period, they will earn the equivalent of the Equity minimum weekly wage for actors in a single day and some storytellers, especially in the United States, may earn several times that. Secondly, storytellers have been able to use this economic advantage, not so much to enter direct competition with theatre companies (although there are some examples of this, especially within education), but to open up new markets. Storytellers have been able to create a work circuit with clients such as libraries, museums, country parks, etc. that, for reasons of finance and/or facilities, would rarely have been in a position to accommodate a visit by a theatre company. In order for this to happen, what storytellers have effectively done is to sell their 'product', as being different, as distinct from other 'products', and so have maintained that economic advantage.

In addition, British storytellers have maintained the distinction between what they do and what actors do in order to access public funding for their work more easily. In the UK, major public arts funding is distributed by regional arts councils (although substantial funding also comes from local authorities and charitable institutions) and these will subdivide their budgets into specific discipline areas such as theatre, music, dance, literature, visual arts, etc. The theatre budget is normally one of the largest, but is also the one that has the greatest demands made on it. The literature budget, on the other hand, would typically be much smaller but is managed around a philosophy of supporting individual artists with relatively modest amounts of money. Whilst storytellers may have an economic advantage over theatre companies in the open marketplace, they are at a distinct disadvantage when competing against them for public funds within the drama budgets. Instead, the funding of storytelling has more usually been delegated to literature panels, with which storytellers have generally been happy, but it has not been without its problems. While some writers have openly embraced storytelling as a way of enhancing the profile of literature, others have seen storytelling as a threat to their own funding and status and have tried to push it back into the theatrical fold. The vitriolic attack on storytelling by Welsh poet Gillian Clarke, in response to storytellers accessing Arts Council of Wales funding through the 'Writers on Tour' scheme, is not entirely untypical:

> Charlatans or virtuosi, are (storytellers) paid from the budget for Writers on Tour? Yes, they are. Why? How much? What percentage of the budget? . . . Yet they're not writers. They draw on, as actors do, creatively, inventively sometimes dazzlingly, our stories. . . . Storytelling is performance, like dancing, acting. . . . With exceptions, storytelling and literature seem to have quite different audiences, and one does not appear to be leading the other. . . . Good storytelling deserves appropriate payment, but not from a budget designed to serve writers.   (Clarke, 2002)

Clarke's letter drew a flurry of responses from promoters, librarians and storytellers, but the debate about whether storytelling should be funded from literature or theatre budgets has had an unfortunate distorting effect on the debate over whether storytelling is a performance or a literary art, by drawing a problematic distinction between the two. For reasons of bureaucratic expediency it has to be one or the other, but of course, it is both. As Billy Teare says:

> I'm probably happier thinking about it in terms of performance but not at the exclusion of the text and words. The literary aspect will come through if it's done right. To me, I'm happier to think of it as performance because I come from this background of wanting to do stand-up and so on.
>
> (Interview)

Clarke's comment about the different nature of storytelling and literature audiences is one that is disputed by storyteller Daniel Morden:

The audiences at these (storytelling) events are literature audiences. I know this because of both the marketing breakdown of other events they have attended, and because of the conversations I've had with them after the shows.   (Morden, 2002)

Debbie Evans, a school librarian, agrees, saying: 'I do not agree ... that storytelling and literature do not have the same audience' (Evans, 2002), although she also qualifies this by recognizing the ability of storytelling to develop new audiences, 'to reach those children that we often feel are unreachable'. Peter Florence, the director of the Hay-on-Wye Literature Festival, likewise expresses his admiration for storytellers' successes in developing new audiences: 'If many of these people are new audiences ... then isn't that wonderful?' (Florence, 2002)

It is perhaps problematic in the first place to try and draw distinctions between 'theatre audiences' and 'literature audiences'. In reality, both these sets of audiences are dominated by the white, educated, and often middle-aged, middle classes. Where the story-telling revival has been particularly successful is in reaching beyond this core 'arts audience' into new venues and new audiences and it has been largely able to do this because of the very form of its production processes. Only rarely have storytellers encroached upon the work of others and this has been mainly within the field of education and at the expense of theatre companies, not writers.

The Education Reform Act of 1988 in the United Kingdom introduced for the first time the notion of a National Curriculum in schools, whereby the curriculum, which all children within state schools in Britain would follow, was prescribed by Government and certain subjects were deemed to be more important than others. Perhaps not surprisingly, English was made part of the core curriculum (high importance), whereas Drama was relegated to a position of low importance. Furthermore, within the English curriculum it was stated, for the first time, that pupils should develop skills not only of reading and writing, but also of speaking and listening, and that to tell a story was something every child should be able to do and a familiarity with world folktales was something to be encouraged and developed. The National Oracy Project, which ran from 1987 to 1991, was also influential in this respect.

A number of Theatre-in-Education companies, such as Theatre Alibi in Devon, already had a long tradition of developing shows based upon folktales and were perhaps in a strong position to meet the challenge, but storytellers, with their flexible repertoires of material and their ability to work in the corner of a classroom with the minimum of disruption, already had the upper hand. Around the same time a system of Local Management in Schools (LMS) began to be introduced, whereby budgets, which had previously been controlled by Local Education Authorities (LEAs), were devolved to the individual schools themselves. Where previously many theatre companies had received core funding from their LEA to work in that authority's catchment area, theatre companies were now having to deal directly with schools and charge for the full cost of a visit. Faced with a choice of paying, say, £600 for a morning with a theatre company or £150 for a whole day with a storyteller who might more directly address the demands of the National Curriculum, most headteachers would not be facing a difficult decision (see Heywood, 1998, pp. 31–2).

In this respect, Theatre-in-Education companies were under great pressure in the UK at this time and many either broadened their spheres of work or ceased to operate altogether, whilst storytelling prospered. If anything, since that time storytelling has increased its grip on work in schools, as successive governments have tightened the education budgets, and there remains significantly more storytelling and less theatre taking place in British schools than before 1988.[1]

If the economic realities of the marketplace were a major factor in determining the need for storytellers to make a distinction between their work and that of actors, then there are also historical reasons for storytellers adopting this position that relate to the origins of the contemporary storytelling movement.

Models of Acting and Storytelling

As previously mentioned, the contemporary storytelling movement grew, at least in part, out of the counter-cultural movement of the late 1960s and early 1970s and, in the UK, specifically the alternative theatre movement. Integral to it was a rejection of the perceived establishment. The alternative theatre companies were challenging conventional production processes by staging plays in new venues to new audiences, dealing with issues which often challenged accepted moral and political codes. For some, especially those within the community arts movement, there was almost a rejection of theatre itself as a viable art form, as they preferred instead to engage with their constituency in ways other than the usual performer–audience relationship. The storytelling movement grew out of this same impulse – a radical rejection of theatre practice and a search for other, more meaningful, intimate and democratic ways of engaging with an audience. In this sense the storytelling movement has distanced itself philosophically from the theatre, and even the alternative theatre. What storytelling often represents to storytellers is something other than theatre, something that, even if it is not always truly traditional, does at least reach out to the past and represents a connection to history and humanity, a sense of continuity.

But what ultimately separates storytelling from acting in the eyes of many storytellers is that they fundamentally *feel* that what they are doing is different from what actors do and, moreover, what they do is more akin to the job of a writer. Again Daniel Morden in his reply to Gillian Clarke's provocative letter makes it clear that he feels his work emerges from a literary tradition, rather than a theatrical one:

> Storytelling is closely related to literature, and at best a distant cousin to drama. I'm not a storyteller because of the plays and television I saw as a child. I'm a storyteller because of books my mother and father read to me. ... When I tell a story to children I'm attempting to recreate the experience I had as a child, an experience that has left me hopelessly in love with the power of words. I consider every visit to school as a Literature Development, bringing on the readers and writers of tomorrow. ... Unlike the actor, a storyteller has to conceive imagery, convert that imagery into language, and communicate his/her vision. Yes, storytelling involves the skills of the performer, but I am not, and never will be an actor.   (Daniel Morden, 2002)

And yet Morden's unequivocal position regarding storytelling and acting is not universal. Michael Harvey, whose background is in street theatre, has a different perspective. Whilst he is aware that his acting background is slightly unconventional, he nevertheless talks of his move into storytelling as being an extension of his other work as a performer: 'It did feel like a natural step, but I didn't feel that I was turning my back on anything as such. ... So, no, I didn't feel that I was turning my back on a way of working, but I was never really in *the* theatre. I was kind of on the fringes of it anyway' (interview). Likewise the Dublin-based storyteller Jack Lynch, who still maintains a successful career as a television and stage actor, clearly traces his development as a storyteller to his work within the alternative theatre movement in the 1970s and 1980s and specifically to his work in a street theatre group, telling stories in a kind of *grammelot*:[2]

there were six in the group, it was a street group, and we took on different characters. One guy told a traditional Chinese folk tale, I made up a story that was anti-religion, about a priest character. It was very simple, but we went out on the street during the Dublin Theatre Festival, spoke no English, and were taken as being foreign clowns and told these stories to people and people began to follow it. We started doing one in a public park in the Garden of Remembrance and the jobsworth started to push us out and we were speaking in broken French and people stood up for us and we told it at the side of the street. People were upset that these visiting performers were being so badly treated by this parks guy, you know. So I look back on that now and see that it was elemental in some way towards a training in storytelling.   (Interview)

This is broadly echoed by Nuala Hayes, who sees the debate between acting and storytelling as partially a false one, whilst also recognizing the fundamental importance of her acting career in determining her effectiveness as a storyteller:

I don't think it really matters, it's ultimately about communication and a storyteller is good and effective if they can tell the story and the audience receives the story. Ok, so what if they come at it theatrically or if they very simply sit there? I think the ability to hold an audience is innate to an actor. I think that probably my acting experience is what makes me the kind of storyteller I am.   (Interview)

What emerges from talking to storytellers is a range of opinions on the subject. Whilst some will reject outright a link between the two disciplines, others will see them as being more closely related. Most, however, would still feel that there was a fundamental difference between the two jobs. What also emerges is that storytellers are, by and large, a thoughtful set of practitioners, constantly questioning their own practice and reformulating their ideas and opinions about it. If the relationship between acting and storytelling is rarely acknowledged by storytellers, then it is certainly not because of a lack of thought about or understanding of storytelling. More usually it is due to misunderstandings about acting, theatre and what these may mean.

For many the job of acting means only one thing and that is a model of acting that has emerged since the end of the nineteenth century and is centred on notions of psychological realism. By and large, actors work not on their own, but in a group, a company or ensemble. The actor does not explicitly acknowledge the presence of the audience (except at the closing curtain call) and instead respects the 'fourth wall', that invisible entity so beloved of Stanislavskian-trained actors, which separates the actors from the audience in a way that prevents the actors from seeing the audience, but allows the audience to peer into the lives of the characters on stage, as if through a one-way mirror. Stanislavski even developed an actor-training exercise, the 'circle of attention', to help actors maintain this façade. Furthermore, the actor works with an elaborate set, costume and sophisticated props, and works from a script written by a playwright, and learned line for line for delivery. Most significantly, the actor subsumes him/ herself within the single character they are called upon to portray, so that the actor's personality becomes invisible beneath the character. These five characteristics of acting are seen to be the key features that differentiate it from the job of storytelling and these commonly held, but ultimately misleading, assumptions might most easily be illustrated thus:

The False Acting/Storytelling Model

Acting	Storytelling
Group/ensemble project	Individual endeavour
Fourth wall	Direct contact with audience
Elaborate set/costume/props	Minimal set/costume/props
Fixed, learned text	Fluid, improvised text
Character-based	Self-based

Rafe Martin's comments, endorsing the above model, are not untypical:

> [Told stories are] not set in fixed text as a book. Unlike theater, no costumed persons move on a stage amidst literal scenery speaking unchanging dialogue ... the story is not so much a performance – a term invested with associations to theater – as a *presentation* or *demonstration* of its own life.   (Martin, 1996, pp. 142–3)

Neither is Ben Haggarty's declaration that, 'I have never been an actor and to this day, though I can tell stories that last three hours, I cannot memorise a single line' (Haggarty, 2004, p. 9). In a similar vein Carol Birch comments that

> Plays depict actors talking as if they were behind a wall the audience can see through, often referred to as the fourth wall. Monologues are still presented to an audience by a *persona* who obscures the actual personality of the one who is speaking, even as the audience is addressed

directly. Storytelling, as an oral medium, is created when the storyteller's point of view weaves through and around the narrator, the events, the characters, and the responses of the audience. This startling reciprocity sets storytelling apart from theater.   (Birch, 1996, p. 119)

What these objective commentators have to say about contemporary storytelling is often incisive and convincing, but comments such as these seem to betray a simplistic understanding of the complex nature of acting. Birch and others refer to these five key aspects of acting as if they were undisputed truths about *all* theatre, but unfortunately there is no such thing as *the* theatre model, anymore than there is such a thing as *the* storytelling model. There are simply a number of equally valid models. What is being referred to here is one such model, namely one based upon the assumptions and philosophies of psychological realism, which has been with us for little more than one hundred years. As Joel Schechter points out:

Before actors were placed behind an imaginary fourth wall by French director André Antoine in the nineteenth century, it was impossible to break through the fourth wall separating actors from audience; it did not exist. The actor could allude to the walls around him ... but the illusion of being a character in a separate world, in a space cut off from the audience, was not actively pursued or sustained.   (Schechter, 1985, p. 12)

If instead we were to consider models drawn from popular theatre, such as Dario Fo's medieval *giullari* (see Chapter 5), the balladeers, the clowns, the travelling showmen, the fairground entertainers, the music hall artists, the street performers, and so on, we would find styles of acting far more in line with the performance of storytelling. We would also find audiences who had much in common with storytelling audiences, feeling free to openly participate in, comment upon and overtly enjoy the performance. In considering Taffy Thomas's performance described at the beginning of Chapter 1, we are reminded of Richard Findlater's description of the famous nineteenth-century clown Joseph Grimaldi as someone who 'radiated great friendliness and great mischief, exuded a fine, frank, confiding jollity ... which at once made friends, and not mere spectators, of the audience' (quoted in Schechter, 1985, p. 14). Indeed, Thomas very clearly places himself within the popular entertainment, rather than the bourgeois theatre, tradition:

As a street performer my roots were in circus and fairground arts, so perhaps that is what informs what I do. For me it's showmanship rather than theatre, because I try to deliver. I'm also not ashamed to be an entertainer. It doesn't mean anything I do is of any less importance or value or seriousness. I think that it operates on all sorts of levels but if you don't entertain, you can't achieve any of the other goals.   (Interview)

Equally we might consider the twentieth-century model of the 'epic actor', as proposed by Bertolt Brecht.

Bertolt Brecht and Storytelling: the Epic Actor as a Model for the Contemporary Storyteller

In her manual on developing storytelling skills, *The Whole Story Handbook*, Carol L. Birch differentiates between storytelling and acting in the following way:

Storytelling is most interesting when the storyteller is not acting out a part, but rather doing *two* things simultaneously. Through verbal and nonverbal clues, effective storytellers bring out the nuances, both large and small, which delineate characters within the story and direct the point of view of an audience toward the characters. Actors may use sense memory to bring a character to life, but they submerge their own *selves* in service of the character. Storytellers are not hidden. Not only are they present, they communicate their love, approval, compassion, contempt, fear, or other direct judgements of, and responses to, the characters in a story ... most of our characterizations share a narrative duality – *simultaneously repeating what a person said while commenting on them*. ... We don't imitate them dispassionately. We communicate attitudes about them so listeners grasp the full import of the personalities involved ...   (Birch, 2000, pp. 20–1)

I have quoted this lengthy passage for two reasons. First, it communicates some rather astute observations about storytelling. Secondly, if you were to substitute the word 'storytelling' for 'epic acting' and 'storyteller' for 'epic actor', then you would end up with a pretty fair description of the central tenets of Brechtian acting.

Bertolt Brecht stands as one of the great figures of twentieth-century theatre. He was born in Augsburg, Bavaria, in 1898 into a middle-class family and died in Berlin in 1956 from an inherited heart condition, which was undoubtedly aggravated, at least in part, by an overindulgence in wine and cheap cigars and an enviably active, not to say complicated, sex life. During his lifetime he became a leading figure in the German-speaking theatre, as both a playwright and a director, but it was not until after his death that his reputation spread more widely to the English-speaking world and his status as a theoretician was established.

Brecht's reputation as a theoretician is based largely on two works, *A Short Organum for the Theatre* (1948) and *The Messingkauf Dialogues* (1939–42), along with the remarkable documentation of Brecht at work as a director, contained in the so-called *Modellbücher* (*Model Books*), where he explores the idea of a theatre and acting style which he terms 'epic'. Brecht may have been slightly uncomfortable in his role as a theoretician, but – as remarkable a playwright as he was – his theoretical writings constitute a major contribution to the development of Western theatre in the twentieth century. If Brecht was often ill at ease with theory, though, then he was completely at odds with the concept of dogma. Brecht's Marxism was one that embraced change, including the right 'to consider each new situation afresh'[3] (Brecht, 1966a, p. 49). His theoretical writings should be seen in the same light, as an often self-contradictory series of theoretical explorations, rather than as a doctrine or blueprint for theatrical production.[4]

Carol Birch's declaration that storytelling is 'all in the attitude' (Birch, 2000, p. 41) is one that would echo true with many storytellers. She is here talking about the attitude to the story and the characters that inhabit it, as well as, through her attitude, exposing the attitudes of the characters in the story for judgement by the audience. Jerome Bruner talks of storytelling as adopting a stance, even if it is a stance against taking stances (see Bruner, 1990). Likewise, in a conversation I once had with the Irish storyteller Jack Lynch, he told me that when he is standing on the stage for a storytelling performance, he is not simply standing. 'It is an attitude that I am adopting,' he told me, and that attitude is conveyed both physically and vocally. Interestingly, Lynch is one storyteller who specifically names Brecht, as someone 'closer to my sensibility' (interview), as an influence on his storytelling.

This notion of 'attitude' is central to the kind of acting Brecht wanted for his epic theatre, although he used another term: *Gestus*. Brecht's development of his dramatic theories was born out of his political commitment and a frustration with the theatre of his time, which he felt duped audiences and lulled them into political inertia. Contrary to popular opinion, Brecht did not want to create a dry, humourless, political theatre, but rather a theatre of *Spaß* (fun), where audiences could smoke, drink, discuss the play in between scenes, a theatre that could 'only be conducted in a cheerful, good-tempered mood' (Brecht, 1965, p. 90) and so refreshing and invigorating audiences, spurring them to social action. Brecht claimed that 'Nothing needs less justification than pleasure' (Brecht, 1978, p. 181).

The prerequisite for this to happen, Brecht believed, was a different kind of relationship between actor and audience, a relationship that was based upon a mutual exploration of the issues raised in the play and, above all, honesty. Brecht ultimately saw naturalism as a spent force by the 1920s. What might have begun as a radical experiment to put the lives of working people on the stage for the first time and to create a theatre that presented life as it truly was (as opposed to the notion of art transcending life), had simply become a confidence trick, presenting as real, what was clearly little more than theatrical artifice, 'coating a sham with as much truth as possible' (Brecht, 1965, p. 29). As an example, Brecht makes reference to

> an account of some well-known exercises for actors, designed to encourage natural acting, which includes the following drill: the actor places a cap on the floor and behaves as if it were a rat. This is supposed to teach him the art of inspiring belief. (Brecht, 1965, p. 14)

The scepticism in Brecht's tone is not difficult to detect here, because it was in that very artifice that he revelled. He saw little point in actors trying to convince audiences that they were characters in real-life situations, when in fact they were clearly actors performing in a play, in a theatre. He did not want his audience to suspend disbelief when they entered the auditorium, because there would be no need to – the actors were not imitating life, but presenting a piece of theatre. Indeed he wanted the exact opposite of his audience, that they should enter the theatre with their critical faculties sharpened, because Brecht's theatre was a forum for debate *and* entertainment, where one was 'free to find enjoyment in teaching and enquiring' (Brecht, 1978, p. 186), famously proclaiming that a 'theatre that can't be laughed in is a theatre to be laughed at' (Brecht, 1965, p. 95). For Brecht, politics and pleasure were not mutually exclusive and the audience

> must be entertained with the wisdom that comes from the solution of problems, with the anger that is a practical expression of sympathy with the underdog, with the respect due to those who respect humanity or rather whatever is kind to humanity in short, with whatever delights those who are producing something. (Brecht, 1978, p. 186)

Brecht wanted his actors to be visible at all times, not 'completely swallowed up by the character' (Brecht, 1978, p. 194), rejecting the idea 'that the actor should be wholly absorbed in his part' (Brecht, 1965, p. 71). He wanted both his actors and his audiences to know that the people on stage were not the characters in the play, but rather actors playing those roles. (In fact, Brecht preferred to refer to actors not as playing characters, but as playing an episode or story (Brecht, 1965, p. 76), or telling 'the story of his character by vivid portrayal' (Brecht, 1978, p. 194)). He adopted numerous devices for reminding his audiences of this fact, including placing actors in view the whole time to observe the action, before entering onto the stage to tell their part of the story. Above all, Brecht insisted upon a separation of actor and character, because without that separation his actors would be unable to comment upon the action. This duality was, for Brecht, a fundamental requirement for the political actor.

> The main reason why the actor has to be clearly detached from his character is this: if the audience is to be shown how to handle the character, or if people who resemble it or are in similar situations are to be shown the secret of their problems, then he must adopt a standpoint which is not only outside the character's radius but at a more advanced stage of evolution. ... There's no A-effect when the actor adopts another's facial expression at the cost of erasing his own. What he should do is to show the two faces overlapping. (Brecht, 1965, p.76)

In effect Brecht was calling for a return to a form of representational acting. Brecht's actors were not to *be* their characters but to 'show', 'present' or 'demonstrate' them and this was to be achieved after 'the actor masters his character by first mastering the "story"' (Brecht, 1978, p. 200). It is not insignificant that these words, used by Rafe Martin about storytelling in the quotation earlier in this chapter, were also used by Brecht about acting. It is similar to Michael Harvey's description of working with undergraduate students on storytelling:

> And then this fantastic thing that happens, even in very casual storytelling, when people 'wear' a character. It astonishes me every time I think about it. They will wear their friend, themselves at another time, their mother, father, policemen, people they meet, whatever. They'll wear it just for a brief second and you're there and you know that's their mother or the policeman or whatever and they just get rid of it, as quick as that, and it's astonishing. (Interview)

Brecht was hugely influenced by the popular theatre of his time. He was a regular visitor to the cabaret and music halls of Munich where acts such as the comedian Karl Valentin (from whom, Brecht later claimed, he learned the most about acting) would perform satirical sketches and monologues. Photographic documentation of these venues bears a striking resemblance to Brecht's own descriptions of his ideal, socially convivial theatre. He regularly attended the annual fairs in Munich (and even performed with Valentin at one), where he witnessed the performances of itinerant ballad singers. He was also influenced by storytelling and folktales, which he considered to be the authentic cultural expression of the agrarian working classes. The influence of the folk narrative is evident in many of Brecht's own short stories (see, for example, Brecht, 1961), as well as in plays such as *The Caucasian Chalk Circle*, which is constructed as a storytelling event, and based upon an earlier short story, 'The Augsburg Chalk Circle' (Brecht, 1961, pp. 11–25).

In the play, the members of two villages meet to settle the ownership of a disputed piece of land. One group of villagers presents their case by collectively telling the story of the Chalk Circle. The story tells of a dispute over the custody of a child – whether it should be looked after by its natural mother, the Governor's Wife, who earlier abandoned it, or whether it should be cared for by its adoptive mother, Grusha, who has risked her own life to save the child from certain death. Azdak, the drunken, corrupt, reluctant, but ultimately humane judge, decides to settle the dispute by placing the child in the centre of a chalk circle and seeing which woman can pull the child out of it, in order to determine the child's true mother. The Governor's Wife greedily grabs the child while Grusha stands motionless, refusing to participate in the competition for fear of hurting the child. The Governor's Wife believes she has won custody, but Azdak decides in favour of Grusha on the grounds

> That what there is shall go to those who are good for it,
> Children to the motherly, that they prosper,
> Carts to good drivers, that they be driven well,
> The valley to the waterers, that it yield fruit.
>
> (Brecht, 1966, p. 207)

Whilst this closing quotation sums up the political attitude of the play, *The Caucasian Chalk Circle* stands as a testament to Brecht's belief in the power of storytelling.

For Brecht, storytelling lay at 'the heart of the theatrical performance', and the story was 'the theatre's great operation, the complete
fitting together of all the gestic incidents, embracing the communications and impulses that must now go to make up the audience's
entertainment' (Brecht, 1978, p. 200). Since he believed that the
greatest problem with naturalism was that it pretended to be life
and, as such, was unable to comment upon life, theatre needed
to celebrate its own artifice. Brecht felt that Stanislavski's 'theatre
seemed far too natural for anyone to pause and go into it thoroughly'
(Brecht, 1965, p. 23). In this sense naturalism is anti-narrative,
because life does not behave like a story, following a beginning,
a middle and an end (Rosen, 1993, pp. 141–2). Story is simply a
structure with which we organize life and attempt to make sense of it.
We divide our lives into episodes or anecdotes, which stand on their
own as significant events but also hang together to make our
autobiography. Brecht's epic theatre, a theatre of social commitment,
works in the same way. Epic theatre is a means by which we seek to
gain greater insight into events, examining, like stories, humanity
within its social and natural environment. It assumes humans to be
primarily social, rather than psychological, animals. The epic play is
likewise structured in episodes which stand alone, whilst also form-
ing part of the whole, challenging the assumption that one thing
necessarily follows on from another.

For Brecht, theatre was to be a force for change and liberation,
rather than stagnation and conservatism. For this reason, he employed
a range of devices which informed the audience of the outcome of a
particular scene at its outset. This was designed to challenge the
audience's assumption that the outcome of a scene or play is inevitable. Brecht preferred his audience to concentrate on the course of
action which leads up to an outcome, so understanding *why* something happened and identifying moments when things could have
turned out differently, if different choices had been made or different
circumstances had been present:

> The main thing was that they acted in such a way that the audience's
> interest was always focused on the ensuing development, the further
> continuation: as it were, on the mechanics of the episodes. On the interplay
> of cause and effect.   (Brecht, 1965, p. 73)

It is not so very different from the technique a storyteller employs
when s/he introduces a story with words similar to, 'Now here's a

story that tells of how ...'. We know from the outset how the story is going to turn out and instead of wondering what happens next, we concentrate on how events unfold and why they unfold in a certain manner. And even if the storyteller does not tell us the outcome at the beginning of the story, the tight and familiar structuring of traditional narrative often allows us to anticipate the story's outcome with accuracy and relish. Either way the audience keeps its 'eyes on the course' (Brecht, 1978, p. 37). From this emerge those moments of laughter so often seen during storytelling performances, sometimes born of satisfaction and enlightenment, when a truth is revealed to and recognized by the audience, or sometimes born of delight in seeing an injustice duly punished, and identical to the laughter described by Brecht in his reflection on a performance of *Fear and Misery of the Third Reich*:

> The spectators didn't seem in any way to share the horror of those on stage, and as a result there was repeatedly laughter among the audience without doing any damage to the profoundly serious character of the performance. For this laughter seemed to apply itself to the stupidity that found itself having to make use of force, and to the helplessness that took the shape of brutality. Bullies were seen as men tripping over, criminals as men who have made a mistake or allowed themselves to be taken in. The spectators' laughter was finely graduated. It was a happy laughter when the quarry outwitted his pursuer, a contented laughter when somebody uttered a good, true word. That's how an inventor might laugh on finding the solution after a long effort: it was as obvious as that, and he took so long to see it. (Brecht, 1965, p. 72)

Storytelling is based upon reported action. As Kevin Crossley-Holland says: 'The staple diet of [the] oral storyteller ... is third person narrative: she said this, he saw that, they did the other' (Crossley-Holland 1998, p. 14). The events are clearly ones that have already happened and what we are witnessing is a reporting of those events through a filter: the storyteller. Even when the storyteller enacts parts of the action, the audience is always aware that they are seeing a demonstration of the events, rather than a pretence that here are the events as they are actually happening.

Likewise, Brecht did not pretend that the audience was witnessing life as it unfolded. This was action that had already happened, a story that the actors were retelling. Brecht himself uses the example of a group of witnesses of a street accident retelling the story to the police to indicate what he means (Brecht, 1978, pp. 121–9) and suggests, as a rehearsal exercise for actors, that they transpose all their directly spoken lines into reported speech. Unlike Augusto Boal's more recent ideas of 'Forum Theatre', Brecht is not inviting his audience to intervene in the action, but rather to respond to the action and then to intervene socially and politically outside the theatre.

At the heart of epic acting and its connection to storytelling, however, is the notion of *Gestus*. It is a complex idea and our understanding of it is not enhanced by the fact that Brecht himself often seems to be unclear about what precisely he means by the term. Loosely speaking, *Gestus* can be defined as 'the socially and historically determined attitude that a character has towards his/her situation and/or the other characters, and the attitude that an actor adopts towards his/her character' (Wilson, 2003, p. 154). It forms what Peter Thomson calls 'the key concept in Brechtian actor training and the defining quality of a truly Brechtian performance' (Thomson, 2000, p. 109) and is closely related to Bruner's idea of 'stance', the attitudinal position that the storyteller adopts towards the narrative (Bruner, 1990).

For Brecht, the actor, the character and even the individual episode or scene has a *Gestus* and the basic *Gestus* for the actor is the *Gestus* of 'showing' (as opposed to 'being', which would be the equivalent *Gestus* for the Stanislavskian actor). In addition the actor must adopt the *Gestus* of enquiry, which means that the actor must be constantly interrogating the text, his/her character and the narrative, both during rehearsal and in performance, in what Robert Lyons calls 'the conscious engagement of the actor on an intellectual plane' (Lyons, 1999, p. 258). Brecht himself encourages actors to 'treat the text as a report which is authentic but has several meanings' (Brecht, 1965, p. 54). The ability of the actor to adopt the interrogative stance leads inevitably to the separation of actor and character; the actor must step away from the character in order to question his/her actions and this, in turn, invites the audience to adopt a similarly interrogative stance. It is *Gestus* and the associated actor/character separation that allows the actor to make political comment upon the play. It is also what lies at the heart of effective and 'genuine' storytelling (Zipes, 1996, p. 9).

Walter Benjamin and the Subversive Storyteller

We might at this point usefully bring another critic into our discussions. Walter Benjamin was an essayist, critic, philosopher and friend of Brecht's. His essay 'The Storyteller' is on one level a critical discussion of the work of the Russian writer Nikolai Lesskov, but Benjamin uses the opportunity to explore the role of the storyteller in society and the nature of storytelling.

On the one hand, Benjamin laments what he sees as the decline in storytelling since the mechanization of society, beginning his essay with the following pessimistic claim:

> Familiar though his name may be to us, the storyteller in his living immediacy is by no means a present force. He has already become something remote from us and something that is getting even more distant.   (Benjamin, 1973, p. 83)

More importantly, the storyteller for him is a political critic with genuine connections to his audience. The storyteller is not a remote performer on a stage, to be admired for their artistry, but someone who is embedded within the community they serve. According to Benjamin, a 'great storyteller will always be rooted in the people, primarily in the milieu of craftsmen' (Benjamin, 1973, p. 101). Benjamin identifies the storyteller as a subversive, an artisan whose job it is to offer meaningful narratives as a way of developing strategies for change. The storyteller is not only a community's link with its past, its history; it is also its connection with its future. The storyteller is located in the *Jetztzeit* ('the presence of the now'), where past and future meet.

For Benjamin, the decline of storytelling (as he perceived it) was due not so much to the mechanization of society, but rather to the obsession with information which he views as being 'incompatible with the spirit of storytelling' (Benjamin, 1973, p. 89). Information, claims Benjamin, is the preserve of the press, 'one of its [the middle class's] most important instruments in fully developed capitalism' (Benjamin, 1973, p. 88) and is characterized by the fact that it 'does not survive the moment in which it was new' (Benjamin, 1973, p. 90). Storytelling, on the other hand, 'preserves and concentrates its strength and is capable of releasing it even after a long time' (Benjamin, 1973, p. 90). Whilst Benjamin's outlook is pessimistic, he sees the job of the storyteller as to use wisdom (the opposite of information)

> to pierce the myths perpetuated by the dominant governmental, religious and social institutions. Since these institutions legitimize themselves by fabricating mythic systems justifying and extolling their power, the genuine

storyteller is by necessity a subversive. Wisdom in a world of lies is subversive.   (Zipes, 1996, pp. 8–9)

In his essay Benjamin is primarily discussing the work of a writer, yet he is keen to make a distinction not between writers and storytellers, but between *novelists* and storytellers. The distinction for Benjamin is essentially to do with the relationship with oral tradition and the sense of community that this engenders. 'Experience,' states Benjamin, 'which is passed on from mouth to mouth is the source from which all storytellers have drawn' (Benjamin, 1973, p. 84), and furthermore:

> What differentiates the novel from all other forms of prose literature – the fairy tale, the legend, even the novella – is that it neither comes from oral tradition nor goes into it. This distinguishes it from storytelling in particular. The storyteller takes what he tells from experience – his own or that reported by others. And he in turn makes it the experience of those who are listening to his tale. The novelist has isolated himself. The birthplace of the novel is the solitary individual ...   (Benjamin, 1973, p. 87)

Crucially, Benjamin also identifies a key characteristic of the oral tradition as being embodied in the fact that somebody 'listening to a story is *in the company of the storyteller*'[5] (Benjamin, 1973, p. 100), which firmly places the act of storytelling in the realm of live performance, rather than literature.[6] He further characterizes the relationship between performer and audience as being democratic and equal, rather than hierarchical. The storyteller is not an individual genius or virtuoso separate from the community, but is of the community, a peasant-turned-artisan (Benjamin, 1973, p. 84). Furthermore, the listener is not merely a listener, but a potential storyteller, whilst the storyteller is also a listener-in-waiting (Benjamin, 1973, p. 97). Benjamin does not go so far as to equate the storyteller with the actor, but he is effectively locating storytelling within a tradition of popular and oppositional performance.

Benjamin, of course, was a Jew, writing at the time of the Third Reich, but it is interesting that, in spite of his lamenting a decline in genuine storytelling, he 'does not wax nostalgic about the decline of counsel, wisdom and storytelling' (Zipes, 1996, p. 7). Rather than proposing a storytelling that wallows in a misty-eyed nostalgia for a pre-industrial past, he proposes that the 'genuine' storyteller is politically engaged, using stories as ways of creating strategies for dealing with the present, subverting injustices and exposing the lies of the powerful. Benjamin wrote of Brecht that 'he reveals the crime latent in business' (Benajmin, 1998, p. 83), but he might just as easily have been talking about storytelling. In other words, the job of the storyteller is not so very different from the job of the epic actor – to show and enlighten, not to conceal and mystify. To quote a favourite maxim of Benjamin's which was supplied to him by Brecht: 'Don't start from the good old things but the bad new ones' (Benjamin, 1998, p. 121). It is a useful motto for both epic actor and storyteller.

Conclusion

We can see, therefore, that the division between storytelling and acting is largely a false one, based upon a narrow understanding of acting, rather than a misunderstanding of storytelling. We might consider storytelling as a legitimate concern of the actor and the model of the epic actor, as proposed by Brecht, is a useful model for the contemporary storyteller, just as the actor, of the *commedia dell'arte* is a similarly useful model for the modern physical clown.

At the very centre of the relationship between acting and story-telling is the presentation of character and the management of identities, and different approaches to acting have dealt with this in different ways. Like storytelling, not all theatre observes the sanctity of the 'fourth wall' and neither is all acting character-based. Presentational and representational styles of acting offer alternatives more akin to the techniques of the contemporary storyteller. Ultimately the storyteller and the actor share similar concerns and a false distinction between the two does neither a service.

3 Platform Storytelling

'Platform storytelling' is a term that is in common usage in the United States, but less so in Britain, where it is more usually called 'performance storytelling', or even 'theatrical storytelling' (Ryan, 2003, p. 45), to describe that which generally takes place on a stage of some kind. Most typically it is the kind of storytelling to be found at most storytelling festivals or major events in the United States, where a storyteller performs a series of stories on a stage, usually with the aid of a microphone, to a sizeable audience of hundreds, if not thousands. The audience will usually be seated in at least a semi-formal configuration, will have paid for tickets and will be expecting a show in which they will generally play the part of a passive audience. It is what the folklorist Richard Bauman calls 'cultural performance' (Bauman, 1977, pp. 27–8).

In Britain such situations are found much less often, and only at some of the larger festivals, as storytelling audiences tend to be more modest in size than in the United States and storytellers rarely need electronic amplification and are able to generate a greater degree of intimacy. These differences are particularly marked in schools' performances. In the States it is not unusual for a storyteller to perform, again on a stage with a microphone, to an entire school of hundreds of students. This would be almost unheard of in Britain, where more commonly a storyteller might be found telling stories in a corner of the classroom to a class of about thirty children or less.

Nevertheless, for the purposes of this book I am using the term to embrace every type of storytelling which places the storyteller, and specifically the gifted professional, at its very core, thus providing a figurative, if not a literal platform. Of course, storytellers who work on the kind of community-based projects described in the following chapter will also work as performers within the context of those projects, but in platform storytelling, the storyteller is placed on a stage to be admired for his or her artistry and it is incumbent upon the storyteller to display that artistry in all its glory. This can, and often does, happen in the small classroom, as much as at the large festival, and it is not necessarily a bad thing. It is less about whether an actual platform exists for the storyteller to work from and more to do with *intention* or *attitude*. Indeed, if we are to talk in terms of *Gestus*, then we might say that in these cases, the storyteller's *Gestus* to the act of storytelling is that of 'displaying' or 'showing' (or sometimes even 'showing off'). Of course this would be only one *Gestus* that a storyteller might show at any time, but this is the one that lies at the heart of platform storytelling.

The Storytelling Event

Whilst it is true that not all storytelling requires a sense of 'event', and that stories can easily and seamlessly be woven into the fabric of everyday life, it is the case that all platform storytelling requires a sense of occasion, of being part of a separately conceived and designed performance event, and it is the event that defines the storytelling in the first instance.

The most obvious examples of self-conscious storytelling events are those organized under the auspices of the burgeoning storytelling clubs and, of course, festivals. Festivals are perhaps the most extreme examples of self-conscious events merely by virtue of their scale and ambition, and the grander the festival, the more extreme. It is at these events that platform storytellers often find themselves most readily at home.

One must exercise some caution when talking about the scale of storytelling festivals. There are a number of community-based festivals which last longer, involve more storytellers and have more ambitious and varied programmes than other, smaller festivals, which may take place over, say, a single weekend. Grandeur, on the other hand, has much to do with intention and a disengagement from the community. A number of festivals and clubs seek purely to elevate and celebrate storytelling and storytellers. These events, which *only* provide platform storytelling at its most extreme, seek to act as a showcase for storytelling, by taking it out of the everyday (some would say, making it special), out of the local community and placing it on a pedestal to be admired as high art. The argument for such festivals is that they provide a much needed forum for the storytelling movement to celebrate its successes and that it is only by laying on such high-profile, almost glamorous, events, that storytelling receives the wider recognition (and sometimes funding) that enables the more invisible, community-based storytelling activities to take place.

There is certainly some truth in this. In Shropshire, the long-established Festival at the Edge receives relatively generous public funding, some of which is used to support a range of community-based events. It is unlikely that these events would have been funded had it not been for the presence of the festival. The festival has, in effect, made storytelling a more attractive proposition for the funders. The argument is that storytelling cannot expect to be treated in the same way by funders as, say, opera or theatre, unless it behaves in the same way.

The same can be said of the Beyond the Border Festival, held every July at St Donats Castle in South Wales. The festival takes place within the private grounds of the castle, now an arts centre and liberal arts college, and has little contact with the local community, beyond placing some of its invited artists in schools during the week preceding the festival, although this seems to be more a way of making the entire venture economically viable (the festival relies entirely on ticket sales at present) than it is borne out of a genuine desire to have an impact on the local community. Admittedly this is not the primary intention of the festival, which aims to bring the very best platform storytelling to Britain. Yet, in spite of receiving no public subsidy, Beyond the Border has been a substantial success as a festival over the past ten years and has played a significant role in the rejuvenation of storytelling in Wales, acting as a focus and inspiration for a range of Wales-based performers.

And yet despite the intention of these festivals to present a high-quality, accomplished profile of storytelling to the wider public, many of the larger festivals find it difficult to reach out to a truly representative public audience. Their audiences largely consist of aficionados of the storytelling scene and the white liberal middle classes that make up the general art-consuming public. It is true that some festivals, such as the Ulster Storytelling Festival in Northern Ireland, have been more successful in engaging with a local constituency, but this is because the festival itself emerged from years of low-key community-based storytelling initiatives.

Where the big festivals have been particularly successful, however, is in establishing an international performance circuit and bringing storytellers from all over the world together and to new audiences.

In the United States the National Storytelling Festival also has the function of replenishing and rejuvenating the movement, celebrating its achievements, honouring its most tireless advocates and reminding itself of its values. It is, as Sobol says, 'a ritual enactment of community' (Sobol, 1999, p. 178). There is no single festival in the United Kingdom that does this in quite the same way.

However, this tendency of the festivals to aspire to high art, to elevate storytelling and storytellers to a pedestal, personifies an intense contradiction that is inherent in all platform storytelling and is articulated in the following comment from Edinburgh-based storyteller Claire Mulholland:

> The bit I really don't like about certain storytelling situations is this whole notion of the storytellers being put on a pedestal. I totally hate that. I was at a festival a number of years ago; it was a brilliant festival, where I heard excellent storytelling. But what irritated me was the notion of having storytellers up on this platform. The way it had been set up was for the audience to all bow down and worship to these Gods, and I just thought it was utter nonsense ... . On my return from the festival I found a great quotation which captured the dehumanizing effect of putting people on a pedestal; it is a less extreme form of what the media do to celebrities. (Interview)

The counter-cultural roots of the storytelling movement lay testament to the fact that many became attracted to storytelling precisely because it is *not* high art.

Storytelling is the ultimate *democratic*, low art and 'genuine' storytelling does not transpose easily or well to the platform of high art. Storytelling is 'the art form of social interaction' (Wilson, 1997a, p. 25), something that *everybody* does and participates in *every day* at some level. It also operates outside the social and class-based hierarchies of 'official' art, even democratizing the performer–audience relationship. As Mary Medlicott says, 'there is a way in which I put myself forward that suggests that we all have stories and that there's a common strand between us. I do like that and I think I want to make storytelling feel like part of our common fabric of our lives' (interview). In other words, the very concept of *platform storytelling* is a contradiction in terms, as it has 'the potential to turn low art into high art, thereby negating the very attributes that draw people to the art form in the first place' (Wilson, 2002, p. 99). As soon as 'genuine' storytelling gets put onto a platform, then it becomes something else. The consequences of this 'platformization' of storytelling has, according to Jack Zipes and others, led to the commodification and commercialization of storytelling and the creation of a self-serving, undemocratic and reactionary (or, at least, non-radical) star system within a storytelling movement that has largely lost sight of its original subversive intentions. Such storytelling, it is claimed, is ultimately self-justifying and self-congratulatory, a non-reflective storytelling that continually fails to question its own validity and interrogate itself.

For Zipes, therefore, the platform storyteller, who places her/himself on a pedestal,[1] is the very antithesis of Walter Benjamin's subversive storyteller, whose roots are in the very community that he or she seeks to serve. As soon as storytellers offer themselves up for admiration, then they are no longer the equal of the audience; the democratic or collective model is abandoned for a hierarchical model, and the storyteller ceases to articulate on *behalf* of the audience.

Perhaps the most intriguing aspect of the emergence of platform storytelling is its effect on those storytellers held in the highest reverence by the storytelling movement, that is those who have been bestowed with the title of 'Traditional Storyteller'. These are storytellers who have lived their lives in relative public obscurity, but have had reputations within their communities as storytellers and are rightly seen as bearers of an oral narrative tradition. The stories they tell will be mainly traditional in the broadest sense of the word, whether they are the tall tales of Texan storyteller Ed Bell or the traditional Jack Tales of Scottish traveller Duncan Williamson or Appalachian mountain man Ray Hicks. Prior to being 'discovered' and plucked out of obscurity by folklorists or the storytelling movement, these storytellers will only have had experience of telling stories to a public audience if there were opportunities for this kind of telling within their own tradition. For example, John Campbell has always performed to large audiences in the village halls around where he lives, but Ray Hicks's storytelling was largely of a domestic nature. And yet when these traditional tellers are invited to perform at large festivals and clubs, they are expected to perform as platform storytellers, to lay their tradition open for admiration.

Certainly it is only right that traditional performance and knowledge should be admired and given its due, but it is not always clear what the audience is admiring. It is usually defined in loose terms as 'authenticity'; here, at least, one is experiencing the real thing. Of course, it is difficult to determine what is authentic and it becomes even more problematic when a vague notion of 'authenticity' is used as a measure of artistic quality and is confused with 'integrity'. For example, the storytellers themselves may be 'authentic', as might their stories, but the performance situation in which they find themselves – often on stage in front of a microphone and a strange audience – is certainly not authentic and fundamentally alters the nature of the performance.

I was struck by a performance by Seref Tasliova, a Turkish Asik, at the Beyond the Border Festival in 2003. According to the festival programme:

> Asiks are Turkish bards, bearers of an ancient tradition of minstrelsy that includes singing, storytelling, poem making and inspired verbal duelling,...
> Seref Tasliova is one of the leading asiks in Turkey – and one of the last of a rapidly declining number. An Azeri shepherd from Kars in eastern Turkey, he has won many gold medals at bardic festival competitions through his skill in spontaneous verse-making and story-making contests. He is hugely respected for his ability to perform sections of the great Turkic epic of Koroglu, accompanying himself on the saz (the traditional long-necked 6 string lute of Turkey).

Tasliova's credentials as a *traditional* storyteller can be in no doubt; his is an *ancient* tradition, he is one of a dying breed, he is non-professional with a rural occupation (a shepherd) and he accompanies himself on a traditional instrument. In other words, everything about his credentials conforms to a particular view of folklore as a relic of a pre-industrial, near-extinct civilization. Perhaps equally significant, Tasliova's tradition is non-Western and, therefore, also contains that vital ingredient – the exotic.

Tasliova was chosen to open the festival and he strode proudly onto the stage in traditional Turkish costume, with a row of medals pinned to his chest. In many ways his performance was quite extraordinary, quite unlike anything I had seen before and he deservedly got a rousing ovation for it. The most remarkable thing, though, was that nobody in the audience had any way of fully understanding what was happening. It is unlikely that any audience member knew the Turkish language adequately to understand the words he was speaking, and I likewise doubt whether anybody had any knowledge of the cultural context from which such a tradition derived to enable them to 'read' the performance. Furthermore, we had no idea *really* whether the storytelling was any good or not. By what standards were we evaluating it? By what criteria would Tasliova's traditional audience have assessed his performance? Of course, I have no reason to think that it was anything but exemplary and I felt enriched by having seen it, but without the means to 'read' a performance, there is always the danger of such an event turning into voyeuristic exoticism.

What was clear was that Tasliova was enjoying himself, had a command of his material and was doing his level best to please the audience. In the circumstances he could probably do little else. As with other traditional storytellers who are asked to perform for prestigious festivals as platform storytellers, the invitation is no doubt issued with the best of possible intentions, and nobody would deny the importance of exposing audiences to a range of unfamiliar cultures. Such initiatives and those that propose them should be applauded, since the alternative can be small-minded Nationalism, but it does raise a number of interesting issues and fundamental contradictions.

Traditional storytellers will react in a number of different ways when courted by the storytelling movement. A minority will shun those advances, preferring relative obscurity to fame within the storytelling world. Most, however, will be flattered and will take the approach in the warm and enthusiastic manner in which it is intended. When confronted with the requirement to perform on stage, however, their performance will be tempered by the nature of the space and the size and nature of the audience (both of which may be quite unfamiliar to them) and the desire to please. Some will manage those situations better than others, but in all cases the storytelling for which they are so admired will be necessarily altered.

In his book *Story, Performance and Event* (1986), folklorist and socio-linguist Richard Bauman analyses a number of performances by Ed Bell, a storyteller from Texas. Some are performances that take place around a campfire, from the days before he was courted by the storytelling and folk movements, and others are performances at major festivals. Bauman notes a number of significant differences between the performances in accordance with 'his growing self-consciousness about the nature of performance, and his developing assessment of the new situational factors bearing on his performance in these new contexts' (Bauman, 1986, p. 80).

Bauman identifies that in the later tellings Bell employs much greater use of metanarration and formal narrative devices, but the most obvious difference is in the length of the stories. Bauman suggests that this is due to the new context of the festival. Faced with an audience that has come to admire his artistry, Bell expands his story to allow him to better display his skill. The context of the campfire, however, demands that stories are told succinctly with the minimum of fuss so as to allow as many tellers as possible their turn. Whilst a festival audience would be expecting Bell to 'hold the floor' with his skills, it would be considered bad form if he were to do this around the campfire. He might then be accused of showing off or *hogging* the floor. As Bauman says:

> Freed from the contextual pressures that favored relative brevity in storytelling at the hunting campfire or fishing camp, such as competition from the floor or the lure of fishing, and singled out to perform at festivals and other public events because of folklorists' recognition of his great talent as a storyteller, Bell has cultivated that virtuosity. (Bauman, 1986, p. 106)

The length of the stories, however, is not the only change in Bell's performances. Bauman also notices a fundamental shift in the relationship between performer and audience. The informality of telling to friends around the campfire is replaced by the necessary formality of a performance to a large, unfamiliar audience. According to Bauman, in the later performances Bell 'has become more distanced from his audience, both interactionally and by culture and background, in the performance situations themselves' (Bauman, 1986, p. 106). Part of the reason for the lengthening of the stories is that Bell finds it necessary to provide the unfamiliar audience with much more background information to the stories, information that he could have taken as being known to his familiar local audience around the campfire, but it is also to do with a change in the way that Bell sees himself in the role of the storyteller and his responsibilities as a performer. In other words, Bell's changing identity as a performer also has a transforming effect on the performance, as 'his view of himself has been transformed from someone who "never used to think of myself as a storyteller" to someone who is preeminently a storyteller, always responsible for the full display of his competence' (Bauman, 1986, p. 106).

It is a convincing argument that by seeking to raise the public awareness of traditional artists and celebrating their artistry by taking them out of their traditional performance context and placing them on the platform at what is an essentially middle-class festival, the nature of that performance is fundamentally altered on many levels. One simply cannot go to a festival and witness a traditional performance – all one can do is witness a traditional performance that is strictly mediated by the structures of the event itself, and so changes the very nature of what is being admired. In conclusion Bauman issues a stark warning:

> Such programs may well provide folk artists with opportunities for a fuller exercise of their artistic virtuosity than they might enjoy in local, more traditional settings, but their art and their lives may also be irreversibly transformed in the process. The assumption that public display of authentic folk tradition fosters its maintenance and preservation is ideologically appealing, but dangerously simplistic. If we are to persist in intervening in folk tradition, we need to look far more closely and carefully at the effects of our efforts on the artists and traditions on whose behalf we claim to be working.   (Bauman, 1986, p. 106)

Bauman's observations of Bell can be seen elsewhere in both the American and the British storytelling scene, most notably perhaps in the case of Ray Hicks, who has been courted and revered as the authentic voice of traditional Appalachian storytelling by the National Storytelling Festival since its inception.

Hicks, who died in 2003, was the kind of storyteller that Joseph Sobol describes as being rooted within 'a place and a particular set of local traditions' (Sobol, 1999, p. 32); his journey from obscure 'old man of the mountains' to 'Jonesborough icon' and his elevation to 'national treasure', what Sobol calls his 'canonisation', are well documented (Sobol, 1999, pp. 104–17). There can be no doubt that Hicks was a quite exceptionally talented performer, who had a profound effect on many who met him or witnessed his performances. The actor and former Wooster Group member Spalding Gray was one who saw Hicks perform in 1985, and Sobol commented that 'none of the performances he saw held much interest for him, until he saw Hicks ... despite his difficulty with the dialect, he was surprised to feel a sense of kinship' (Sobol, 1999, p. 113).

Gray is not the first to comment on Hicks's dialect and accent, which was almost impenetrable to the unpractised ear. Coupled with his striking physical appearance (Hicks was almost seven feet tall), this only added to his exoticism for the festival audience. Sobol, however, is quick to point out that the reverence in which Hicks is held is not entirely due to this exoticism: 'They would pay for the exotic, sure enough – but not if the exotica couldn't put on a show' (Sobol, 1999, p. 111). In other words, the attraction was Hicks's exoticism along with his skill as a performer and ability to adapt his performance to meet the needs of the festival audience. And yet

Hicks's first appearance at the Jonesborough Festival gives a hint of how much his performative style had to change to make him a festival star. As Sobol tells us, 'he had never before told stories outside of his local area or at any kind of outdoor festival' (Sobol, 1999, p. 104). Barbara Freeman recalls:

> Ray was so nervous that he looked at the sky the whole time. And that microphone, and his voice, he was just shaking, you know; and his mouth was dry, and he was scared to pieces. And I thought to myself ... this seems cruel, you know, to bring somebody who is a front-porch storyteller out of their environment and subject them to a big microphone and big speakers and a great crowd of people.   (Sobol, 1999, p. 101)

By the following year Hicks had adapted to the demands of the festival and was much more at ease. Freeman, rather interestingly, suggests that Hicks's initial difficulties were due to 'growing pains' (Sobol, 1999, p. 101), as if it were his responsibility to grow up to meet the needs of the festival, rather than the festival recognizing that the result of changing the performance context of these traditional tellers would make a potentially significant impact upon the very performance traditions that the festival held in such high esteem. What is clear from Freeman's testimony, though, is that Hicks's performance *did* change because of his engagement with the storytelling revival and that it was his skills as a performer that enabled this to happen and made his survival of this first tricky encounter possible.

In Great Britain, the storyteller to have achieved near-similar iconic status to that of Ray Hicks is Duncan Williamson. Williamson has been likewise adopted by the British storytelling movement as an authentic icon of traditional storytelling. He has an astonishingly large repertoire of traditional stories, learned around the travellers' campfires and, more recently, no doubt, around the storytelling clubs and festivals. These clubs and festivals, as well as community-centred venues, form the mainstay of his performance work and, whilst these are much smaller than their American counterparts, they still present a performance context that is a far cry from the intimacy of the traveller's tent. More recently Williamson has been courted by the international circuit and has begun to adapt his style to suit the larger American venues. Like Hicks, Williamson's success can be attributed to a combination of exoticism and a high degree of performative skill, which is easily recognizable and at the same time has allowed him to adapt and flourish within the new contexts of the storytelling revival. In other words, he has fulfilled a need within the British storytelling movement, as he embodies the very notion of authentic folk performance, to which so many revival tellers aspire. In addition his natural sociable and gregarious nature has endeared him to the storytelling movement, as he is often ready and willing to continue the storytelling in the bar long after the formal proceedings have finished. It should be noted that the storytelling revival in the United States is known for being a far more abstemious project than its British and Irish counterparts, where many storytelling clubs take place on licensed premises and alcohol is often considered as a necessary lubricant for the throat and loosener of the tongue.

Nevertheless, observers have not failed to notice that Williamson's storytelling style has changed over the years of his engagement with the storytelling movement, displaying an increased (and necessary) sense of detachment (Ryan, 2003, p. 239). This is not necessarily a bad thing – it is a sign of a *living* tradition that it can adapt to new circumstances, but it has certainly had an effect. Not only is this due to new performance contexts, it is also due to the fact that Williamson is so *busy* as a storyteller. He arguably does more storytelling now, as a professional, than he did before, and any artists will develop and evolve through the very practice of their art – traditional artists are no different in this respect. It is ironic, though, that the apparent timelessness of Williamson's storytelling, so attractive to the storytelling movement, is the one thing that is most vulnerable to an engagement with that movement.

'Mega-identity'

As argued elsewhere, the understanding of and attitude towards tradition is a key factor in understanding not only the contemporary storytelling movement, but also the individual storytellers within it. It is not coincidental that the movements in both America and Britain have created icons out of their foremost traditional storytellers, but the obsession is particularly strong in Britain. In America, debates around the appropriation of traditional stories from other cultures (especially from Native American cultures), alongside concerns about the ownership and copyright of material, have led many storytellers to draw largely on autobiographical and original stories for their repertoires. In Britain it is far more usual for storytellers to draw on traditional material (often from a range of cultures) and the traditional story is seen to have greater currency than the non-traditional tale. There are very few storytellers in Britain whose repertoires do not largely consist of traditional material. In Ben Haggarty's recent survey of storytelling in England and Wales, out of the thirty-nine respondents, only one had no traditional stories in their repertoire and thirty-five claimed more than 50 per cent of their repertoire consisted of such stories (Haggarty, 2004, p. 25). For some storytellers this may be because of a belief in the intrinsic value of traditional story and reinterpreting it for a contemporary audience. Others may wrap themselves more fully in the cloak of tradition, laying claim to their own place (rightly or wrongly) within a tradition and modelling themselves as genuine tradition-bearers.

In his recent doctoral study into contemporary storytelling in context, Patrick Ryan (2003) discusses a concept that he calls 'mega-identity' (see especially pp. 109–23). Essentially, mega-identity is the storyteller-identity that individuals create for themselves and which manifests itself most obviously in a stage persona (which may be the same, pretend to be the same, or be very different from their actual everyday persona), but is also part of how a storyteller presents him/herself offstage to the audience, potential bookers, etc. Fundamental to this is the storyteller's attitude towards tradition and this is of particular relevance in the matter of platform storytelling, because it is here that the storyteller's mega-identity is most openly and publicly on display.

The storyteller's *Tradition-Gestus* will pervade his/her publicity material, which in turn will influence the kind of events that she or he is booked for and the kinds of audiences played to. It will affect the storyteller's choice of repertoire, the manner in which they organize the space (if indeed they are given the opportunity to do so), the way that they dress and, of course, the way in which the stories are performed.

By way of example, let us compare some contrasting mega-identities, beginning with the Devon-based environmental storyteller Spindle Wayfarer (real name Chris Salisbury). In the August 2003 edition of the magazine *Devon Life* there is a short feature article profiling this storyteller and the Westcountry Storytelling Festival that he organizes (p. 116). Included is a publicity shot (used on the festival's publicity) of him dressed in a loose-fitting seventeenth-century style shirt with a leather waistcoat. He is striking a suitably dramatic pose, leaning forward towards the camera, full of urgency and import, a candlestick thrust forward in one hand and an oversized, worn, leather-bound volume held underneath the other arm. Everything about the photograph lays claim to this being a storyteller steeped in tradition and possessing a knowledge and wisdom that only a true tradition-bearer might have. Furthermore, it is a complete rejection of modernity and the present, being utterly located within an imagined pre-industrial past. Even the storyteller's stage name, containing suggestions of spinning and travelling (two activities traditionally associated with storytelling), is dripping with 'olde worlde charme'.

A contrasting example would be American–Irish storyteller Patrick Ryan, whose website (www.telltale.dircon.co.uk) is free of all traditional imagery. Instead there is a photograph of the storyteller in an animated, but conversational pose, dressed in a sports jacket and teeshirt. The accompanying text concentrates on the kind of work that Ryan specializes in (mainly non-platform telling) and his experience to date. The only reference to tradition is in a short paragraph that refers to his own family traditions of storytelling and the eclectic nature of the traditional stories in his own repertoire. It is not that Ryan (and others like him) reject notions of tradition, but rather his relationship to it is quite different – what he rejects is what he sees as an indulgent wallowing in a false sense of tradition. Coming as he does from Irish ancestry, he is especially critical of the selective way that New-Ageism has plundered traditional Celtic culture and reinvented it with a bogus spiritual veneer and then presented it as an authentic, superior and separate cultural tradition – that is, superior to and separate from a modern, post-industrial cultural tradition. Such misuse of Celtic imagery is widespread and is a way of creating a mega-identity that is validated by tradition.

Perhaps the most extreme example of this can be found at www.ansgeulaiche.co.uk, the website of Scot AnSgeulaiche (Scot, the Scottish Storyteller), who describes himself as a Traditional Highland Storyteller – Seanachaidh', the evidence for which seems largely to be web pages ornately decorated with Celtic scrolls and many pictures of a plaid-bedecked Scot striking suitably meaningful poses against mountain landscapes. The text itself serves to present the storyteller as a wise mystic. Of his credentials, we are told that, about this time, he

> took up training with the Ehama Institute of California, who are Keepers of the style of Earth Wisdom found amongst the indigenous people of America. Through his training, [his] understanding of Celtic Wisdom has been expanded.

For Jack Zipes this kind of approach epitomizes the folly (as opposed to the wisdom) of storytelling, presenting a façade of non-conformity, but actually being ultra-conservative because in

[S]triving to fill gaps in their lives left by a technological society that discounts human feelings ... they are often unaware of the extent to which their behavior conforms to market expectations and unknowingly helps sustain a myth of freedom ... (Zipes, 2001, p. 145)

What may seem to be subversive and oppositional actually sustains the status quo, since an attitude of there being virtue in existing on the edge of society, only exists and defines itself in terms of its relationship to the status quo and has, therefore, an interest in maintaining it. As such it is tolerated by society as an entertaining distraction and reinforcement of the preferentiality of the way things are, and not of alternative systems.

We should, however, be extremely careful of condemning all storytellers' engagement with tradition. The case above is an exception and the examples of Patrick Ryan and many others show that revival storytellers can engage sensibly and creatively with traditional stories and give due acknowledgement to the influence of traditional storytelling practices within their work. The problem arises, of course, when the lure of tradition and the desire for a sense of authenticity are so great that unsustainable claims are made by storytellers about their 'traditional' credentials.

To some degree there has always been an element of this right across the storytelling movement. In the early days of the revival, a notion of tradition was used by storytellers to explain to potential clients what it was that differentiated their work from that of, say, writers, or even actors, and so justify their being booked. In turn this often led to an expectation by bookers that storytellers should be traditional in their practice and material. Billy Teare, a storyteller from Northern Ireland, freely admits the rather cynical use of a picture of himself as a child sitting on his grandmother's lap, in an early publicity leaflet, in order to gently exploit the market's expectations of storytelling. At the time, Teare was just beginning to establish himself as a storyteller and he confesses that he was hoping to suggest, by the picture, that he was steeped in, and a bearer of, a tradition of Irish storytelling that had been passed down through the generations, whereas the tradition to which his storytelling owes most (and which he now acknowledges) is that of Music Hall and stand-up comedy. I, too, remember an early publicity leaflet of my own which made probably rather too much of the traditional nature of the stories in my repertoire rather than concentrating on the real purpose of the work I was doing. When tradition is used as a yardstick of quality, it can turn many genuinely motivated people into charlatans and it is a particular irony that the greater one strives for authenticity, the less authentic one becomes.

The importance of the storyteller's relationship to tradition in establishing the mega-identity is of particular importance to platform storytelling, where the stage persona/identity helps determine the audience's expectations of the performance. This can be an important tool, of course, but it is not always in the control of the storyteller and when the publicity is determined by the booker or festival organizer, it can lead to false expectations and problems for the performer. As one of the few Welsh language storytellers, Michael Harvey is often frustrated by the use of this for marketing purposes, as it can create a false mega-identity:

> When I market myself, I don't market myself as a Welsh storyteller. I understand that marketing's a game and I understand it's the label and you kind of need it and it's PR and it's not really what you do, but I don't market myself as a Welsh storyteller because culturally the most important thing for me in the work I do is what happens between me and the audience. ... I love all the big festivals and everything, but it does sometimes feel a bit like *It's a Knockout* when you have your name and your biog and then you're from somewhere. ... I have a feeling it has to do with what PR and marketing are, because it's necessarily unreflective and flashy. It's also prone to exoticism. So you've got to exoticise your product. (Interview)

For Harvey, his cultural identity is integral, yet also incidental, to his mega-identity, which he feels is informed more by what he does than by what he is. Of course, mega-identity is primarily determined by the performers themselves (working either with or against the expectations the audience have received through the publicity and marketing) and is particularly established during the performer's preamble, that is the introductory remarks and business that precede the actual telling of the stories. The mega-identity is also supported by the organization of space and use of costume, in so much as the performer has control over these.

Space and Platform Storytelling or How Storytellers Use Space and Why They Do it in Certain Ways: the *Gestus* of Space

The way the space is set out, for platform storytelling in particular, is not always under the control of the storyteller. Very often festival organizers will understandably design spaces (and not allow those spaces to be manipulated) with economics, rather than storytelling, in mind. The festival organizer will want to sell as many tickets as possible and will, therefore, arrange the space in a manner that maximizes the size of the audience. This almost always means a stage for the performer, facing rows of seats – in other words a model that mimics conventional, proscenium arch theatres. The less formal the event (that is, the more it moves to the left-hand side of the Performance Continuum, see Chapter 1), the more scope there is for the manipulation of space. A storyteller performing in a school or library may well face some restrictions due to desks or book-shelves, but will, within reason, be allowed to transform the space. The festival organizer, on the other hand, may claim that space is configured in order that as many people as possible who want to see a storyteller perform can do so, yet the fact is that it has a profound effect upon the actual storytelling.

Since purpose-built theatres first appeared in western Europe in the sixteenth century, the stage and auditorium have been designed principally to divide performer from the audience and the audience amongst themselves. Moreover, this audience segregation has been on a basis of social class and status – *who* you were would determine *where* you sat (or stood) in the theatre. Although the storyteller may be able to manage some modest decoration of the stage, they are still stuck with a hierarchical space, rather than a democratic one.

The separation of performer and audience is often reinforced by the use of a microphone. Again the organizer may legitimately claim that voice amplification is necessary for large audiences to hear the storyteller, but it cannot be denied that, in the hands of all but the most accomplished performer, the storytelling becomes less intimate and less capable of building a sense of community. Not only does the microphone present a physical barrier between stage and auditorium, but the voice becomes electronically mediated and, therefore, more distant. Joseph Sobol notes that the microphone has become standard in the American storytelling scene, irrespective of the context in which the storytelling is to take place (see Sobol, 1999, pp. 100–2). This is an observation that is borne out by Patrick Ryan who told me that, faced with a small group of participants at an informal 'story-swapping' session at an American festival, he suggested that they pull their chairs into a circle in a corner of the large room. Instead the participants insisted on telling their stories on stage through a microphone to a mere half a dozen people. The festival scene and its insistence on a particular way of organizing space had led to expectations from these participants that denied them the experience of a more informal, more intimate and ultimately more meaningful storytelling event.

However, even when storytellers themselves control the organization of the space, they often do so in ways that are both complex and informed by political, as well as aesthetic decisions. For many the ability to tell stories in any place and at any time, taking it out of the centres of bourgeois cultural production, such as the theatres, concert halls and arts centres, is what marks storytelling out as a truly democratic art form. Consequently the decoration of the space in any way, let alone its organization along hierarchical lines, can be considered an unnecessary diversion, a way of leading the audience into enchantment and, ultimately, a way of depoliticizing the storytelling act.

Such an attitude is not a rejection of the consideration of space. In fact, these storytellers are making very clear decisions and statements about the way a space is used – for them storytelling should appropriate non-performance environments, since storytelling traditionally takes place in social areas (for example around the kitchen fire or in the pub) and contemporary storytelling ought to take place in contemporary social locations. Liz Weir is typical in not wishing to decorate or transform a space, whilst still giving its arrangement careful consideration:

> You must have an eye for the space and see what works best in terms of seating. You sometimes make the best of a very bad situation. You have to create a comfortable space. ... I always like to define a space, even if I've got a group of children coming into a library. I define my space by setting out two chairs for the teachers at the side to make them a part of it. That's a technique that you have to learn, nobody taught me that.   (Interview)

Alternatively other storytellers will often try and transform the space in any way possible, beyond simply arranging the chairs in a particular way. They may bring drapes (often 'ethnic' in character) to hang on the walls as a backdrop, or rugs to place on the floor.[2]

Sometimes they may decorate the space with props or musical instruments, which they may or may not use. Sometimes it is done in order to enhance the storytelling experience and illuminate the stories so that the audience is enlightened. At other times it is not always clear why it is being done other than to homogenize the space (and so homogenize the performance and the audience's experience from performance to performance by that storyteller) and to pay lip service to a particular view of what is authentic in terms of storytelling.

The issue, however, is not really whether to 'dress' the space or not, but more about how the decisions about space are made and to what purpose and effect. Indeed these are intensely political decisions that concern themselves with how individuals view the function of storytelling, whether as an act of enchantment or one of enlightenment.

What we are really talking about here is the *attitude* to space, and specifically the socio-political attitude to space. This spatial attitude or *Gestus* (to borrow the Brechtian term) is informed by the storyteller's overall *Gestus* towards the very act of storytelling itself. In other words, the way the decisions that a storyteller (or storytelling event organizer) makes about space are informed by their attitude towards space, which in turn betrays their overall approach to storytelling, reinforcing their mega-identity.

For example, some years ago, in an early edition of *Fact and Fiction*, a British storytelling magazine, a reader wrote of her experiences of setting up informal storytelling evenings in her own home. She wrote that in the first instance the sessions took place in the living room, but that they soon changed rooms, because it was felt that storytelling could not take place in the same room as the television (which was not switched on at the time). It was a statement that clearly said that storytelling has no place in the modern technological world, and that if effective storytelling is to take place, we must construct spaces that are free of technology and, as much as possible, harp back to a golden age of pre-industrial simplicity. What at first we might have thought was a progressive initiative to explore contemporary social space as a space for storytelling actually turns out to be driven by an ideology that denies contemporaneity in storytelling.

On the other hand, some of the site-specific storytelling which takes place in museums and historical sites (English Heritage have been particularly pro-active in using storytellers to enhance the visitor experience) might seem to be guilty of the same attitude, but rather, actively encourages an informed and critical stance towards the past. The annual Ulster Storytelling Festival which takes place every June at the Ulster Folk and Transport Museum in Cultra, County Down, Northern Ireland, is particularly interesting in this respect. On the surface it might seem that the festival has two opposing aims – to stage a high-profile festival of storytelling, and to engage creatively and educatively with the historical sites that make up the museum, and yet the success of the festival has shown that both are indeed possible.

It is an open-air museum located in the grounds of a large estate in Cultra and consists of a substantial array of genuine examples of vernacular architecture (cottages, farmhouses, schoolrooms, shops, etc.) from all over Ulster, which have been dismantled, relocated and rebuilt, brick by brick, at the museum. The weekend-long festival, which consists largely of platform storytelling from local, national and international storytellers, takes place in and around the museum buildings. As part of the festival programme, there is one large concert, held in a venue large enough to accommodate a couple of hundred people, with the storytellers positioned on a low stage and performing with the use of a microphone (although many will decline the offer to use it). Most of the festival, however, consists of story-tellers being located in buildings around the site and being visited by groups of about a dozen or so audience members. The groups are necessarily small, as some of the venues will accommodate no more than this at any one time.

One might, of course, argue that to locate storytelling in the peat-smoke-filled kitchens of the museum's cottages is simply pandering to a romanticism of storytelling, yet these *are* authentic buildings, albeit relocated to the museum. They provide a context that is more than merely decorative and artificial, but actually facilitates a different quality of communication than that afforded by the larger venues. It is rare for platform storytelling to achieve such levels of intimacy and it is done simply by a rethinking of what constitutes performance space. Under such circumstances it is hard for the storyteller to assert the superiority of the performer that so often accompanies platform storytelling and the event consequently becomes a more democratic one. Ultimately, there can be no such thing as a perfect space for storytelling, as different types of storytelling will demand different types of space and different storytellers will have different ideas about what constitutes a perfect space for them. Liz Weir, who established and, for many years, organized the festival is very conversant with the debates surrounding it:

I've heard people criticize the festival by saying it's perpetuating the myth of the old people sitting by the fire telling a story and this isn't part of the modern world. To me it's every bit as valid doing that. If I was only doing that, I would take criticism of it. . . . It's very much about trying to recreate the atmosphere. But that's only one way. . . . I honestly do think that stories can be told anywhere.   (Interview)

One notable example of an attempt to create a perfect storytelling space is the Celtic Roundhouse built by storyteller Eric Maddern in the ground of his home in North Wales. Maddern has returned to the architectural model of the roundhouse to create a more intimate and democratic space for storytelling and it also reflects his interest in pre-industrial (indeed pre-Christian) Celtic culture. It is an impressive construction and there is no doubt that it represents a special, dedicated and focused storytelling space. Entering the roundhouse, the audience gets the feeling of being imaginatively transported back in time, as the contemporary world is completely shut out, which provides for a more intense experience for them. It is unapologetically not a modern storytelling space and so brings with it a set of messages about the storytelling that will take place there. It is ideal for some types of storytelling, but not for others.

It is significant that most storytelling clubs in the UK take place in pubs. Here the organizers have placed greatest emphasis on the storytelling event as a social occasion and one that is enhanced through the drinking of alcohol. In many ways pubs make ideal storytelling venues because of this, promoting an all-inclusive, informal mode of telling – with the clatter of glasses and the low-level chat at the bar, it is difficult for storytellers to succeed if they try and retain pretensions about the preciousness of their art. The pub venue promotes a certain honesty in the storytelling, but it again sends out certain messages and attracts a certain kind of audience. In spite of the changes seen in society over the past twenty or thirty years, pubs (and here we're talking about pubs as opposed to the recent explosion of bars-cum-cafés-cum-clubs) remain predominantly adult and male institutions. Storytelling clubs in pubs effectively exclude most families, many elderly people (especially women) and those who, for whatever reason, do not drink alcohol. For others, these clubs are also redolent of the folk clubs and viewed as amateurish and unfashionable. On the other hand, many of the 'Yarnspinners' Clubs set up by Liz Weir and others in Northern Ireland are located in the local libraries. In many ways these are more neutral spaces and are already seen as appropriate to literary and cultural events. These certainly draw larger audiences than many of the pub-based clubs and significantly larger numbers of elderly people. Clearly, the different kind of venue attracts and caters for a different kind of audience.

Dressing the Performer: Costume and Physicality

Just as storytellers will often choose to dress or decorate the performance space in order to confirm their mega-identity and raise certain expectations within the audience, storytellers will also dress themselves for the same purpose; sometimes to distinguish themselves from the audience, sometimes to associate themselves with the audience, but always to present a certain identity and lay the ground for their performance. At the National Storytelling Conference in Chicago in 2003, there were a number of clothes stalls, specializing in 'ethnic fashions' proclaiming their suitability for storytelling performances. It was not clear exactly which ethnicities were being represented by these fashions, but that did not seem to matter, as long as they transmitted the exotic, colourful and home-spun message supposedly appropriate to storytelling.

Other storytellers may wear items of clothing that suggest their own ethnicity, especially if their repertoire derives primarily from their own cultural background. For example, Scottish storyteller David Campbell always wears a kilt, both for performance and for everyday use. Many other storytellers reject the concept of costuming as a way of declaring one's cultural identity, choosing instead to dress in a manner appropriate to the social occasion of the storytelling event, dressing smartly, if not formally. Others may take a more radical approach, viewing any decoration of the performer as both unnecessary and a betrayal of the everyday nature of genuine storytelling, underplaying any sense of occasion and dressing as 'ordinarily' as possible. Daniel Morden and Hugh Lupton's work on *The Iliad*, *The Odyssey* and *Metamorphoses* is interesting in this respect. Their attempt at neutral costuming is an attempt to play down their own personalities. Morden says,

> We dress very neutrally and ... we try all the time to be neutral, to appear to be as neutral as possible, so neither the artistry nor our personalities are present. We hope the audience is left with the images from the story ...   (Interview)

At the same time the space is organized in a very formal way, echoing a formal style of presentation:

> We have some of the trappings of theatre, which establishes a certain kind of relationship with the audience, such as a darkened auditorium and stage lighting and seating in ranks rather than around tables. These elements contribute to a formality which means that the story is being served by its presentation. It's more heightened than one might have in a pub, for example.   (Interview)

In this sense, storytellers will usually use costume, and consequently their bodies, in different, more gestural and less mimetic ways than actors often will. On the surface this appears as if storytellers are less physical – and certainly less physically aware – than actors. It is almost as if there exists a denial of body. It is certainly true that storytellers will tend to be more physically restrained than actors, but this doesn't quite mean that they are being less physical.

Storytellers will often root themselves physically in a spot, either standing or sitting, with movement primarily emanating from the hands and/or the head. In part this is to do with our expectations of storytelling as a sedentary activity, and those domestic storytelling traditions. In part it is due to the legacy of the library story-telling session, which is a necessarily sedentary (and often book-based) event. In the United States, at least, the legacy of the large festivals and the limitations of using a microphone, must also have had an effect. Most of all, though, storytelling is largely considered to be the kind of thing that requires quiet contemplation, rather than a burst of physical energy.

Many storytellers, especially those with an actor's training, talk of their need to learn a different kind of physicality for storytelling,[3] to resist the actorly impulse to mime, or play out, the actions of the story, but rather to develop a language of gesture. In reality this tends to be a slightly exaggerated and more considered use of the kind of hand and facial gestures that a particular storyteller will use in every-day speech, but it becomes more mannered and serves largely to *emphasize* moments of spoken text (and indicate the *Gestus* of the storyteller), rather than *replace* it. This means that most storytelling audiences will focus on the hands and face of the storyteller in order to look for physical clues to help them interpret the text. I would argue, therefore, that storytellers in performance are not *less* physical than actors, but *differently* physical.

Of course, there are exceptions to this. Irish storyteller Eddie Lenihan is well known for the frenetic physical energy of his performances. He will leap around the stage, stand on tables, almost throw himself into the audience, using both gesture and mime to create the world of the story. Both language and physicality are delivered with such high energy that both teller and audience are left exhausted. Franco-American teller Michael Parent's physicality is more mellow, but he will still use the entire stage to create the world around him. He will start to act out entire scenes and sections of dialogue, showing the audience the different characters as they appear in the story, in a way that is not common amongst storytellers generally, and British storytellers particularly. In many ways his performance style is more reminiscent of Dario Fo in *Mistero Buffo* than traditional tellers such as Ray Hicks, but where Fo is a skilful mime, Parent's physicality is still largely gestural (and gestic). It is more a case of Parent extending his face and hand gestures into the rest of his body to create a physical language that supports the narrative text.

In the main, even for those storytellers who deliberately understate gestural language, physicality – that is posture, stance and the way they move onto, off and around the performance space – is closely related to mega-identity and particularly status. A storyteller who wants to exude a sense of authority will adopt a certain kind of physicality. Likewise storytellers who wish to present themselves as spiritual beings will most likely have an exaggeratedly slow and relaxed physical demeanour. It is the case, therefore, that contrary to first impressions, physicality plays an important part in the story-telling experience.

Repertoires, Stories and the Positioning of the Performer

One key determining factor as to how storytellers develop their repertoire is their understanding of 'tradition', especially in Britain and Ireland. In the United States the situation is rather different, as storytellers have cast themselves in the role of tradition-bearers of their own communities, reinventing autobiographical stories as mytho-logical tales of those communities. In this sense, when Carmen Deedy tells stories of her childhood as a Cuban immigrant, she is also telling them as stories of the entire Cuban immigrant community. The same applies to Michael Parent's stories from the French-speaking communities in Maine. Ethnicity becomes a synonym for tradition and they become spokespeople for those ethnic communities. The debates in America have forced many storytellers to look at themselves in terms of *their* communities, *their* traditions and *their* ethnicities in a way that has not happened in Britain and Ireland to the same extent.

Just as Richard Bauman is critical of how the storytelling movement has intervened in the lives of traditional tellers such as Ed Bell, folklorist Barre Toelken asks similarly uncomfortable questions about storytellers' use of material outside of their own culture. Toelken challenges many of the assumptions that he sees widespread within the storytelling movement concerning folktales, including the theories of the universal mythic meaning of stories, as expounded by Joseph Campbell, Robert Bly and others (Tolkein, 1996, pp. 41–4). He also challenges the notion that folktales are in some way superior to other kinds of stories:

> Folktales ... are stories whose meanings grow out of and reflect the values of the groups in which they are told. Folktales are not 'better' or 'older' or 'more genuine' than other stories; their primary characteristic is simply that they are formed and polished by those who tell them among themselves over time. (Toelken, 1996, p. 37)

Instead Toelken argues that the meanings of stories are rooted in cultures and when 'such a story is taken out of the group and "retold" on a stage or to the rest of us who may not be members of that group, most of the richness of meaning ... usually falls away' (Toelken, 1996, p. 38). Of course, the meaning of a story is primarily rooted in the moment of performance, but Toelken's point is well-made and he is particularly critical of storytellers who use folktales as if they were 'a single articulation of some network of meaning shared by all mankind' (Toelken, 1996, p. 41). He describes such behaviour as 'performative colonialism' (Toelken, 1996, p. 60) and suggests that these issues cannot be ignored by the storytelling movement 'by simply reciting platitudes of intercultural lore, intergalactic archetypes and the power-of-a-story-to-heal-all-wounds-and-bridge-all-chasms' (Toelken, 1996, p. 61). But Toelken does not propose that storytellers should not tell folktales from other cultures, because 'good stories deserve and demand' to be told. Instead he argues for sensitive, respectful and informed engagement with the materials of other cultures (Toelken, 1996, p. 61).

As may be expected from an American academic, Toelken is particularly critical of the way Native American culture has been misappropriated, but, as already suggested, these arguments are as relevant, if not more so, in Britain where folktales are the staple of the storyteller's repertoire. Just because a British storyteller tells British and European folktales this does not mean that they are not being taken out of their cultural context. Few storytellers today have genuine connections with the cultures that produced such stories, and they often come to the stories through the literary medium of the nineteenth-century educated, middle-class antiquarian.

Although there are very noticeable differences between the repertoires of American storytellers and their British counterparts, there are some stories that are regularly told on both sides of the Atlantic because they express a shared ideology about the very importance of storytelling itself. These are what Joseph Sobol calls 'totemic stories' and he quotes three examples in his book *The Storytellers' Journey*, the first of which is as follows:

> When the great Rabbi Israel Shem-Tov saw misfortune threatening the Jews it was his custom to go into a certain part of the forest to meditate. There he would light a fire, say a special prayer, and the miracle would be accomplished, and the misfortune averted.
>
> Later, when his disciple, the celebrated Magid of Mezritch, had occasion, for the same reason, to intercede with heaven, he would go to the same place in the forest and say: 'Master of the Universe, listen! I do not know how to light the fire, but I am still able to say the prayer.' And again the miracle would be accomplished. Still later, Rabbi Moshe-Leib of Sasov, in order to save his people once more, would go into the forest and say: 'I do not know how to light the fire, I do not know the prayer, but I know the place and this must be sufficient.' It was sufficient and the miracle was accomplished.
>
> Then it fell to Rabbi Israel of Rizhyn to overcome misfortune. Sitting in his armchair, his head in his hands, he spoke to God: 'I am unable to light the fire and I do not know the prayer; I cannot even find the place in the forest. All I can do is to retell the story, and this must be sufficient.' And it was sufficient. God made man because he loves stories. (Elie Wiesel, *The Gates of the Forest* (New York, 1966), pp. 6–10, quoted in Sobol, 1999, p. 63)

Most storytellers will have in their repertoire stories about stories, stories of 'self-affirmation and self-reaffirmation that embody the shared ideology of all those involved in the storytelling revival' (Wilson, 2004a, p. 92). In other words, these stories emphasize the importance of stories, and therefore, by implication, storytellers, to human existence – they raise the status of story, storyteller and storytelling event.

These stories have an important function within the story-telling movement, in that they help the movement define itself both to those within and those outside the movement, which is their totemic function. Each totemic story, however, will also say some-thing specific about storytelling in addition to the general reaffirma-tion of its centrality to our lives. In the case of the story of 'The Story Was Sufficient', the story underpins a commonly held belief amongst storytellers about the relationship between performer, text and audi-ence, particularly in reference to platform storytelling. The story tells us that the most important part of that trialogue is the story. As Michael Parent says, 'I think the story always has to have the upper hand' (interview). The storyteller remains a vehicle for the story and the audience remains a repository for it, and the storyteller in particular must not allow his/her artistry or ego to get in the way of it. As Nuala Hayes says, 'I believe effective storytelling is when the audience remembers the story clearly afterwards, whereas the flashy, showy stuff puts the focus on the performer rather than the story' (interview). Additionally Daniel Morden inists that the storyteller's main task is to become invisible in order to allow the story to work its magic (interview). Morden's position is extremely common, but not unanimous. Carol Birch criticizes this approach as a 'submersion of self in deference to the story' (Birch, 1996, p. 112) since it fails to acknowledge the difference between the author and the narrator of a story. Principally, Birch's argument is that a storyteller can and should never remain invisible because that would disallow the storyteller taking an attitude towards the material, or having a point of view. Morden's argument, on the other hand, is against self-aggrandizement where the story becomes lost and the performance becomes about the cult of the storyteller. And yet Birch is also right that the invisibility of the storyteller is ultimately a myth. The text exists in performance and so story, storyteller and audience are indivisible (and, therefore, to separate them is to distort our understanding of the storytelling process). It is the visibility of the storyteller and his/her *Gestus* that make the story worth listening to.[4]

Nevertheless, Morden is absolutely right that the successful story-teller needs to position himself or herself in a way that best suits the performance. In most cases, in the opening introductory moments the storyteller will seek to lower his/her status, to befriend the audience and to present a persona that is at ease, unmannered and relaxed. In his work with actors and storytelling, Peter Brook talks about being 'carried along through the play with a good friendly relationship with the audience' (Croyden, 2003, p. 215). Perhaps this is what Morden really means by invisibility, because a genuine sense of community between performer and audience is established when the audience is entirely focused upon the storyteller and his/her artistry, and the performance becomes seemingly natural and effortless. There is no sense of strain and yet the audience is simultaneously aware and unaware of the skill and technique at play. It is the kind of effortlessness that can be readily seen in the work of actors such as Dario Fo and Ken Campbell in their one-person shows, and of comedians such as Billy Connolly, Mark Thomas and the late Dave Allen. It is an ease which helps create the necessary familiarity between performer and audience for effective storytelling and one in which the performer does not become invisible but might *appear* to be so.

There is perhaps an interesting irony here. If platform storytelling results in a situation where the performers are separated from the audience and placed upon a literal or figurative stage to be admired for their artistry, then it appears that the most effective platform storytelling works against those very assumptions, deformalizing the event and creating familiarity and *communitas* between teller and listener. The more prestigious and formal the storytelling event, the harder the storyteller has to work against it in order to succeed.

> The successful storyteller needs to create that same sense of intimacy, not by some artificial means, but simply through the presentation of an identity that befriends the audience, rather than enchants it. The storyteller needs to be the audience's equal, not its better, a fellow student, not its teacher. It is not the case of distinguishing between those storytelling performances that are seemingly well-rehearsed, scripted and highly polished and those that seem to be spontaneous, improvised and flawed, but rather between those whereby the story is used as a vehicle for the performer to openly demonstrate his/her skills and those whereby the skills of the performer become embedded into the performance of the story, serving it and thereby becoming invisible.   (Wilson, 2004a, p. 97)

It is a rare performer that can succeed in storytelling by formalizing their performance. Abbi Patrix is perhaps one of those performers.

Case Study 1: Abbi Patrix

I would here like to refer to Patrix's performance of his show *To the Ends of the Earth*, which premiered at the Beyond the Border International Storytelling Festival at St Donats in South Wales in July 2003. Patrix's background is that of an actor, having trained at the Jaques LeCoq School and worked with Peter Brook in Paris, from where his 'Compagnie du Cercle', an eclectic mix of actors, musicians, singers, writers and storytellers dedicated to creating new versions of stories from world mythology, also operates. Writing in 1996, Ben Haggarty, co-artistic director of the Beyond the Border Festival, said the following about his work:

> If anyone wants to see hope for the authentic western revival of a professional storytelling tradition then make an effort, go to France and follow the sophisticated theatre work that Abbi Patrix and his Compagnie du Cercle are doing on rhythm and pitch.   (Haggarty, 1996, p. 23)

According to the 2003 festival programme, Patrix's 'powerful, rhythmic work has earned him an international reputation as the greatest of Europe's performance storytellers'. Whilst there may be some of the usual hyperbole one would expect to find in festival publicity present in this statement, Abbi Patrix's reputation as a consummate performer is well established. He is not a traditional performer in the sense of Duncan Williamson or Ray Hicks, but he is the one revival performer who is held in similar esteem by the story-telling movement. His performance at the first Beyond the Border Festival in 1993 had a strong impact on Michael Harvey, who describes Patrix as 'the man who actually blew me away' (interview).

For his solo shows, Patrix, unlike most storytellers, works not from repertoire as such, varying the content from one show to another, but more like a one-man theatre company, presenting a full-length fixed programme based around a single story or cycle of stories. *To the Ends of the Earth* is such a show, thematically based around stories which feature a journey to the World's End, a not uncommon motif in European folktales. One such episode in the show is based upon a story very popular in contemporary storytelling, 'The Man in Search of his Luck'.

In the story, a man sets off to find God at the World's End to ask how he can find his luck. On his way he meets a starving wolf, a dying tree and a lonely woman and he promises each in turn that he will, on their behalf, ask God to solve their problems too. When he finally arrives at the World's End, God tells him that if he continues searching, he will indeed find his luck. He also furnishes him with answers for the wolf, the tree and the woman. When he tells the woman that she must find a companion to share her life with, she asks the man to marry her, but he says he is too busy searching for his luck. The tree is dying on account of its roots being crushed by buried treasure, but the man has no time to dig the treasure to save the tree. Instead he moves off in search of his luck. Then he meets the wolf and tells him that God has said that he should just eat the first fool who comes along, and so the wolf eats the man.

This story is the first item in Patrix's highly stylized performance and begins with the sound of a repeated single drumbeat from the back of the auditorium (in this case a large marquee), interspersed with chanting. After about a minute Patrix emerges, still drumming and chanting, from the back of the auditorium, making his way through the audience to the stage. The stage itself is carefully arranged with a dulcimer on one side and a microphone centre stage. Patrix is casually, but smartly dressed, as neutrally as possible.

It is interesting that there is no preamble to Patrix's performance, no attempt to deformalize the event, no effort to befriend the audience. Instead the drumming and the chanting represent a very stylized opening that legislates against the familiarity on which storytelling so often relies. The performance has, of course, begun off stage and once it has begun, Patrix will only lower his status as performer briefly in between the stories. The moment he is on stage, the story begins and Patrix launches into his script.

I use the word 'script' advisedly here, since most storytellers would deny the use of a 'script' or fixed text of any sort, claiming instead that each performance of a story is improvised anew. According to Ben Haggarty, storytelling 'is an interpretative improvisation; it is Jazz; it is primordial, immediate responsive *theatre*' (Haggarty, 1996, p. 21). I suspect that most storytellers' texts are less fluid than they would assume them to be, having become more fixed and less improvised over a relatively limited number of performances, until there is very little discernible difference between the texts of two separate performances of the same story by the same teller. The main difference is that with storytelling, the text becomes fixed during the process of performance by the storyteller, rather than being scripted by a writer prior to rehearsal. Jack Lynch maintains that the storytelling text remains fluid because of the element of performance, stating that 'it never does get fixed, and the reason it never does get fixed is because of the audience, because of the listeners' (interview). Taffy Thomas, on the other hand, is less convinced about the notion of an improvised text, but stresses the importance of its *alterability*, its potential for change, claiming, 'I would rather say it's not improvised, but it's possible for it to change in performance, if the performer is feeling especially creative' (interview). With Abbi Patrix one gets the impression that his performance has the quality of being scripted, rather than improvised.

During the two performance of *To the Ends of the Earth* performed at the 2003 festival, there was little variation in the two scripts, apart from a short improvised comic dialogue between characters in the middle. Words, intonation and gesture all changed very little from one performance to the other.

This seems to be different from his first Beyond the Border performance in 1993, when Michael Harvey noted:

> There was rapport with the audience, complete familiarity with the *material*, because obviously he wasn't working from a script, he was telling you the story. Also he was using *informal* presentation, he was just a guy on a stage. (Interview)

The 1993 performance was in French, which may account for his 'complete familiarity with the material' and his ability to be not working from a script, but it was not only the text that showed lack of variation in 2003, but also the physical language that accompanied it. If it was Patrix's *informality* that impressed Harvey in 1993, then the 2003 performance was a more *formal* performance altogether, something significantly higher up the Performance Continuum. This may simply have been an artistic decision made for this particular show, of course, but Harvey's further comments possibly suggest a gradual drift away from informal simplicity to a more consciously stylized approach in Patrix's work over the years:

> Well, I'm glad I saw him do 'The Companion' first because I've since seen him do several things where he was more self-consciously theatrical. If I'd seen one of his other things I think I would have been less interested. What was interesting for me was that it was completely pared down. There was a theatrical consciousness there, but it was used for the benefit of the story. Whereas I've seen him do the same story – it must have been five years later – and it was much more overtly theatrical. And I didn't enjoy it as much. (Interview)

What does seem to be present in Patrix's work, however, is the remarkable rigour which Harvey refers to and the rapport that he is able to build with the audience in spite of the formality and styliza- tion. Patrix's style is not unlike that of Dario Fo, clearly emanating from a popular theatrical tradition, but Patrix 'plays' to the audience less than Fo and does not make use of the long introductions used by Fo in *Mistero Buffo*, which enabled him to familiarize himself with the audience. Patrix retains a certain formality in his style, although he will also occasionally address the audience directly in the middle of a story. His performance may be highly skilled, but it is not effortless – we are very aware that Patrix is working very hard on our behalf. It is a testament to Patrix's artistry that in spite of this formality, he is still able to generate a high level of *communitas* with his audience. He is, of course, fortunate that his reputation goes before him – his audience *expects* him to be good and that is half the battle won. Nevertheless it is that very rigour and focus that allow him to bring the audience in, and he creates a rare sense of intimacy, even when telling into a microphone.

Case Study 2: Mary Medlicott

In contrast to Abbi Patrix's festival performance, I would now like to discuss a performance given by Mary Medlicott at Bennett's Well Primary School in Solihull, Birmingham, on 14 July 2004. Bennett's Well is a relatively typical suburban state primary school in the UK, drawing from a mixed catchment area in terms of affluence and ethnicity, catering for children aged four to eleven with an attached nursery unit for children aged three and four.

The storyteller had been booked by the school for a whole day, the arrangements having been negotiated between the organizing teacher and the storyteller by telephone and letter in the weeks preceding the visit. Although this was to be a memorable day for the children, there was no publicity or programme material generated for the event and the children were merely informed that there was a special visitor in school. A number of sessions, each between thirty minutes and one hour in length, were planned for the day and were conducted on a class-by-class basis, ensuring a limit on the audience size of about thirty. On this particular occasion the storyteller was asked to con- centrate on the nursery and Key Stage 1 classes, that is, in the British system, children aged between three and seven. I was present for the afternoon, which included three storytelling sessions.

The first session was for the nursery children, about fifteen in total, and three teachers, and it is where the most noticeable contrast exists between Medlicott's and Patrix's approach. The first thing worthy of note is the arrangement of space. There is no formal performance area here. Medlicott is seated on a small, low chair, raising her only slightly above the level of the children, who are seated informally around her on the carpeted floor of the classroom. The other adults are seated on similar low chairs or on the carpet with the children. The teacher introduces Medlicott as the visiting storyteller and there is a buzz of anticipation amongst the children. They may not know what is in store for them, but they know they like stories and they are fully aware that this is a special occasion. But the storyteller is not over-hyped in any way by the teacher's introduction and its purpose is merely to help focus the children's attention. Medlicott, however, appears to be aware that such an introduction has inevitably raised the children's expectations and placed her on something of a pedestal. Unlike Patrix, though, who uses that pedestal in the service of his performance to formalize it and engender a sense of awe, Medlicott actively works against it. In fact, so important is it to her to dismantle any barrier there may be between herself and the audience, that the first fifteen minutes of the thirty-minute session are devoted to establishing the right kind of relationship between performer and audience, and it is one that as much as possible is based on an equal status. Whereas much as Patrix's performance may be located at the right-hand end of the Performance Continuum, Medlicott's may be placed much more to the left-hand extremity.

It is noticeable that there is a sense of calm about the way in which the session is conducted. There is no hurry to start the telling of the story, which will only begin when Medlicott is quite certain that the relationship between her and the children has been established at the right level. The first part of the session is, in fact, conducted as a structured, but informal and relaxed conversation. Medlicott intro-duces herself again, this time by her first name, and some of the children respond by telling her their names and often other items of personal information (such as ages, names of siblings and pets, and favourite stories). The children are encouraged to respond to Medlicott's comments and are given the time to do so. She also has with her a large colourful bag which contains a number of items such as small musical instruments, glove puppets and brightly coloured cloths. She takes a couple of these out for the children to look at, hold and comment upon. Among the items she shows the children is a frog puppet (deliberately chosen because by this time she had decided to tell a story about a frog) and some time is also spent practising frog noises with the children. Again this is all conducted with no sense of haste and it is only when Medlicott feels ready that she begins to tell the story. It is done without a formal announcement that the story is beginning, but is seamlessly woven into the introductory banter. Gradually one is aware that the story has begun. Clearly to make any kind of formal announcement would formalize the performance and undermine the careful preparatory work.

At first glance it may seem that this lengthy conversational introduction is inconsequential, but it is, in fact, part of a skilfully employed strategy designed to help the storytelling itself meet its objective. Not only is Medlicott carefully negotiating the nature of her relationship with the audience – that is, one that is largely informal and equal, whilst allowing her to retain the authority of the performer – but she is also establishing the ground rules for the performance. These are rules that allow her to retain control of the session and remain its focus (thus also establishing the importance of listening for the audience), but also, crucially, to grant permission to the audience to join in, question and generally contribute to the telling. It is noticeable that when the story begins, the children join in with verbal repetitions quite naturally, without any prompting whatsoever, and even begin adding physical gestures to illustrate the story. This is genuinely a piece of communal storytelling, where the roles of storyteller and audience become partially blurred. Medlicott herself describes this relationship as evidence of a particular mode of practice adopted by the storyteller:

> I have a mode in which I can talk which seems terribly simple and terribly relaxed, as if I've never thought about it at all, probably. Of course I've thought about it a great deal. ... You've got to tell a story in a way that gives the message, 'You too can do this. You're part of this. You can comment on it. You can work on bits of it. You can tell a story of your own, if you want.' So that has always been a very, very important part of my mode of storytelling. It's that sharing of creativity, it's not showing off that I want to do, it's not being better than others.   (Interview)

Most tellingly, at the end of the session, one of the children raised her hand and declared that she had a story to tell. Such occurrences are not that unusual for storytellers used to working with children and in most cases result in a very short retelling of a favourite fairy tale, film or television programme. In this case, however, the girl improvised a three-minute narrative (perfectly structured with a beginning, a middle and an end) involving the characters in Medlicott's story in a new adventure. This remarkable piece of storytelling from a particularly able four-year-old may well be the exception, rather than the rule, but it is difficult to imagine it having taken place, had it not been for Medlicott's carefully managed session.

The next session was with a class of Year 2 children (6–7 year olds) and was one hour long. Again Medlicott employed the same sense of calm and lack of haste, using a similar series of techniques to establish a democratic relationship with the audience. This session comprised a number of stories from her international repertoire[5] – some of them chosen in direct response to a comment from a child. It was clear that the stories were also being chosen and delivered with the children's age in mind. These stories were longer and more complex in narrative terms than that told to the nursery children and were interwoven with comments to reinforce the listeners' existing knowledge of story and narrative structures. For example, one story began as follows: 'One day ... because there's always a "one day" in stories, isn't there?' Such asides may seem to be coincidental but are, in fact, carefully considered. The Year 2 children were equally quick to recognize repetitive verbal and gestural patterns with which they could join in.

The final session took place with Reception children (four- to five-year-olds in their first year of compulsory education), although some of the nursery children also joined the group. This was a short session at the end of the school day and likewise comprised a series of activities whereby the children were encouraged to join in and even to contribute to the stories. The session, and the whole day, culminated in a sense of hilarity and celebration.

Conclusion

Bearing in mind the radical roots of the storytelling movement, one question that might legitimately arise from an observation of both Patrix and Medlicott is the extent to which their work is governed by a political stance. Although Patrix's work may be compared to that of Dario Fo in performance terms, Patrix's show contains none of the explicit class-based politics of *Mistero Buffo*. Patrix's political stance is more an implicit and gentle internationalism, demonstrated in the stories by the multicultural nature of his material and a general concern for and sympathy with the underdog. Unlike Fo, Patrix is not interested in using his art as a weapon in the service of class struggle, but sees it rather as an international language promoting understanding across all cultures. Patrix's politics certainly owe more to Brook than to Brecht.

Medlicott too is an internationalist, but that is merely the foundation to a more radical approach to her work, although she would not describe herself as a political storyteller *per se*. Many of her stories more directly address issues of empowerment and that is very much reflected in the way she works. Where Medlicott is most overtly political is in the way she concerns herself with storytelling as a vehicle for empowering the individual audience member, particularly in her educational work. Hers is much more the politics of the contemporary community arts movement, with a keen impulse to democratize storytelling.

The examples of Abbi Patrix and Mary Medlicott could, in many ways, hardly be more different. They are both examples of performative or platform storytelling, yet in Medlicott's case the platform has become all but invisible. Of course, much is determined by the context of the performances – Patrix is performing to a large, predominantly adult audience at a festival, whereas Medlicott is working with small groups of young children within an educational environment. No doubt if Medlicott were performing at a festival and Patrix at a school we would be talking about very different things. Nevertheless, we can still detect a fundamental difference between the approaches of the two storytellers towards their art. The audience leaving Patrix's performance are in no doubt that they have witnessed a 'cultural performance', a highly skilful performance by a virtuoso performer. On the other hand, Medlicott's performance has been far less about a display of skill. In fact, it has been almost effortless, with the storyteller's skills almost invisible. The audience members have been active participants rather than passive consumers, and are encouraged to go and tell the stories for themselves, in what Medlicott herself describes as 'a democracy of participation' (interview). It is not that Medlicott dislikes being cast in the role of formal performer, but is more about establishing the right kind of performer-identity:

I love being a performer in the appropriate circumstances. I love to put my show on and have people come and be there, but there is a way in which I put myself forward that suggests that we all have stories and that there's a common strand between us. I do like that and I think I want to make storytelling feel like part of our common fabric of our lives.   (Interview)

In many ways, it has more in common with some of the practices described in the next chapter, on 'Applied Storytelling', than it does with most platform storytelling and is perhaps the point at which both sets of practice meet.

4 Applied Storytelling

The term 'applied storytelling' is being used here to mean everything that is not platform storytelling. It covers a huge range of work and it is the intention of this chapter to give an overview of that range. In fact, applied storytelling often involves some platform storytelling, but it is usually at a low intensity and rather informal and it is never the central part of the work. It is sometimes used as a catalyst, but never anything more, and its aim is not to place the storyteller on a platform to be admired, but rather to engage the interest of the audience in participating in their own storytelling.

'Participation' is a key word here. After a fashion, it could be argued that the early storytelling pioneers from the public libraries and education boards on both sides of the Atlantic (such as Marie Shedlock, Ruth Sawyer, Eileen Colwell and others) were involved in applied storytelling since their work was not following a perform-ance agenda, but integrated into literacy programmes to encourage children to read. However, the central impulse for applied storytelling emerges from the community arts movement, which itself emerged from the counter-cultural movement of the late 1960s.

Underpinning the community arts movement was the political drive to reinvent the relationship between artist and audience, whereby the audience was effectively the passive consumer of the product of the individual creative genius. The community arts movement sought to bring about a far more egalitarian relationship between artist and audience, where they became equal partners in the making of art. On one level this resulted in theatre companies producing shows that spoke directly to their audiences (rather than some notion of high, worthy art) and dealt with the issues that affected them. This still, however, retained the audience in the role of passive consumer and soon another principle of the community arts movement had been established, namely a belief in the absolute creative potential of all human beings and that, by participating in the arts, everybody could have their creativity unlocked and become makers of art, rather than consumers. The role of the artist was no longer simply to produce art, but to enable others, through participation, to make their own art – the ultimate act of democratization.

The fact that storytelling was rooted in the everyday – it is something that everybody does at some level – and its love of the amateur[1] made it a popular form amongst those artists inspired by the politics of the early community arts movement. Ever since the early days of the revival, storytelling has been applied to a whole range of projects that have sought to democratize the means of cultural production, by either giving people the due acknowledgement for their own storytelling or providing them with the skills and confidence to become effective storytellers themselves. Other projects have used storytelling as a tool to address other agendas, such as health and social inclusion. The examples included in this chapter are wide-ranging and typical, but not exhaustive.

The primary form for applied storytelling is the 'workshop', although we should be prepared to use the term very loosely to mean any forum whereby the performer acts as a facilitator and the audience become active participants. Workshops are designed to suit the aims of the particular project and a workshop for a project working with prisoners can be very different from a workshop for a project with the confused elderly. It is also important to different-iate between workshops which are part of a broader applied story-telling project (even if those are skills-based workshops) and those workshops run by eminent platform storytellers, whose participants are already involved in the storytelling movement, and the purpose of which is to make the participants better platform storytellers. These follow what we might call the masterclass model and involve a very different, hierarchical relationship between workshop leader and participant. Approaches to applied storytelling necessarily reject the 'star' system that has begun to develop around platform story-telling – politically speaking it is the intention of applied storytelling forms to dismantle the very platform on which the performer is placed. Indeed, applied storytelling can often be non-performative.

Whilst most professional storytellers will be involved in both platform and applied storytelling, it is also clear that the two forms can at times be fundamental opposites in the way that they define the storyteller–audience relationship and the creative process and it is hardly surprising that most storytellers prefer one or the other.

Storytelling in Education

The storytelling movement has been remarkably successful in establishing storytelling as a mainstream activity within schools. Regardless of a particular storyteller's preference for a particular way of working, there are very few storytellers for whom work in schools does not fill a significant part of their diary. It is the kind of work for which storytellers are most in demand. Nevertheless, there is a wide variation in the kind of work that a storyteller may be asked to undertake within a school and, even though it will all seek to address the educational agenda, it could not all be identified as applied storytelling. In fact, because applied storytelling always works best in the context of a *series* of engagements with the storyteller, budgetary restrictions within public education mean that most storytelling in schools is simply a one-off visit for a special occasion, such as a Book Week, in which case the platform storytelling model invariably applies. This is particularly the case in the United States, where it is not uncommon for a storyteller to be asked to perform on stage, with a microphone, to the whole school of several hundred pupils. Even in Britain, where the more usual model is for a storyteller to spend a whole day in a school, travelling from classroom to classroom, telling to much smaller audiences in more intimate surroundings, the storyteller in schools is employed primarily as a performer who, it is hoped, will enthuse and inspire the pupils to greater reading and storytelling themselves. Occasionally, the storyteller will also be asked to run a short skills workshop, usually with the older children.

This is very different, however, from applied storytelling, which usually is planned around a series of visits by a storyteller over a period of anything from a few weeks to a whole school year and will typically address a broader agenda than simply trying to make the pupils into more enthusiastic readers and better storytellers. The storyteller will not primarily be held up as an exemplar of excellence for the pupils to emulate, but rather will be employed as a facilitator attempting to unlock a child's creativity. Such projects are expensive to fund because of the often lengthy nature of the work and require significant planning on the part of the storyteller, so are usually left to those storytellers particularly dedicated to the broad application of storytelling in education.

Jack Zipes, in addition to his career as Professor of German at the University of Minnesota, also organizes storytelling programmes at public schools with the Minneapolis Children's Theater, which are documented in his books *Creative Storytelling* (1995) and *Speaking Out* (2004). These hugely successful projects are driven not by a desire to turn all the children into expert storytellers, but to enable them to develop strategies for taking control of their own lives, through encouraging creative independent thought – what Zipes calls 'becoming storytellers of their own lives'. These are projects inspired by the need for social action, projects that attempt to equip children with the necessary tools for creative survival and the building of meaningful communities. The Italian Marxist educator Gianni Rodari's maxim that ' "Every possible use of words should be made available to every single person". ... Not because everyone should be an artist but because no one should be a slave' (Rodari, 1996, p. 4) was never more appropriate. Not coincidentally, Zipes is also Rodari's English translator.

Creative Storytelling and 'Neighborhood Bridges'

The Neighborhood Bridges Project is a year-long programme of storytelling that has developed out of Zipes's previous work within education and has been running successfully in Minneapolis/St Pauls since 1998 (see Zipes, 2004, pp. 63–83, for a full description). Zipes describes the project's guiding principles as follows:

> The overall tendency in the mass media and advertising is to make good consumers of children. In contrast, we seek to enable children to take control of their own lives. Not that they won't consume. But they may reflect more about their own commodification. We do not, therefore, dismiss or denigrate popular culture. We try to use it against itself by exposing contradictions. We do not offer solutions or resolutions but alternative ways of thinking and acting.   (Zipes, 2004, p. 66)

Zipes's work has had a profound effect on the storytelling movements on both sides of the Atlantic. He has always remained connected to, but ultimately separate from the storytelling movement, which he often criticizes as becoming increasingly commercial and less subversive, especially in America, in spite of its radical and idealistic roots. Instead he has positioned himself firmly within the tradition of the public scholar, providing support and authoritative constructive criticism to both American and British storytellers, alongside the production of his many scholarly translations of collections from the European fairy tale tradition.

The involvement of theatre companies in the projects devised by Zipes is by no means accidental. Creative drama is an indispensable partner to storytelling for projects such as Neighborhood Bridges to be at their most effective:

> The sense of storytelling that we try to instill in children cannot be accomplished if we do not explore and use all the arts, especially creative drama, which involves all the skills and talents of the children and opens their eyes to their potential. (Zipes, 2004, p. xviii)

Furthermore, it is within the sphere of much children's theatre that he recognizes the continuing radical ethos that is a prerequisite for producing work that effectively challenges the social, political and economic orders that shape children into becoming good consumers and well-balanced, compliant citizens, rather than independent, self-confident thinkers. Zipes is particularly admiring of the work of Berlin-based Grips Theater[2] in this respect, whose work he describes as 'politically subversive or threatening, and thus enlightening and empowering' (2004, p. 256). Furthermore, Zipes acknowledges the central role of creative drama in allowing children to experiment with narratives and attain an almost Brechtian 'distancing effect that enables the children to step back from themselves, to step out of themselves and to become someone new' (Zipes, 1995, p. 11). In this sense the division of storytelling from acting becomes both false and unhelpful.

The job of the storyteller, according to Zipes, is principally 'to demonstrate how the ordinary can become extraordinary' (Zipes, 1995, p. 6) and to 'intervene with teachers in schools to instill confidence in children so that they can readily acquire the instruments and skills they will need to determine their destinies' (Zipes, 1995, p. 5). To this end Zipes is insistent on two things – first, the importance of a sustained project and partnership between storyteller and school, so that the work takes place over a whole term or more, with the storyteller visiting the school on a weekly basis, which he sees as crucial to successfully meeting any educational and developmental goals. In contrast to this, the more usual format of a one-off storyteller visit is of little value, claims Zipes, as it effectively works against the storyteller making any lasting impact on the culture of the school community. To do so the storyteller must intervene regularly over a prolonged period.

Secondly, Zipes calls for a redefining of the role of the storyteller as performer, a role which is further encouraged by the one-off visit model. For Zipes, 'Storytellers are not just performers. They may perform, but they are first and foremost listeners and animators' (Zipes, 1995, p. 7). In addition, storytellers should not simply enter the school and deliver a set programme determined by themselves, but should be negotiating the project with the teachers in advance, in order to harness *their* expertise and knowledge, as well as securing their commitment to any project and its aims. Here storytellers are not selling products to consumers, but generally collaborating with a range of other professionals to achieve real and lasting change.

Zipes's programmes typically involve a range of creative exercises which revolve around variants of well-known folk and fairy tales, designed to equip children with a knowledge of the structures and common motifs pertaining to the fairy tale genre. Pupils are encouraged to act out stories, create new endings and twists and turns in well-known tales and to create new stories from a range of familiar and unfamiliar characters and motifs. Fundamentally the children are taught the possibilities and the liberating potential of the folktale form, rather than the restrictions of genre. They are encouraged to subvert conventions at will, exploring alternatives and transformations through a creative mix of drama, writing, drawing, speaking and listening. The aim is to allow children to become masters of the genre so that they can then use that skill to articulate and determine their own aspirations and futures. If the primary function of storytelling is to make sense of our experiences, then this kind of work is a rehearsal for the challenges that lie ahead, equipping children with the ability to be critical and questioning observers and empowering them to make their own choices and decisions.

Moreover, this work is not designed to produce a sense of *wonder* at 'traditions' or the skills and artistry of the storyteller – it is not to demonstrate the 'wisdom of the ancients', but to illuminate the necessity of our own wisdom for 'an age when lies often pass for truth in the mass media and the public realm' (Zipes, 1995, p. 225). The measure of success for Zipes is not the volume of applause at the end of a performance or the observation of a roomful of engrossed children, mouths agape in wonderment and eyes transfixed as they are transported to an enchanted world. Instead it is that teachers and children will take the place of the storyteller to become their own storytellers. As Zipes says of the Neighborhood Bridges Project: 'we have a slogan, borrowed from Bertolt Brecht, that keeps us fairly honest: we do our best to make ourselves dispensable' (Zipes, 2004, p. 68).

The Developing Schools Project Storytelling Residency

The Developing Schools Project (DSP) Storytelling Residency is not unique in its scope and ambition as a storytelling project, but it is, on the one hand, unusual for a dedicated storytelling-in-education project to be able to operate at such an ambitious level, yet also typical of the kinds of demands that the education sector had increasingly begun to make of the storytelling movement by the mid-1990s. The residency involved a resident storyteller, Patrick Ryan, supported by a team of visiting professional storytellers (Liz Weir, Billy Teare, TUUP[3] and myself) across six secondary schools (ages 12–18) in Derry, Strabane and Omagh in Northern Ireland in the summer and autumn terms of 1997. The rationale and methodology of the project drew heavily on Zipes's work in the United States, and the fact that the official report on the project (Ryan, 1997) begins with a lengthy quotation from Zipes's translation of Rodari's *The Grammar of Fantasy* lays testament to this.

As a storytelling project, the residency was significant in two ways. First, it was to be a residency of a substantial length, a radical departure from the usual model of the one-off visit by a storyteller, in order to allow a much greater degree of developmental and participative work. As Paddy Ward, the English Advisor for the Western Education and Library Board, states, the project was 'a wonderful opportunity to provide **sustained** emphasis over a lengthy period – something which has not been possible before' (Ryan, 1997, p. v). Secondly, it was to be a project that worked across the entire curriculum, whereas it was normal for storytelling in secondary schools to be located entirely within the English and Drama departments. Arguably the most interesting aspect of the project was the use of stories in new curriculum areas. For example, in history, students who were studying the Second World War might collect reminiscences from grandparents and elderly members of the community; science students might look at cyclical or cumulative stories (such as 'The Old Woman who Lived in a Vinegar Bottle' or 'The Old Woman and the Pig'[4]) and then apply these narrative principles to natural cycles (such as the Water Cycle) or to, say, the Food Chain or the chain of events in a chemical reaction. Alternatively, they might look at traditional myths that offered some explanation of natural phenomena and compare those explanations with those offered by modern Western science;[5] mathematics students might concentrate on the logic of riddles, especially number riddles, and deconstruct the mathematical principles behind them.[6] The Northern Ireland context is also significant in that the project was innovative in working across a range of schools from both sides of the community divide.

In the days immediately after the introduction of the National Curriculum into British state schools,[7] professional storytellers were still enough of a novelty for schools to limit their use of them to a one-off visit. However, as storytelling became more common in schools and teachers saw the possibilities of using storytelling (and storytellers saw the possibilities of working in education), the schools began to be more demanding of storytellers. No longer was it enough to be able to sit in the corner of the classroom and tell a good story well; teachers began to ask how storytellers might actively help to develop the curriculum. It became a case of asking storytellers to apply their storytelling to a much broader educational agenda.

Even now the one-off visit remains the standard model for storytellers working in schools, but this is more often due to financial restrictions rather than a lack of vision on the part of the schools or the storytellers. The DSP Residency was a significant step in developing the role of storytellers in education and its resounding success, all thoroughly documented, helped secure funding for further innovative projects of this nature. The project formed part of a three-year-long wider initiative to raise standards across the curriculum in disadvantaged schools, and its principal aim was 'to use a storyteller to raise students' self-esteem and confidence, and to motivate them in their studies, through oracy' (Ryan, 1997, p. 6). In addition the project aimed 'to model new or different practices' that would have a *lasting* impact on the pupils and the delivery of the curriculum. It was the intention that the storytelling would not end as soon as the residency finished. The residency itself took place over a twenty-week period, with each school receiving twelve days of contact time with a storyteller to work towards previously negotiated objectives. In effect, the twenty weeks were divided into two ten-week periods with the first period concentrated within the English curriculum and the second period operating across a much wider range of subjects. The work of the storytellers covered concerts, workshops, guidance (that is, further development of pupils as storytellers) and consultancy (that is, the provision of advice and resources to teachers) (Ryan, 1997, p. 7), although the exact programme of work inevitably varied significantly from school to school.

The project was considered a substantial success by all concerned, from pupils to members of the Senior Advisory Service, and culminated in a storytelling event involving almost forty young storytellers from the schools involved, at a conference to discuss the wider Developing Schools Project across Northern Ireland. One of the most significant outcomes of the project was the positive response of teachers in maths and science subjects who had previously not seen the relevance or value of storytelling to their own subject area. The residency's lasting legacy was the establishment of

> a culture of storytelling in all the schools. Not all students and staff may be telling stories. But all of them are now aware of the art form, when they may not have been before, and more importantly they are aware of its potential for use in education.   (Ryan, 1997, p. 15)

The DSP Storytelling Residency remains a model of good practice for much storytelling-in-education work that has followed.

Storytelling and Therapy

Much of the work in this chapter might be justifiably described as 'therapeutic', or at least as having some kind of therapeutic benefit. If therapy is about improving or maintaining mental and physical well-being, then much storytelling work that seeks to culturally empower people can be described as therapeutic. Furthermore, the telling and retelling of personal-experience stories can promote self-esteem or even purge some demons, and, in the field of geriatric care, reminiscence work has proved to be beneficial to the health of the elderly, and in particular to those suffering from the early stages of dementia. Jack Zipes acknowledges that 'storytelling has indeed its therapeutic and cathartic moment, and storytellers must be aware of that moment' (Zipes, 1995, p. 224), but he also warns that they 'cannot and should not pretend to be therapists, gurus or social workers. They should not pretend that stories have a magic power of healing the woes of children and the community, that stories can work wonders for each troublesome situation' (1995, p. 223). It is the difference between accepting that storytelling has therapeutic value and can be a useful tool in therapy, because stories 'can powerfully communicate what it is like to be in the world and can provide opportunities to change our view of reality' (Crawford, Brown and

Crawford, 2004, p. 1), and claiming that the stories themselves are endowed with the power to heal, cure and mend. It is certainly important, in any discussion of storytelling and therapy, to differentiate between the work of a therapist working long-term with story as a tool, storytelling as a technique or a storyteller as a colleague, and the kind of 'prescription' approach occasionally seen, whereby the storyteller becomes the healer, diagnosing and treating all manner of complaint by dispensing the 'right' story.

Both the Society for Storytelling and the National Storytelling Network have special interest groups devoted to storytelling and healing, which embrace an appropriately wide range of work. Lapidus, an organization whose membership includes artists, health care professionals, academics and teachers, and that is funded by the Arts Council of England, exists 'to promote the use of the literary arts ... for personal development' (www.lapidus.org.uk), not limiting itself to storytelling, but also embracing fictional writing, poetry, autobiography and journal writing. It is a highly professional organization which supports regional networks, holds conferences, publishes research and promotes 'appropriate training and ethical research in the field' (www.lapidus.org.uk).

It is important to recognize the extremely broad church that is 'storytelling and therapy', from the anti-bullying work of Raymond Chodzinski in Canada (see Chodzinski, 2004), who uses personal storytelling as a tool to address 'this insidious form of school and community-based violence' (Chodzinski, 2004, p. xii), to the Waldorf-inspired personal and spiritual development work of American psychotherapist Nancy Mellon. Among some storyteller-therapists, especially those who make use of myth and traditional, rather than autobiographical, stories, it is not uncommon to find a neo-Jungian outlook, sometimes influenced by aspects of New-Ageism. In addition to Jung, the main influences on this particular school of thought are Joseph Campbell, Bruno Bettelheim and (to a lesser extent) Sigmund Freud, and find some level of scholarly legitimacy and expression in the writings of people like Robert Bly (*Iron John*) and Carlissa Pinkola Estes (*Women Who Run with the Wolves*).

It comes in for particular criticism from Zipes and others because it is a school of thought that can ignore the social, political and social dimensions to stories and storytelling, suggesting instead 'that fairy tales can heal all of our wounds and solve all of our problems if we learn how to read them and follow their symbols' (Zipes, 1995, p. 223). These symbols are essentially Jungian archetypes, which rest on the assumption that fairy tales and myths are repositories of a *universal* meaning and wisdom. In other words, such analysis ignores any scholarship that suggests that meaning in stories is variable and negotiated in the moment of telling between teller and listener, and instead insists that at its core a story must have the same meaning and resonance for everyone, irrespective of the age, race, gender and class of teller and listener, and the context in which the story is told. It is also based upon two further questionable tenets, namely that all stories can be traced back to some authoritative *Ur-text* from which all other variants worldwide have emanated, and that this original text is the purest, most unadulterated and *truest* text and that consequently all variants of a story have been in terminable decline ever since.

To be fair, whatever criticism may be levelled at the scholarship of Bly (who comes in for particular censure from Zipes for his misrepresentation of the highly edited and modified Grimm Brothers' version of 'Iron Hans' as the authoritative text, which forms the basis of *Iron John* (see Zipes, 1994, pp. 96–118)) and even Campbell, the changing understanding of folklore scholarship is unlikely to be of much concern to the trained Jungian therapist, who will measure the success of therapy on a patient-by-patient basis. Nevertheless the tendency to decipher the significance of stories as if they were codes to be broken by endowing narrative symbols with unchangeable meanings, can lead to a kind of 'story by prescription' mentality whereby a person's health can be ensured by simply prescribing the correct story. Ultimately that can only lead to a neglect of the social and political meaning of story and its *real* power and potential to effect change. That may be the business of therapists but, it is argued, should not be the business of the storyteller.

To develop the argument further, let us briefly consider two specific examples of the use of storytelling within therapy. The first is quoted in Dick Leith's incisive *Fairy Tales and Therapy* (1998) and the second is from Alida Gersie's *Earthtales* (1992). Leith approaches his subject as both a storyteller and a patient of therapy and raises a number of important questions, including why it is that fairy tales, rather than any other kind of story, are considered to be of particular value in therapy. To do so attaches the therapeutic power to the story itself, rather than the act of storytelling. It is clear, therefore, that the Jungian approach does not take into account the therapeutic benefits of storytelling practices, such as reminiscence, in their own right. Leith rightly claims that the 'notion that the fairytale is essentially oral has influenced the thought and practice of many psychoanalysts and therapists, particularly those of a Jungian persuasion' (Leith, 1998, p. 11) and that *oral* stories are 'associated ... with humanity at its collective and most *primal* levels' (Leith, 1998, p. 11). It therefore follows that fairy tales and stories from 'primitive' cultures, which are furthest from the risk of contamination by literate cultures, are most open to accurate interpretation through the means of archetypes. Leith also points out, however, two key problems with such an assumption; first, that it is wrong to assume that stories only change in literate societies, as if pre-literate societies are somehow more homogenous, and secondly that many of the stories used by therapists (and storytellers) are sourced from highly edited literary collections made by nineteenth-century folklorists, such as the Brothers Grimm. The case study with which Leith chooses to open his discussion, illustrates the point well.

It tells of a non-communicative patient who was lured out of her (ultimately destructive) inner world by means of the therapist using the story of 'Sleeping Beauty'. The therapist is likened to the character of the prince, struggling to find a way through the forest of thorns in order to free the sleeping princess (the patient) from her prison of enchantment. Like all good fairy tales there is a happy ending and the story is the magic kiss that allows the therapist to waken the patient. There is an assumption that the *story* of 'Sleeping Beauty' has had a curative effect upon the patient, and this is true if we are to believe this version of events, and we have no reason not to. Indeed we must acknowledge that the therapist has done a good job and we must be pleased for both the therapist and the patient. However, for the story to have had this effect, we must also assume that both therapist and patient have understood the story in the same way – that there is a shared universal meaning. Leith, however, is quick to point out that there is no evidence to support such an assumption. In fact, there is no evidence that any storytelling has actually taken place. The therapist and patient have merely exchanged observations as to how their situations and feelings correspond to characters in the story. As Leith says:

> The therapeutic process seems to need only parts of the story, not the story as a whole. It is questionable whether either participant could have readily re-told the story without much memory-searching and perhaps creative re-composition. Indeed the account hints at the possibility that the participants may have first encountered the story in very different ways.
>
> (Leith, 1998, p. 9)

In other words, the therapist's work is based on a highly selective use of certain aspects of the story. In a way, there is nothing wrong with this if it results in a clinical success. On the other hand, however, it has little to do with storytelling, as such, and it is dangerous to make claims about the therapeutic value of storytelling or the meaning of stories based upon it. As Leith concludes, 'we need to see fairytales as offering us no more, but also no less, than a source of metaphor' (Leith, 1998, p. 19). The real danger is, says Zipes, that 'by focusing on childish enchantment and happy ends' (Zipes, 1995, p. 222), we avoid tackling the difficult and uncomfortable issues that fairy tales offer us the opportunity to confront. According to Zipes, we forget that 'Hansel and Gretel' deals with child abandonment, or that in 'Sleeping Beauty' the princess is not simply woken by the prince, but is raped by him.

Alida Gersie is a highly respected dramatherapist and academic who has published widely on the uses of story within therapy programmes, as well as having practised extensively in the field. Her book *Earthtales* is at face value less to do with therapy than it is to do with helping us re-evaluate the relationship between humanity and the environment. The techniques covered in the book, however, belong to the same school of thought and include the use of story as a tool for personal and group development. Once again the stories are 'drawn from the culture of tribal people' (back cover). In other words they are afforded greater value because of their (supposed) antiquity and the fact that they have emanated from tribal (i.e. pre-literate) societies. Stories (especially old and oral ones) are presented as a cure-all for the world's problems – in this case, 'for understanding the many ways in which we value and devalue our beautiful green and blue planet' (Gersie, 1992, p. 1). Gersie's central claim is that she and others are 'using ancient folktales and myths to enable people from different cultures and backgrounds to reach out towards each other' (Gersie, 1992, p. 1).

Of course, the central purpose of Gersie's work is to empower individuals and effect change, and in this sense her work is not dissimilar to many of the projects described in this chapter. Furthermore, there is a clear political agenda to her work, even if it is more concentrated on personal (and in this case, environmental) change, rather than social change – empowering the individual to flourish within society, rather than empowering the individual (or community) to *change* society.

I am not offering up this analysis as a criticism of Gersie's undoubtedly effective work, but to highlight its differences from other forms of applied storytelling. At the beginning of *Earthtales*, she offers the reader three case studies to illustrate her technique. The first concerns an eight-year-old girl who is the victim of bullying and having fought back against the bullies, has lost the fight. Arguably more importantly, the girl is surrounded by the brutality of poverty in her everyday life. She lives, we are told, 'in a flat on (a) tough housing estate' (Gersie, 1992, p. 2) and is responsible, even at such an early age, for the after-school care of her two younger brothers. From what we know of her social situation, it is hardly surprising that the girl's 'face showed a perpetual frown' (Gersie, 1992, p. 2). When faced with the taunts of the bullies, she responds in the only way she knows how – with physical violence. When she enters the centre where Gersie works, she is not only wearing the physical scars of her fight, but the emotional ones too – she is crying, but so is her brother who is still clinging to her. Gersie's solution is to tell the girl 'an ancient Bushman myth' (Gersie, 1992, p. 2).

The story clearly has the desired effect on her by calming her down to the point that she can go off and play, calmly returning to inform Gersie when the bullies arrive at the centre. This enables all concerned to sit down, talk through the issues and bring an end to the bullying. This is clearly a success and Gersie's skills as a counsellor and facilitator should not be underestimated here. Furthermore, the story has a lasting effect on the girl – she remembers the story and refers back to it in conversation some time later. The story has no doubt provided the girl with a useful tool for understanding the situation that arose and how best to deal with it.

It is an interesting example, because, unlike the Sleeping Beauty example, it involves the telling of a complete story previously unknown to the listener. The story is not being used so much as a source of metaphor to unlock a process, but rather the storyteller is presented as a guardian of the wisdom that is contained in the story, which is then revealed to the listener, who is consequently enlightened. Without the intervention of the storyteller with the story, the listener would have remained in ignorance.

The counter-argument, however, might question the extent to which the story has actually effected change or even resolved a conflict situation. The story seems to deal with the immediate problem – that of two young hysterical children. It calms them down and allows them to start functioning again normally. However, it could be argued that the bigger issue of the bullying is actually solved by the skilled negotiating of the counsellor, involving all parties in a dialogue. The story illustrates the importance of standing up to bullies, but it simply makes the girl feel a bit better about herself and restores to her some degree of personal dignity. As important as that is, it is not a story that is addressed to the bullies or even that offers solutions to bullying – that is done in later discussion. Perhaps most importantly, neither does it offer any hope for change to the social situation in which *all* the children find themselves. In fact, it tends to suggest that injustice is something that the children must learn to endure, rather than change. This approach, therefore, actively ignores the social context of storytelling and what fails to be recognized is that the real problem here is not bullying alone – although that has to be dealt with – but social deprivation. Far better, it could be argued, to use the Bushman myth as a way of allowing the children to tell their *own* stories so that they can better understand their situations and change them.

It is not difficult to see why the writings of Jung, Campbell, Bettelheim, Bly et al. should hold a particular attraction for many involved in storytelling. They appear to offer simple and alternative solutions to the many ills of modern society by purporting to access an ancient, forgotten wisdom that lies encoded in traditional stories. Furthermore, this approach seems to reaffirm the importance and power of storytelling; not only the power to entertain, but the power to heal society's and the individual's wounds.

Having said that, many therapists and psychologists are certainly doing good and important work using story as a way of breaking down barriers with patients or approaching problems from different perspectives. The power of *metaphor* is ever strong. Furthermore, much of the neo-Jungian work that takes place in self-help groups and the like, is largely harmless at worst, and at some level probably beneficial to many of the participants. However, it is still an area fraught with problems and controversy.

Leaving aside the question of the sustainability of the scholarship that underpins it, there is often an ethical minefield to negotiate. If storytellers present themselves as great repositories of wisdom with special healing powers, then not only do they run the risk of being exposed as charlatans and mountebanks, but they come dangerously close to encroaching on the territory of trained and skilled professionals of a different order. Storytellers are not necessarily therapists, any more than therapists are necessarily storytellers. Alida Gersie is, unusually, both, but not everyone is Alida Gersie.

The greatest irony, though, is this. By presenting storytelling as the panacea for all our ills, it would seem that it is elevated to the highest possible level of significance as a human activity. Its importance may be undeniable, and it is certainly not the job of this book to argue otherwise (or even to undermine the excellent work done by trained therapists and psychiatrists), but by ignoring the political and social dimensions of stories and storytelling, it may ultimately end up by *undervaluing* it.

One of the most interesting pieces of work in this field in recent years, precisely because it bridges the gaps between the therapeutic and social aspects of storytelling and also between applied and platform storytelling, is *Take These Chains from my Heart*, performed by Taffy Thomas and Janet Russell and written by singer-songwriter Jim Woodland. In 1984, while still in his thirties and in the middle of a performance, Thomas suffered a stroke which left him unable to speak and with partial paralysis. Thomas turned to storytelling as a kind of self-therapy, which enabled him to regain the power of speech. *Take These Chains from my Heart* is a show that is based upon the story of his own recovery, whilst also addressing the wider issues of disability and illness for audiences of both patients and their carers. It is at once autobiographical *and* depersonalized through the use of folk story and song, taking 'the form of a narrative linking traditional tales and newly written songs round the theme of physical and psychological recovery from a stroke' (www.harbourtownrecords.com/Russell.html). The show played to great critical acclaim in a range of public and institutional settings. What is important to note, however, is that Thomas did not use the show as part of his own therapy (the show did not tour until the mid-1990s), nor did he target the show at individuals or groups as part of their therapy programmes. Nevertheless, he is fully aware of the therapeutic aspects of the show. By telling the story of his own illness and recovery, he is not only attempting to break the taboo and prejudice surrounding disability and illness, but also publicly declaring solidarity with those who have also suffered in this way, offering a message of both hope and defiance. The show, claims Thomas, 'has more laughter than tears and is heartening for anyone who has suffered major illness' (www.taffythomas.co.uk), and it is this laughter in the face of adversity which ensures that the social context of illness is not forgotten.

Community Storytelling

In 1992, when I was still making my living from being a storyteller, I was invited by Sally Tonge, then Literature Development Worker for

Cornwall, and Phil Webb of Restormel Arts (the arts promotion agency for the district of Restormel in mid-Cornwall) to become involved in a storytelling project based around the china clay villages of the area. This was partly as a result of an intergenerational project I had developed on the Ernesettle housing estate in Plymouth, where young people (who were routinely blamed for the vandalism that was occurring on the estate) would collect the stories and experiences of the older residents (who generally did the blaming and felt intimidated by the young people). The plan for the clay villages was similar, but on a more ambitious scale.

We would begin working with the teenagers through the schools and youth clubs, whilst at the same time talking to other community groups and (considering that these were communities defined by the industry that has left, and continues to leave, its physical mark on the landscape) the local trades unions. The result was a project that lasted three years and generated two modestly produced books of stories, collected and edited by a group of mainly young people from across the community, a number of 'concerts' involving local storytellers, a series of short broadcasts on local radio and a teachers' pack for use in schools.

I am not for one moment suggesting that the Clay Stories Project is an exemplar in any way, nor am I suggesting that it was particularly innovative, but rather that the beliefs and values that underpinned and drove it were typical of a certain type of storytelling work. It was certainly not a project without its faults and problems, but it none the less serves as a useful example. Besides, it is a project that I know intimately.

The Clay Stories Project was by no means alone in attempting to engage meaningfully with communities and fundamentally redefine the relationship between storyteller and audience. There were, and continue to be, many similar, and equally worthwhile projects, on both sides of the Atlantic (for example Jim May's work in Illinois with local senior citizens, or the intergenerational and cross-community work of Liz Weir and others in Northern Ireland), and each is innovative in its own way, seeking to push back and redraw the boundaries of what storytelling does and can do. There is often a political rationale sustaining this kind of work, whether that is simply a desire to build bridges across divided communities by the sharing of experiences, or whether it is another small step along the road of cultural egalitarianism, through blurring the distinction between the producers and consumers of art.

Certainly that was the feeling amongst those of us working on the Clay Stories Project. On one level the work was innovative in that there were few storytellers in Britain who were working in this way with teenagers at this time, but we were also very aware that we were working within a variety of traditions, and that we owed much of our methodology to ways of working that had been established by others. In a way, the project could be firmly located within the tradition of community arts practice that had grown up since the late 1960s, whereby the artist's role was to become embedded within a community, giving voice to its concerns and aspirations, but also to act as a facilitator. In this role, by teaching the skills of cultural production, the artist would enable the community to act as its own spokesperson. The artist would no longer act on behalf of the community but would *empower* the community to act on its own behalf. Ultimately the aim of the community artist was to bring a community to a point where the artist was no longer needed, where the community had the tools to express itself culturally – or at least to the point where professionally produced art existed alongside and on an equal footing with community-produced art. This spirit of democracy ran through the Clay Stories Project and many other similar projects as well.

The Clay Stories Project was, however, also informed by other traditions, most notably those of youth workers, reminiscence workers (especially the work of reminiscence theatre companies such as Medium Fair in the 1970s and Age Exchange in the 1980s and beyond), educationalists (especially the work of Harold and Betty Rosen, who have worked extensively with autobiography), folklorists (such as Sandra Dolby-Stahl, who has argued convincingly for the consideration of personal experience stories as legitimate expressions of folklore), writers (for example, the poet and photographer Leon MacAuley, who had worked with the Verbal Arts Centre in Derry, Northern Ireland, in the early 1990s, to collect oral testimonies from residents of the Fountain area of the city, and which were then transcribed and published as blank verse) and, perhaps most importantly, oral historians. Here the names of George Ewart Evans in Britain and Studs Terkel in America most readily spring to mind.

Ewart Evans was born in Abercynon, South Wales, but made his name as a recorder of oral history from the rural working classes of his adopted Suffolk. Although he coined the term 'prior culture' to refer to a centuries-old culture that he felt was dying out as a consequence of mechanization, his work was never 'in danger of lapsing into *floral*[8] history, a flowery indulgent nostalgia perpetuating the calendar and chocolate-box image of a timelessly tranquil country-side. The village was an occupational community, not a setting for smock and straw whimsy' (Williams, 1991, p. 55). Neither was this 'prior culture' a culture that had remained unchanged for centuries; it was in a constant state of change, most recently as a result of mechanization. The impetus for much of his work was driven by a lifelong commitment to the political left, born of his experiences as a young man in the depression-hit 1930s, when he developed a 'savage contempt for the monied class, the leisured capitalists he held responsible for the economic and political crisis' (Williams, 1991, p. 11).

Studs Terkel (1912–), on the other hand, has lived his life in Chicago, but has not restricted his documenting of oral history to a particular geographical region, preferring instead to focus on particular issues or historical periods, such as the Great Depression, and collecting testimonies from across America. Terkel has broadcast daily on Chicago radio for over thirty years and has been a winner of the Pulitzer Prize. In common with Ewart Evans, his work is driven by a political commitment to give voice to, and allow history to be influenced by, the under-represented majority.

Like the work of Evans and Terkel, what the Clay Stories Project attempted to do was not so much to empower the community to become more skilful storytellers, but to give recognition to a high level of artistry in storytelling that already existed, albeit latently, within the community. It was not about creating a storytelling culture, but about providing a forum for a storytelling culture that already existed and giving this its due recognition and value. Neither was it about creating a 'star system' within a community, whereby certain individuals are 'discovered' and then raised up as examples of authentic, but previously unrecognized, folk artists. It is perhaps inevitable that this happens to some degree and I could name a number of people who emerged from the Clay Stories Project as first-class storytellers, but our aim was to give voice to a community, not to individuals.

Shortly after the project was completed, I wrote:

> The motivation behind recording and collecting these stories is not one of preservation, but one of celebration. We are not of the opinion that we had better get collecting quickly otherwise there'll soon be no folklore left. Folklorists and story collectors have always felt that they have been capturing the last vestiges of a fast-disappearing way of life. However, folklore and tradition are not specifically to do with the past, but are about deconstructing and defining the present ... and by giving value to the oral

> narrative currently in circulation within a community, we create a snapshot
> of that community at a particular time of its development. This is something
> worth celebrating.   (Wilson, 1997b, p. 151)

Quite simply our starting point was a belief that communities (in whichever way one might like to define that term) express themselves culturally by the stories that they tell to themselves and about themselves. The collection and publication/broadcast/performance of those stories is a way in which a community is able to say something about its collective identity. There was no hierarchy afforded to either the storytellers or the stories. Everybody was welcome, irrespective of whether they were a senior citizen or a primary school child, had lived all their lives in the community or had recently moved into the area. All stories were acceptable too, whether they were personal experience stories, local ghost stories, family tales or even jokes.

As the main storyteller employed on the project, there were times when I found myself working as a platform storyteller, but these were few and far between and were very low key in nature. There were times, for example, in the early stages of the project when I would perform in schools and at pensioners' lunch clubs, but this was not done for the sake of the performance in its own right, but to raise awareness of the project and to enthuse people about becoming involved. Likewise, at later stages in the project, evenings with local storytellers were arranged, which would involve my telling stories as a kind of warm-up act, an icebreaker before the main feature. For the main part, the time was spent visiting people in their homes (or other social space) with a tape recorder or training and encouraging members of the community to do the same. All this material was then transcribed and catalogued for future reference. In this way, much of the work was indistinguishable from that of the folklorist or oral historian. In one key sense, though, it did differ. The folklorist or oral historian collects stories and testimonies as artefacts in their own right, as ways of better understanding folklore or history, whereas community storytellers collect those stories with an artistic purpose, and concern themselves less (perhaps wrongly so) with issues of accuracy or contradiction between different tellers. Everything is valid and *what* is said is sometimes less important than *how* or *why* it is said.

It could be said that the Clay Stories Project owed much to Ewan MacColl and Charles Parker's *Radio Ballads* or the subsequent work of the Birmingham-based Banner Theatre. When they were first broadcast in the 1950s, the *Radio Ballads* attracted unprecedented audiences. MacColl and Parker collected the oral testimonies of ordinary working people and used these to create a series of radio programmes, each one focused around a different industry, which interwove the actual recordings with newly written music and song. Banner Theatre's overtly political work adopted the same technique, using 'actuality' to interweave and comment upon dramatic action which explored a specific political issue or campaign. Unlike many reminiscence theatre companies, Banner did not take the interviews as raw material from which to devise, but turned the 'actuality' into a kind of performer in its own right, interacting with all the other actors. Its status was thus raised from that of valuable source material that needed to be filtered, interpreted and rewritten, into that of valid cultural expression that did not need to be reworked to earn its place on the stage. In the same way, the stories collected for the Clay Stories Project earned their place as items of artistic currency in the books, broadcasts and performances that emerged from the project.

Both these examples were born of a political engagement with working-class culture, a desire to give due voice to communities whose voice had hitherto remained unheard, the same political commitment indeed that inspired both Evans and Terkel. Community storytelling projects, such as the Clay Stories Project, were similarly motivated. Those involved were, at least in part, driven by a radicalism that wanted to put the emerging art form of storytelling to a social and political use. Not content to simply be platform tellers, those involved have sought to fundamentally alter the hierarchical relationship between performer and audience. The mantra that '*everybody* tells stories' is one that is often quoted by all kinds of storytellers. I have even used it myself a number of times. Community Storytelling attempts to put it into action.

Further Examples of Applied Storytelling

One of the problems with writing about aspects of applied storytelling is that it covers such a diverse range of practices. Admittedly, the examples of educational, therapeutic and community work described so far in this chapter represent some of the most common types of practice, but as storytelling develops, increasingly inventive applications are devised and tested. For example, storytelling projects have been run with some success in prisons (in this respect, the work of

English storyteller Clive Hopwood is of particular interest), including work amongst paramilitary prisoners in Northern Ireland. Storytelling has also been used as a tool for conflict resolution across divided communities and has been an important tool in working with migrant and refugee communities.[9] In the early 1990s, midlands-based story-teller Graham Langley successfully ran an anti-bullying programme which used storytelling as its central tool. A number of storytellers have also worked with disaffected and disadvantaged young people through the youth services. And the list of examples goes on.

One of the most unlikely and successful initiatives has been the Kick into Reading project, which has seen Patrick Ryan working with local schools and professional football clubs. The project grew out of a highly successful pilot in 2000 which involved Ryan telling stories in libraries alongside Peter Rhoades-Brown, Community Officer at Oxford United Football Club (see Ryan, 2002). Two years later, with a grant from the Esmée Fairbairn Foundation, the project was modified and became Kick into Reading, part of the National Literacy Trust's Reading the Game initiative, which was particularly aimed at addressing the underperformance of boys in key skills such as reading. The aim was to provide positive role models for boys by engaging footballers to promote reading in schools and libraries. Ryan began working within three London football clubs (Brentford, Charlton Athletic and Queen's Park Rangers) and their local libraries, training 'Football in the Community' officers and apprentices from the clubs to become storytellers. Ryan and the trainee storytellers would then tell stories (both traditional and autobiographical) in local libraries and on special family days at the football clubs themselves prior to a match. The results were extraordinary, with the football clubs promoting a positive image within their local communities, libraries recording increased membership and book issues from children and schools reporting a marked increase in interest in reading from boys. In addition the apprentice footballers were picking up important communication skills which would help them in the world of work, regardless of whether or not they ended up in a career in football (apparently only 1 per cent of apprentices on the Football Academy scheme make a successful professional career in the sport) (source: 'Kick into Reading Activity Report, March–May 2003'). Following the award of what is probably the largest grant given by the Arts Council of England to a storytelling project, the project now looks likely to be expanded to several other football clubs and to include a number of other professional storytellers, who will be trained in

Ryan's techniques. It has even attracted the interest of the Professional Footballers' Association. According to Ryan the work 'confirmed the power of oral narrative to enthuse and engage reluctant readers, and reluctant narrators and creators of narration' (Ryan, 2002, p. 161). It is the inventiveness of projects such as this, the ability to envisage and demonstrate the wider applications of storytelling, beyond simple performance and skills workshops, that are giving storytelling the solid foundations it needs for the future and enabling *all* forms of storytelling to thrive by creating new contexts and audiences.

Another area that has witnessed significant growth over recent years is in the use of storytelling as an organizational tool. Increasingly, storytellers are being asked to apply their skills to the organizational and staff-development programmes within businesses. Naturally enough some storytellers are politically reluctant to engage so readily with the world of big business, but it is undoubtedly an area where there is demand and there are others willing enough to develop their work in this area. The websites of numerous storytellers advertise their services to business organizations,[10] and other storytellers have teamed up to create companies with a focus of delivering training to businesses and corporations, alongside their other work. For example, A Word in Edgeways (www.awie.moonfruit.com) is a partnership between Philippa Tipper and storyteller Katy Cawkwell and boasts clients as diverse as Pfizer, the BBC, the Royal Bank of Scotland and the Home Office.

The philosophy of such work is largely based upon the ideas contained in books such as Peg C. Neuhauser's *Corporate Legends and Lore: The Power of Storytelling as a Management Tool* (1993) and has a longer history in the United States from where it has been imported to Britain and Ireland. The work uses 'the tribe' as a model for the business organization and much of its discourse is conducted in the neo-Jungian language of Joseph Campbell et al. Whether or not one concurs with such philosophy, it is undoubtedly the case that business organizations, like all kinds of communities, develop their own folklore, which is expressed through narrative. Beneath the imagery of the tribe, Neuhauser is merely suggesting that such folklore can be used to encourage a culture of storytelling, which in turn can lead to more effective communication within organizations, teambuilding, shared visions, a deeper common sense of purpose and better staff relations, all key to creating a successful business. It is simply a case of recognizing the existence of organizational folklore and creating opportunities where a storytelling culture can flourish.

Nevertheless, the reluctance of many storytellers, for political reasons, to engage so overtly with big business is firmly rooted and many storytellers would be highly selective about the organizations they would choose to work with, and seek reassurance that any initiative was benevolently aimed at increasing the voice of the employees, rather than the profits of the shareholders. Their suspicions would appear to be well-founded since it is the large corporations, and not trades unions, that are listed as clients on the websites of those storytellers who do this kind of work. When the Society for Storytelling (SfS) was approached by The Body Shop in 1997 to work with its staff, there was much fierce debate within the Society. Many saw the negotiations with a commercial organization as a betrayal of its principles of simply promoting the art form, whilst others saw this as a way of exploring and piloting, on behalf of members, an emergent way of working that might prove to be an important source of employment for storytellers, as well as taking storytelling itself into relatively uncharted waters. In the end the project went ahead and a number of storytellers who were interested in exploring such possibilities were engaged to work with Body Shop staff. The project was no doubt made easier because of the Green and Fair Trade credentials of the company, to which most SfS members were sympathetic. Doubtless the debate would have been much fiercer if another company had been involved. Charlene Collison, who managed the project on behalf of the SfS and now is a partner in Oracy, a storytelling consultancy organization for businesses, claims that 'story is on the verge of becoming a buzzword amongst communication professionals' (Collison, 2001, p. 8) and there is little doubt that this represents a new, potentially lucrative field of operation for storytellers. Nevertheless, many feel that this move into the corporate world is yet a further step away from the radical and oppositional beginnings of the storytelling movement. For some the progression from using storytelling as a tool of empowerment with community groups to using it with business corporations is a small and inevitable step; for others it is a monumental leap and one that must be resisted. Even those storytellers who welcomed the Body Shop initiative with some curiosity would be less happy with selling their services to Coca-Cola, Nike, IBM or Hewlett-Packard,[11] especially at a time when large sections of the storytelling community are debating how their art form can best be used to promote internationalism and resist globalization.[12]

Conclusion

As has been seen, the range of work that might be defined as 'applied storytelling' is hugely wide and varied. It ranges from small-scale half-term workshops with children on council estates through to staff development programmes with employees of business organizations. What brings this work together, however, is a willingness to look beyond storytelling merely as a performance art, and to consider its wider applications and uses within society as a tool for cultural empowerment, education, social regeneration, therapy, reconciliation, raising of political awareness, and so on. The possibilities are almost limitless and new, exciting work continues to emerge from committed storytellers who are willing to push the boundaries of their art.

5 Theatre and Storytelling

To attempt to write a comprehensive history of the relationship between storytelling and theatre would necessarily require writing a comprehensive history of theatre itself, which is far beyond the scope of this book.[1] In saying so, I am, of course, assuming a constantly close relationship between storytelling and theatre, but rather than exploring that relationship in its entirety, this chapter proposes to outline the work of a sample of twentieth- (and twenty-first-)century practitioners who involve themselves closely in the notion of story and whose work deliberately blurs the distinction between storytelling and acting. The examples have been selected either because of the distinctive significance of their contribution (for example, Dario Fo's *Mistero Buffo* would be difficult to ignore in a discussion on theatre and storytelling because of its international impact) or for the typicality of their contribution. I am, for instance, not suggesting that Theatre Alibi have been the only company producing storytelling shows for a family audience, but their work is worthy of consideration because it is typical of the high-quality output of many small and medium-scale companies in this field.

If the rise of storytelling in the late twentieth century is linked to popular (and resistant) acting traditions, and emerged from the post-1968 alternative theatre movement, then the work of Bertolt Brecht once more appears in the frame, as one of the key influences on that movement. The work of Brecht and many of his contemporaries (such as Erwin Piscator) represents a return to a narrative-centred tradition after the anti-narrative stance of naturalism. Viewed from our twenty-first-century perspective, the plays of writers such as Ibsen and Chekhov may appear to be dramas that are built around a strong sense of narrative, especially when compared with contemporary experimental and post-dramatic performance, which seeks to work beyond what it sees as the restrictions of conventional narrative structures; but naturalism is, as previously discussed, effectively an anti-narrative form. This is partly because narrative is an artificial structure that is imposed upon a series of events in order to give them meaning. Inevitably, therefore, narrative seeks to interpret events and will distort 'truth' to some extent in the process. In this sense *all* narratives are, to a greater or lesser degree, fictions, whereas naturalism attempts to present a 'slice of life', as if holding a mirror to reality. In other words, naturalism reflects reality, narrative refracts it.

Furthermore, naturalism is character-based drama. Individual characters are driven by a psychology, rather than a narrative, and are thus presumed to have an existence outside of the play. They have histories and futures, meaning that the play is a mere snapshot, rather than a self-contained narrative with a beginning, middle and end. It is, however, interesting that nowadays[2] we are able to see that nineteenth-century naturalism was still largely unable to tear itself away from the five-act structure and the Scribean principles of exposition, development, climax and dénouement.

The documentation of Brecht's rehearsal techniques, on the other hand, lays testament to his continual striving for clarity in terms of the play's story, or *Fabel*, as he called it. For Brecht theatre was an act of collective storytelling (Eddershaw, 1994, p. 255) and each actor, therefore, a storyteller. Much has already been said in this volume concerning the relationship between storytelling and Brecht's concept of epic acting, but it may also be worth considering why Brecht was particularly attracted to a narrative theatre in the first place, if only to clarify the influence he has exerted on the subsequent forms of storytelling theatre outlined in this chapter.

Whilst trying to resist the simplistic approach that locates Brecht's dramatic theories in direct opposition to those of Stanislavski, it should be said that Brecht was partly responding to his own dissatisfaction with the inadequacies of naturalism to deal with large social and political issues. Naturalism, claimed Brecht, attempted to hoodwink the audience into believing it was witnessing something that it was clearly not – that is, that it was witnessing real life, when it was actually witnessing a piece of theatre. Brecht saw little point in denying the artificiality, of theatre and particularly thought that a theatre that sought to enlighten its audience was unsustainable if it was built upon a fundamental dishonesty concerning its own nature. Brecht recognized that not only was narrative an artificial structure, but it was a form that self-consciously celebrated its own artificiality and he wanted to create a theatre that was unashamed of itself and would celebrate its own artifice. Furthermore, Brecht saw that the purpose of story was not to present reality, but to enhance our understanding of it. He wanted to create a theatre that acted as a prism through which life could be seen in a new light, and 'story' presented that very opportunity.

Brecht's concept of *Verfremdung* is born of the idea that we become blind to the injustices and inequalities of society as we become more used to them. Familiarity breeds acceptance and discourages a questioning attitude. Naturalism, by simply presenting life as it is, is unable to effectively question what is familiar, whereas the very artifice of story invites the audience to question, interpret, evaluate and judge. More than that, it insists upon it.

If Brecht was particularly drawn to the form of the folktale as an 'authentic' cultural expression of a peasant class, then no doubt he also recognized the emancipatory nature of the form: that the concept of change and transformation is inherent within the folktale – and that would have been attractive to Brecht as a committed Marxist. Folktales do not simply present life as it is (or was), but as it might be, often alongside a social critique of reality. They encourage the audience to think not that life, however tragic or unjust, is inevitable and unchangeable, but rather that anything is possible, offering hope for a changed and better future. Furthermore, Brecht recognized the importance of folktale structure in allowing the audience to anticipate the outcome of a story. In this way the audience is able to focus on *how* events unfold and, consequently, to understand that events do not *necessarily* follow on from each other, but occur as a result of a series of choices (or lack of choices).

It is clear that storytelling was the key to the kind of theatre Brecht wanted to create, a theatre that enlightened its audience, yet entertained them too as part of a communal social event, a theatre that encouraged its audience to make judgements by retaining an objective distance from the events on stage, and a theatre that prompted its audience into action by showing the possibilities for change. Story was the filter that allowed this to happen.

Dario Fo

The Italian actor, playwright and Nobel Laureate Dario Fo is often described as the epitome of a modern epic actor and 'Europe's most popular political satirist' (Schechter, 1985, p. 142). His approach to acting is vehemently non-naturalistic and he reserves most criticism for 'the self-absorbed method actor' (Hirst, 1989, p. 23). Clearly Fo's work owes much to Brecht's ideas of the epic actor who presents a character objectively for critical analysis, rather than identifying with it subjectively (Hirst, 1989, p. 128), but Fo also shares with Brecht the belief that storytelling, rather than character, lies at the heart of effective theatre. As David L. Hirst says, 'Fo ... had come to realize that the basic element which was key to his reanimation of popular theatrical forms was a skill in storytelling' (Hirst, 1989, p. 24), and Fo's approach to performance and rehearsal is strikingly similar to the working methods of many storytellers. Nowhere is this more obvious than in his one-man show *Mistero Buffo*, which reworks traditional stories for a modern audience.

Fo was born in 1926 in San Giano in northern Italy, near the border with Switzerland. His father worked for the railways and his mother 'came from a tradition of oral storytellers' (Behan, 2000, p. 5). As a child Fo spent hours listening to the stories of the local fishermen and the travelling *fabulatori*. As Tom Behan says, 'What Fo absorbed at a very impressionable age was the art of storytelling, without the use of a theatrical cast and props' (Behan, 2000, p. 6). By the time Fo first performed *Mistero Buffo* in 1969, he and his wife Franca Rame were already well-known performers on Italian television and in the bourgeois theatre, but they chose to abandon the bourgeois, commercial circuit in 1968 in order to devote themselves to political theatre in the service of working-class audiences.

Mistero Buffo, whose evolution coincides with the beginnings of the alternative theatre movement in Britain and America and the foundations of the contemporary storytelling movement, is readily comparable to a storytelling event in a number of ways. Fo performed this show without costume or props at the end of the 1960s, throughout the 1970s and into the 1980s, playing in venues ranging from workers' canteens to huge stadia to worldwide audiences estimated at 40 million (Mitchell, 1984, p. 10). In Italy it remains the single work for which he is most famous and is rightly considered his most significant contribution to theatre.

Mistero Buffo is essentially a storytelling show in which Fo tells, or acts out, a number of traditional stories from folklore, biblical sources and ecclesiastical history. Each story is preceded by an often lengthy introduction or *interventi* (some of these are even longer than the stories themselves) where Fo, as himself, will furnish the audience with contextual information for the story, suggest its contemporary relevance and provide it with a political framework. Thus he will establish his *Gestus* as a performer. The stories themselves are 'acted out' by Fo, with his adopting one or more characters, although we remain aware of his critical detachment from the character(s) he is playing. As a performer Fo would effectively be working from a repertoire that if played continuously would, it is estimated, 'last an entire day' (Mitchell, 1984, p. 17), although a single performance of *Mistero Buffo* would typically last in the region of four hours.

The two most distinctive features of *Mistero Buffo* are the lack of a fixed text to allow for (and as a result of) a significant degree of improvisation and the breaking of the fourth wall to allow *direct* interaction between performer and audience. Both of these are key characteristics of contemporary storytelling and are often used to differentiate storytelling from acting. In fact, for Fo both of these features are crucial aspects of his theatrical aesthetic. Fo maintains throughout *Mistero Buffo* a distinct separation between actor and character, which allows him to step outside the action and pass comment upon it. It also allows him to improvise around the stories to include references to contemporary events or issues of particular relevance to a specific audience. As Tom Behan rightly says, 'if you are to break down the fourth wall then you should comment on recent events' (Behan, 2000, p. 108), and like both Brecht and the con-temporary storyteller, Fo is not so much interested in the psychology of a character, as in how the character behaves in a given situation. Situation always takes precedence over character and Fo, the political observer and documentary clown (Schechter, 1985, p. 142), is always visible beneath the myriad characters in the stories. Fo, like most contemporary storytellers, can justifiably claim that no two *Mistero Buffo* performances are the same.

One particularly interesting aspect of Fo's work on the show is revealed in the following quotation from Franca Rame:

> Gradually Dario worked out the right rhythm and structure through public performance, and began to perform individual pieces, talking about where he had found them, the significance of popular theatre, popular culture, and popular language, and how it had been continually stolen and mysti-fied by the powers-that-be ...   (Quoted in Behan, 2000, p. 99)

Unlike most theatre companies, who will rehearse a play to performance standard during an intensive rehearsal period before the opening performance, Fo admits to the development of material being an ongoing process in the sense that new stories are constantly being added to the repertoire and, most significantly, these pieces are developed not in the rehearsal studio, but in performance in front of a live audience. For Behan (and arguably for Fo as well) this places him in the tradition of the *giullari* (Behan, 2000, p. 101), travelling players who 'performed as themselves, by themselves, with no other actor on the board – or table – even when they produced "two-handers" ' (Fo, 1991, p. 84) to the common people, as opposed to the courts of the aristocracy and royalty in medieval Italy. According to Fo the *giullari*

> was a mime who, in addition to gestures, expressed himself in word and song but who, for the most part, would not bother to write out his own scripts. He improvised and worked from memory, so the tradition was transmitted orally.   (Fo, 1991, p. 84)

What Fo and Rame are describing is precisely the working practice of the vast majority of contemporary storytellers and indicates the centrality of the performer–audience collaboration to the creative process and the making of meaning. To develop material without the benefit of the audience's input would be a betrayal of a fundamental principle of effective storytelling, namely that the teller puts himself or herself at the service of the audience.

In many ways, Fo's *Mistero Buffo* can be seen as an exemplar in the debate concerning the relationship between acting and storytelling. It is Fo's ability to locate himself simultaneously within the traditions of the popular actor and the oral storyteller that lends further clarity to the proposition that contemporary professional storytelling is best understood within the historical context of the popular, resistant and oppositional performer.

John McGrath

In an undated essay emanating from the late 1950s, John McGrath wrote the following:

> Also we must turn to the story-tellers of the past. Because the theatre must tell a story, even if it is most slender, it must be a story, not an amorphous collection of disparate experiences, which seems to me to be the inevitable cul-de-sac in which capitalist art will end in a fine frenzy of schizophrenic activity. So we must turn to the story-tellers of the past and ransack their collections for outlines that bear meanings to us now. And from these, and

from our own deeper narrative springs, we must create new stories that speak clearly and truly.   (McGrath, 2002, p. 4)

This essay, with its clear emphasis on the necessary relationship between storytelling and theatre and written while McGrath was still a student at Oxford, sets out some of the guiding principles that were to characterize a career in theatre, film and television that was to span over forty years until his death in early 2002. Arguably the most influential figure on the political theatre scene in Britain in the second half of the twentieth century, McGrath had a career as a playwright and director that bears some parallels with that of Dario Fo, not least because of their shared belief in the central function of comedy in popular theatre (DiCenzo, 1996, p. 157).

Born in 1935 into an Irish Catholic family in Birkenhead, Merseyside, McGrath had already built the foundations of a successful career as a writer by the end of the 1960s. Most notably he had worked for the BBC and had been a key player in the ground-breaking *Z-Cars* police drama series, but he also had a number of film credits to his name, including adaptations of *Billion Dollar Brain* and *The Virgin Soldiers*, as well as several plays for the Royal Court, the Hampstead Theatre Club and the Royal Lyceum in Edinburgh.

As with Fo, it was the events of 1968 that marked a turning point in McGrath's career and, as with Fo, in the politically charged climate of the aftermath of the Paris demonstrations, he chose to turn his back on a successful career within the theatre, television and film establishment in order to join the fight to redefine theatre and reconnect it with popular, working-class audiences. In the first instance this led to a number of projects at the Liverpool Everyman, including a radical reworking of Brecht's *The Caucasian Chalk Circle*. Ultimately, however, the Everyman, with its policy of supporting projects that aimed to take account of working-class communities, still proved too limiting and unable to create the kind of theatre envisaged by McGrath. In 1971 he founded 7:84 Theatre Company with his wife Elizabeth MacLennan, in what Nadine Holdsworth describes as 'a determined rejection of metropolitan-centred, bourgeois and universal concepts of culture' (in McGrath, 2002, p. xvi). That the company took its name from the statistic that 7% of the population in Britain owned 84% of the wealth, has become part of the folklore of the post-1968 alternative theatre movement and lays testament to their revolutionary political position. With its collective and democratic working practices, 7:84 had some early success at the Edinburgh

Festival and with touring productions of plays by Trevor Griffiths, John Arden and McGrath himself, but it was in 1973, after the decision to divide 7:84 into two sister companies, one operating in England and the other in Scotland, that McGrath produced the work on which his reputation as a radical theatre-maker was established.

The Cheviot, the Stag and the Black, Black Oil was 7:84 (Scotland)'s first production and toured successfully around village halls throughout remote Highlands communities, telling the story of the Highlands from the nineteenth-century clearances, when thousands were forcibly evicted from the land by the landowners to make room for more profitable sheep farming, to the discovery of North Sea oil.[3] The production was a sensation, playing to packed houses and proving, against the expectations of the theatre establishment, that there was a working-class audience for high-quality, politically aware theatre that did not compromise artistic integrity for radicalism, but addressed audiences on its own cultural terms and in its own language. In many ways *The Cheviot* was to McGrath what *Mistero Buffo* was to Dario Fo, 'a landmark in popular political theatre in this period' (DiCenzo, 1996, p. 152). Like *Mistero Buffo*, *The Cheviot* reached a national audience when it was filmed for television, being broadcast as part of the BBC's flagship series for new drama, *Play for Today*.

The Cheviot can be read as a straightforward piece of politically charged storytelling and it is a reading that is supported by the fact that the show was structured around the form of the ceilidh, 'a social event which combines storytelling, singing and dancing, but ... is also relevant in political and cultural terms' (DiCenzo, 1996, p. 153), even finishing with a public dance as the actors transformed themselves at the end of the play into an impromptu dance band. The drawing upon the ceilidh as an appropriate popular form for 7:84's Highland audiences was no coincidence and, as McGrath says: 'I wanted to keep this form – an assembly of songs, stories, scenes, talk, music and general entertainment – and to tell through it the story of what had happened and is now happening to the people' (McGrath, 2002, p. 63). It is clear that McGrath deliberately chose a form that was particularly suited to the act of storytelling, a form in which storytelling traditionally played a large part, in order to tell the epic story of *The Cheviot*. The play was arguably the accomplishment of the ideal he had first expressed as a student more than a decade previously.

The work of 7:84 and much other political theatre in the 1970s was the creation of a storytelling-led theatre concerned with

reconnecting with working-class audiences and reflecting and recognizing as legitimate their own culture and history. The reinterpretation
of history through the telling of the stories of working-class communities is an essential part of the kind of theatre McGrath created
with 7:84 and the use of direct address to establish a new, more
democratic relationship between actor and audience was at the heart
of it. It is the kind of relationship that is very familiar to the contemporary storyteller and Elizabeth MacLennan's remarks on the performance style adopted for *The Cheviot* is interesting in this respect:

> There was a tangible sense of involvement as well as 'a good night out'.
> They were, I suppose, part of an ancient story-telling tradition which is an
> act of sharing with the audience. We were quite aware of this and deeply
> affected by the confidence played [*sic*] in us.   (MacLennan, 1990, pp. 54–5)

It could be argued that 7:84 (in either country) never repeated the
success of that first show, which 'is widely acknowledged as one of
the most successful radical theatre pieces Britain has ever produced
and is credited with redefining the nature of Scottish theatre's subject matter, aesthetics, context of production and modes of reception'
(Nadine Holdsworth, in McGrath, 2002, p. xvii). McGrath and his
colleagues undoubtedly made an enormous impact on the development of political theatre, which in turn made them rather obvious
targets for the financial cuts imposed as a result of the arts policies of
successive Conservative governments in Britain under Margaret
Thatcher in the 1980s. Grants to politically committed theatre companies were cynically cut, resulting in the demise of 7:84 (England)
and the removal of McGrath from the board of the Scottish company.
Consequently, 7:84 (Scotland) was brought back from the brink of
oblivion under new management to produce work of a less politically
challenging nature. As McGrath said of the new company in an
interview for a television documentary in 1993:

> I felt very positive about the different thing and it *was* different from what we
> were doing and I just wish they'd changed the name and not called it 7:84
> because they were doing a good job and one that I valued, but it was
> different. It wasn't the same. It's another theatre company.

There is perhaps an irony in the fact that it was in the midst of the
crisis that British political theatre found itself in the mid- to late
1980s, the final, but most vicious years of Thatcherism, that a new

kind of storytelling theatre, that of the solo professional storyteller, enjoyed its biggest surge in popularity and secured its position on the British arts scene.

Ken Campbell and Spalding Gray

If similarities can be drawn between the work and careers of John McGrath and Dario Fo, then a similar comparison can be made between the work of the English actor Ken Campbell and the American Spalding Gray. Both Campbell and Gray emerged as figures of some significance on the post-1968 alternative theatre scene, Campbell primarily because of The Ken Campbell Roadshow, a pub theatre troupe who worked initially out of the Bolton Octagon, and Gray through his involvement with the highly influential Wooster Group in New York. Likewise, both are familiar faces in television and film for a range of minor roles – Campbell played the part of Alf Garnett's neighbour in the hugely successful BBC sit-coms *Till Death Us Do Part* and *In Sickness and in Health*, whilst Gray played the role of an ambassador's aide in Roland Joffe's *The Killing Fields*.

However, it is as solo performers that they have both received the greatest critical acclaim. Their one-man shows are very different from the usual kind of one-man show, where an actor takes on the mantle of a person from history, which is then presented to the audience as a fully developed psychological character through a series of monologues and recitations, such as Simon Callow's successful portrayal of Dickens in the *The Mystery of Charles Dickens* by Peter Ackroyd in 2002 (Callow had previously played Oscar Wilde in Michael MacLiammoir's *The Importance of Being Oscar*) and Dave Ainsworth's *Oh! Hello!* (2002), based upon the life of *Carry On* actor Charles Hawtrey. Certainly this type of show remains popular – at the time of writing, two such one-man productions, *The Tragedian: The Rise to Fame of Edmund Kean* and *To Be Frank*, based upon the life of comedian Frankie Howerd, are successfully running on the London stage. Instead Campbell and Gray both draw heavily on autobiographical material and present *themselves* on stage – or at least a version of themselves. Neither are their one-man shows of the *An Audience with* … variety, where a celebrity recounts a series of amusing and significant anecdotes in an unapologetic act of self-glorification. Campbell and Gray's performances are carefully crafted acts of storytelling, where the actor takes a backseat to the story and where a series of life experiences are woven together in whatever unlikely fashion to form a larger, more significant narrative.

Ken Campbell's first one-man show, *Recollections of a Furtive Nudist*, was initially performed in 1988, but Campbell's own interest in storytelling is evident in his much earlier work with the Ken Campbell Roadshow. The hugely popular Roadshow presented collections of stories, songs, stunts and magic tricks to pub audiences in north-west England from 1969. For the Roadshow, Campbell was joined, among others, by Bob Hoskins and Sylvester McCoy (who later went on to play Dr Who in the BBC television series) and much of the material drew upon contemporary legend, as Campbell recalls in a 1991 interview with James Nye:

> I was into modern mythology and urban myths around 1969. The Roadshow was based on things like FOAFs (friend of a friend stories) like the vanishing hitch-hiker and so on that get reported in the Fortean Times. ... So that's the sort of thing I did as a show. I dramatized large numbers of these things.   (www.frogboy.freeuk.com/ken.html)

What is particular about Campbell's work, though, is his delight in the extraordinary. The three plays that comprise *The Bald Trilogy* (*Recollections of a Furtive Nudist* (1988), *Pigspurt* (1992) and *Jamais Vu* (1993)), are a celebration of the moments when everyday, mundane life is invaded by the unusual, the inexplicable and the 'weird'. It is this that clearly places Campbell within a *popular* theatre tradition (and particularly a nineteenth-century popular theatre tradition). Campbell is arguably most at home in the world of the magician, the stuntman, the fairground mountebank and the freak show. It is these traditions and Campbell's innate sense of playfulness that much of the Roadshow drew upon, and this has continued in his one-man shows. The material for these shows has a basis in autobiography but Campbell is also careful to distinguish between the overriding interests of the *story* and those of the *truth*.

> It's basically autobiographical, but I had no worries about putting things in the wrong order. It's irrelevant whether it's true or not. It's just whether it adds up in the story sense. The way it goes whacking off in various directions is just for a sensational story – the dictates of what you set up seem to demand something of that order.   (www.frogboy.freeuk.com/ken.html)

Referring to the 'various directions' in which Campbell takes his narratives, James Nye describes *Furtive Nudist* as 'a network of sychronicitous [*sic*] events and disturbing thoughts that leaves the mind in unassailable (but joyful) knots' (www.frogboy.freeuk.com/ ken.html) and it is this seemingly random and chaotic structure, whereby the greater narrative will shoot off in unrelated directions, only for all the strands to be miraculously tied together in the closing few minutes, that is served by the understated, low-key performance style that Campbell adopts.

He comes on stage dressed in his own casual clothes – he has made no attempt to dress for the occasion, but appears to have simply walked in from another room to pick up a conversation he has previously been having with us. The stage itself is furnished with a collection of books and bric-a-brac that Campbell will occasionally refer to in the telling, or even chance upon in the middle of a particular story, which will then seemingly sidetrack him into a different story. The apparent informality supports the notion that we are simply engaged in an improvised conversation, albeit a rather one-sided one, and that there is no order or shape to the show at all. Indeed Campbell doesn't *seem* to be doing anything beyond simply having a chat with the audience. However, as the show ends we suddenly become aware that this is a complex and tightly structured piece of narrative performed with a high degree of expertise. It is almost as if Campbell the magician has led us to believe that he has no artistry, only to astound us when the complexity of the linked narratives is revealed at the end.

If Campbell's one-man shows are a joyous celebration of the unpredictable and unpredicted, then Spalding Gray's autobiographical monologues are 'born of grave distress' (www.hno.harvard.edu/ gazette/2002/01.17,03-gray.html), where the very source of Campbell's joy becomes something threatening and unnerving. Humour is certainly a key element in Gray's work, but he links this more to the absurdities of his life rather than to his gifts as a comedian or a deliberate attempt to be funny (www.chronogram.com/backissues/ 2002/0502/current/viewfromthetop/conversation). These absurdities in which Campbell delights are ultimately seen as sinister by Gray and his work constantly hovers between comedy and tragedy. In an interview with Kate Miller, Gray explained that 'I think that what an audience doesn't see is the enormous amount of pain that the humor comes out of. And they laugh right over it' (www.altx.com/io/gray3. html). Not surprisingly, perhaps, Gray suffered from sporadic bouts of severe depression and finally committed suicide in early 2004.

Like Campbell, Spalding Gray's performative style for these monologues, the most famous of which is arguably *Swimming to Cambodia* (1988), which tells of his experiences in Thailand while filming *The Killing Fields*, is one that is low-key. Again Gray appears as himself, in casual clothes, with no set except a table and a glass of water. Where Gray's work differs from Campbell's is in the sense of a fluid text. Campbell's text may appear fluid, and even contain brief moments of improvisation, but it is very tightly structured and written prior to performance. Gray, on the other hand, develops his text through improvisation in performance. In a 2002 interview with Liza Weisstuch from the *Harvard University Gazette*, he explains:

> I'm making the sentences, they're not [always] pre-written. There are the keywords and then I speak it, so it's a form of oral writing. It's definitely an oral composition, storytelling in the Irish sense of first-person present talking about your own life. ... Although I do act, when I perform I'm acting myself.
> (www.hno.harvard.edu/gazette/2002/01.17.03-gray.html)

Both Campbell and Gray have achieved great critical acclaim for their brands of autobiographical storytelling theatre and yet have remained virtually unacknowledged by the storytelling community. Gray himself was invited to perform at the National Storytelling Festival in Jonesborough in 1985, but his show was not warmly received and both parties were left dissatisfied by the experience (Sobol, 1999, p. 198). It is perhaps due to their respective television and film profiles that Campbell and Gray have always been classified as 'actors' (i.e. 'not one of us') by the storytelling community. At the same time neither has engaged particularly, if at all, with the contemporary storytelling movement and that is certainly storytelling's loss.

Storytelling Theatre Companies

The examples considered so far in this chapter have all been solo performers, but a number of theatre companies have also responded to the rise in interest in storytelling over the past twenty or thirty years. In 1975, when the storytelling revival was in its infancy, Shared Experience 'focused on experimenting with storytelling' (Craig, 1980, p. 109), producing shows based on collections such as *The Arabian Nights* or even on substantial works of narrative fiction such as *Bleak*

House. In Britain, though, the storytelling revival has had the largest impact within the field of Theatre in Education (TIE) for primary school children (ages 4–11). As shown in Chapter 1, the introduction of Local Management in Schools and the National Curriculum in the 1980s both privileged storytelling over theatre within the curriculum and solo storytellers over theatre companies, for financial reasons. Understandably, TIE companies had to address the demands and priorities of the new curriculum and many began to develop specific storytelling shows. These were different from pieces of theatre that were *narrative-centred*, but specifically drew on the great folktale collections (such as those by the Grimms and Calvino) to create shows that were structured around a series of tellings of individual stories, sometimes by individual members of the company and sometimes by the whole ensemble. In other words, they were retaining the model of the theatre company, along with its production practices and rehearsal and touring patterns, but were drawing on the same material and performance structures as the new, emerging breed of solo professional storytellers, who were experiencing a very rapid expansion in work opportunities and numbers at this time.

To give an example, one such company, Theatre Alibi from Exeter, was able to develop a strong reputation for their storytelling shows based on lesser-known folktales. This reputation ensured their survival and allowed them to continue to develop other programmes of schools work and to develop into other areas of community-based theatre, especially targeting family audiences. As a result, Alibi was one of the few companies who enhanced their standing and financial security at a time when Theatre-in-Education companies in Britain were generally becoming increasingly financially unstable.

In fact, Alibi were in a strong position to respond to the challenges of the Education Reform Act of 1988 because they already had a history of producing storytelling shows, but their storytelling output and the popularity of these shows certainly increased during this time. Theatre Alibi was formed in 1982 by Ali Hodge and Tim Spicer, graduates from Exeter University's Drama Department (the current artistic directors are Nikki Sved and Daniel Jameson, later graduates from the same department), with a commitment to producing theatre for children and families, primarily throughout Devon. Whilst the company now tours both regionally and nationally, for children and adults, the philosophy upon which the company was founded, still underpins their work: a belief in 'the actor as a storyteller with a bagful of theatrical skills' (www.theatrealibi.co.uk).

Theatre Alibi describe themselves as 'contemporary storytellers' who 'look for the right stories to tell and the right way of telling them to question the modern world'. For Alibi, storytelling is also a form that provides a means of 'reaching the broadest possible audience'. On the one hand, Alibi's *modus operandi* is firmly within the traditions of small-scale touring companies, rather than storytellers. The company will tour two shows per year, each developed with a team of actors, writers, musicians and designers. There is no sense that the actors are developing a repertoire of material from which to draw for any single performance, in the way that a storyteller would often develop work. Whilst the performance style might embrace the notion of simplicity, these are also shows with a high degree of technical support and design. It is certainly not the minimalist staging of a chair and a microphone that might be expected at a storytelling performance. At one level, therefore, the work of Theatre Alibi might seem to have little connection with contemporary storytellers beyond a shared sense of the importance of story, and the company has little direct contact with the storytelling movement.[4] Nevertheless, Theatre Alibi is in fact much closer to the work of storytellers than many storytelling-theatre companies.

Back in the mid-1980s Alibi was already creating shows based upon the retelling of folktales by a small ensemble of actors. These shows retained most of the trappings of small-scale theatre production, but consisted of individual retellings from a limited repertoire of material. The method of telling was also varied; the story of 'Crystal Rooster' from Calvino's collection of *Italian Folktales* was told by a single actor, playing the narrator and all the individual parts, not unlike Dario Fo's piece based on the rising of Lazarus, where he plays up to fifteen separate characters (Fo, 1988, p. 64), whereas other stories were told by the entire ensemble, alternating between narrators and characters. Although the performances themselves were not improvised, Alibi's way of working towards a script is not unlike that of many storytellers working towards a fixed text, using stories as a 'starting point rather than scripts'. The difference is mainly that for Alibi, the script becomes fixed during rehearsal, rather than during performance.

In a way, what these early storytelling shows enabled Alibi to do was to respond to the National Curriculum in the way that storytellers were able to do, by addressing the demands of the English *and* the Drama curricula. Just as storytellers will find schools and libraries making use of their services in the context of literacy and literature promotions, such as Book Weeks, Theatre Alibi have more recently taken children's literature as a starting point for their particular brand of storytelling-theatre, with adaptations of popular modern classics such as Michael Morpurgo's *Why the Whales Came* (2004) and *You Can't Catch Me* (2003), based on the poetry of Michael Rosen.

What is particularly interesting about Theatre Alibi is that the company has continued to develop its own brand of story theatre, whilst remaining quite separate from the storytelling movement. Their work is clearly different from that of most solo storytellers, yet there is one significant point of contact that they have with the best in contemporary storytelling, and that is a shared belief in the primary function of the storyteller as a performer who, through a meaningful engagement with the audience, is able to cast the world in a new light. According to Alibi's website:

> The company is still interested in telling stories, in actors making real sparks of contact with their audience, still excited about integrating live music, film, puppetry, anything that helps tell stories well, and still fascinated by this endlessly necessary thing called theatre.

The interest in storytelling theatre was not restricted to the world of Theatre in Education, however. Writing in *The Independent* (28.11.2001) upon the occasion of the revival of Brian Friel's play *Faith Healer* (1979) at the Almeida Theatre, Paul Taylor credits the play with starting a trend in Irish theatre for storytelling (what he calls 'this much-in-vogue mode'), leading ultimately to Conor McPherson's hugely successful *The Weir* (1997), where a group of men in a remote pub engage in a round of competitive ghost storytelling, but 'are eventually silenced by the quietly horrific true tale that is delivered by the female newcomer they have been trying to impress' (Taylor, 2001).

The impact of the storytelling revival on the mainstream commercial theatre sector is further evidenced, for example, by the collaborations between the poet Carol Ann Duffy and directors Melly Still and Tim Supple with their two shows, *Grimm Tales* (1994) and *Beasts and Beauties* (2004), the latter being an ensemble show based upon the separate (i.e. not connected or held together by some wider narrative structure) retelling of eight relatively well known stories from the broad European cannon of folk and fairy tales, including Hans Christian Andersen's 'The Emperor's New Clothes', Charles

Perrault's 'Bluebeard' and the Grimms' 'The Juniper Tree'. Here the actors adopted many of the techniques of epic theatre and contemporary storytelling, drifting effortlessly between myriad personalities (self, narrator and characters), albeit with a lavishly designed set and costumes. In many ways, what the ensemble was doing in this critically-acclaimed show was simply using the kind of theatrical inventiveness that companies like Theatre Alibi and their colleagues in Theatre-in-Education and Children's Theatre have, out of necessity, been doing for a long time, but applying it to the creation of storytelling theatre for adult audiences. The result was an audience that was both amazed and delighted by the sense of *communitas* created in the auditorium by the performers and their material.

The increasing influence of storytelling on theatre is further evidenced by Susannah Clapp's review of Kneehigh Theatre's production of *A Wooden Frock* (2004), a reworking of 'Cinderella':

> Time and again, fairy tales are proving a sly but ferocious way of telling hard stories. At Bristol Old Vic, trees sprout magically, unwanted stepchildren are dismembered and an emperor's knickers become weapons of mass destruction.[5] Meanwhile Kneehigh ... are showing incest while performing a variation of the Cinderella story.
>
> (*Observer*, 18 April 2004, p. 12)

Kneehigh Theatre are certainly no strangers to storytelling, having built their reputation as a major touring company on shows that have drawn extensively on Cornish folklore, and have adopted a straightforward and 'expressive, visual narrative style' (www.hca2005.com). In 2002 the company won the prestigious Barclays Theatre Award for best production with *The Red Shoes*, based upon the Hans Christian Andersen story of the same name.

Like Still and Supple, Kneehigh are aiming their work at predominantly adult audiences, establishing storytelling theatre within the mainstream, whereas most theatre companies aim their storytelling shows primarily at children and/or family audiences. This is partly due to the perception of storytelling as first and foremost an activity for children, and partly due to the economic conditions this creates with opportunities in the lucrative educational market. The storytelling movement has made significant progress over the years in challenging this attitude, but storytellers will regularly complain that adult audiences who have never witnessed a storytelling performance, and armed only with images of library and school storytelling sessions, will still perceive storytelling exclusively as a child-centred activity. For many the further development of adult audiences for storytelling remains the largest single challenge for the movement in the coming years.

It might, at this point, also be worth mentioning the work of Vayu Naidu, whose work could arguably be discussed in any of the chapters of this book, so wide-ranging is it. Naidu, who has a doctorate in storytelling from the University of Leeds and now teaches at the University of Kent, was a key figure in the British storytelling movement in the 1990s with her distinctive and stylized perform-ance style based upon Indian narrative dance traditions. She was a founding director of the Society for Storytelling, but has more recently maintained a more distanced relationship with the storytelling move-ment, concentrating instead on her work as a playwright (*There Comes a Karma* (1999), *Playboy of the Asian World* (1999), *Nine Nine Nights* (1999), *Future Perfect* (2000), *When* (2002) and *Guess Who's Coming to Christmas?* (2003)), her academic research (she is currently engaged in an applied storytelling project, using narrative to explore the dynamics of the relationships between asylum seekers and their host (and often host*ile*) communities) and her achievements in establishing a forum for the development of 'performance storytelling that is new work' (www.kent.ac.uk/sdfva/vvn/vvncompany.htm).

To this end, Vayu Naidu has set up the Vayu Naidu Company, which has undertaken a number of projects in recent years. What is particularly interesting about this work is that, whilst it is driven by the impulses of storytelling, its means of production and dissemina-tion more recognizably belong in the world of theatre. The company is, like Peter Brook's Paris-based company, manifestly multicultural, drawing on the skills of performers from all continents, and one of its stated aims is to develop 'culturally diverse audiences' (www.kent.ac. uk/sdfva/vvn/vvncompany.htm). *South* (2003),[6] for instance, a 'piece of cross-genre theatre, which draws on multi-cultural inspiration to make compelling storytelling theatre that weaves narrative with live music and dance' (www.britishtheatreguide.info/news/south.htm), was developed with the help of a theatre director (Chris Banfield, who also directed a number of Naidu's plays) and toured mainstream and prestigious theatre venues, rather than the community-based venues in which even platform storytelling can often be seen to operate. The radicalism of such work may lie primarily in its aim of producing formal storytelling performances that are relevant to a contemporary multicultural Britain, made up of various diverse diasporas, and in its approach to working with both innovation and tradition. *South*, for example, has been described as 'storytelling at its finest, based on traditional myths and legends, told in a modern context, which delivers a contemporary vision of our multicultural society in a witty approachable form' (www.indielondon.co.uk/ theatre). Its choice of venues, however, suggests that it safely exists within the theatre establishment, rather than shaking its walls and rattling its doors, by challenging the existing and dominant relationships between performer, audience, text and form. It arguably draws more from classical, rather than popular and vernacular, traditions of theatre and performance, more from 'high art' than 'low art'. Nevertheless the work of the Vayu Naidu Company is unique in that it is a fusion of storytelling and theatre that has evolved from storytelling, rather than theatre, and as such continues to make a significant and important contribution to the future development of storytelling.

Peter Brook's *Mahabharata*

Perhaps the most significant and ambitious, if not controversial, exploration of storytelling theatre in recent years has been Peter Brook's production of the Indian epic *The Mahabharata* (Carrière, 1988) which was premiered at the Avignon Festival in August 1985, but which had been many years in the making. It subsequently toured internationally and was made into a film. The impetus behind this colossal project (the original is fifteen times the length of the Bible, taking six months in the telling, and Brook condensed it to a cycle of three plays lasting a total of nine hours) would appear to be two-fold, namely the quest for an international language of theatre and the importance of storytelling. These, indeed, have been features of Brook's work at the International Centre for Theatre Research, which he founded in Paris in 1970, and therefore, *The Mahabharata* can be seen as 'a full reflection and realization of all Brook's Paris-based research work' (Williams, 1988, p. 355).

Informing Brook's work is a belief that theatre is an international language which can overcome ultimately divisive cultural differences and this is reflected in the multicultural company of actors he works with – *The Mahabharata* was performed by 'a company of twenty-one actors from sixteen countries, as well as five musicians ... who played dozens of Oriental and African instruments' (Croyden, 2003,

p. 206). In this sense *The Mahabharata* 'did nothing less than attempt to transform Hindu myth into universal art, accessible to any culture' (Croyden, 2003, p. 206). Brook states his position thus:

> When one speaks of culture, culture isn't the last word. We're not all simply defined by our culture; this is already secondary. I think that if one doesn't accept that, all the rest becomes totally confused. If one believes that a person's identity, a person's definition, and consequently a person's reality, is his culture, then one's denying something much more important. The living person is a living person; this is what the entire humanity has in common. From that ground, cultural differences slowly develop and become more and more pronounced, and eventually become highly sharpened by every form of the inevitable conflict.
>
> (Quoted in Moffitt, 2000, p. 130)

This is in stark contrast to the position adopted by theatre-makers such as John McGrath, who condemns such a stance as an attempt to homogenize theatre and culture according to the interests of those in power and to deny working-class cultural expression. McGrath rejects the notion that 'art is universal, capable of meaning the same to all people' (McGrath, 1981a, p. 3), claiming that any universal language will inevitably be the language of the powerful and that meaningful and effective theatre must acknowledge that *different* audiences from *different* parts of the world and *different* social classes will necessarily interpret any piece of theatre *differently*. Whilst Brook's attitude may be well-intentioned, with his goal being to use theatre to promote global harmony amongst culturally diverse peoples, it is also the source of much of the criticism that has been levelled at Brook's work generally and *The Mahabharata* in particular.

Brook's critics accuse him of cultural appropriation (or, worse, theft and piracy) and of adopting the attitude of a colonialist towards other cultures. His fiercest critic is perhaps the Indian critic and director Rustom Bharucha, who accuses Brook of orientalism and creating a 'trivialised reading of "Hindu Culture"' which was then sold back to India as a commodity in the form of the film version of the production (Bharucha, 1996, p. 199). Bharucha's main criticisms of Brook are that, rather than creating a universal piece of theatre, he has ripped the cultural heart out of *The Mahabharata* by creating a version of the story according to Western cultural tastes. Specifically he stands accused of decontextualizing the text, imposing a chronology upon the narrative, that does not exist in the original, cutting out some of the characters and editing out key sections of the narrative, and avoiding many of the more problematic aspects of the text, such as the justification of the caste system, all in the name of creating a piece that is understandable and palatable to a Western audience (and indeed, as McGrath would argue, a Western bourgeois, theatre-going audience). Certainly comments from Brook such as, 'We would find a way of bringing this material into our world and sharing these stories with an audience in the West' (Brook, 1988, p. 161), and Williams's observation of Brook's belief that 'it (*The Mahabharata*) belongs to the world, not only to India' (Williams, 1988, p. 354), would seem to confirm his critics' accusations of cultural colonialism, whilst Brook's comment that

> It was as though the *Mahabharata*, which had lain asleep for so many centuries, suddenly awoke. It had needed to come out and cross the world. Luckily for us, we were there to help it on its way.   (Brook, 1998, p. 211)

betrays more than a hint of Western arrogance. Likewise his regular descriptions of *The Mahabharata* as 'Shakespearean' (Brook, 1998, p. 218; Croyden, 2003, pp. 215–16) may be intended as compliments, but suggest a distinctly European understanding of cultural merit. One is left to wonder whether he would describe Shakespeare as 'Mahabharatian'.

In his defence, however, Brook draws a distinction between the intercultural work of his own company and that of an Indian storyteller, claiming that 'we were ... refracting the Indian work through the many nationalities of our company' (Croyden, 2003, p. 222), and

> We knew that we could not, and should not, imitate Indians or Indian art, but suggest it. We did not pretend to reconstruct ancient India of three thousand years ago. We did not pretend to present the symbols of the Hindu philosophy. In the music, costumes, and movements, we tried to suggest the presence of India.   (Croyden, 2003, p. 220)

Arguably, though, Brook's mistake is to assume that in working with such an internationally diverse company to create what Irving Wardle called a 'performance [which] is a melting-pot of national differences', all cultures are automatically respected. Whilst no one can deny the immensity of Brook's achievement in staging *The Mahabhrata*, the diversity of opinion and the fierce controversy it has sparked, illustrate that the issues are more complex than he supposes. Interestingly, they are the very same issues that continue to be debated within the storytelling movement.

Where Brook and McGrath would agree, however, is in the centrality of storytelling to the kinds of theatre they are trying to create. In the case of *The Mahabharata*, Brook recognized that 'first of all, the actors had to be terrific storytellers, with many different faces' (Croyden, 2003, p. 223). In fact, storytelling had always been at the heart of Brook's work in Paris, his first work there being a version of a fairy tale from the collections of the Brothers Grimm (see Moffitt, 2000, pp. 132–3), but this idea very much came to maturity in his work on *The Mahabharata* and informed the whole creative process. As Brook states, he has 'always considered a theatre group as a multi-headed storyteller, and one of the most fascinating ways of meeting *The Mahabharata* in India is through the storyteller' (Brook, 1988, p. 162). In the first instance, Brook refused to read the text in order 'to remain true to its oral tradition' (Vallely, 1989), instead preferring to have the story told to him over several weeks by the Sanskrit scholar Philippe Lavastine.

On one level *The Mahabharata* can be seen as a vast theatrical testament to the traditions of oral storytelling and an example of theatrical storytelling at its most daring and most ambitious. Nevertheless, it has not been without its difficulties and controversies and has been the centre of a debate that is of great relevance to the whole storytelling movement, as it is currently grappling with almost identical issues. To some it stands as Brook's master work, the worthy legacy of a theatrical genius and a great supporter of storytelling, whilst to others it is the embodiment of misguided Eurocentrism.

Conclusion

For the storytelling movement to have distinguished and separated itself from the theatre is perhaps a necessary thing to have happened in order for it to have thrived. Attention can be drawn to any number of differences between the work of contemporary solo storytellers and that of actors and theatre companies. A strong case can be argued that storytellers and actors train, and prepare and create work, in different ways; that storytellers have a different relationship to their material and engage their audiences in different ways from those of actors; and that storytellers work in a different economic market from that of actors. There is undoubtedly some truth in all of these statements.

However, there are sufficient examples from theatre to draw an equal number of similarities and to argue that both actors and storytellers are, at the end of the day, simply approaching the same activity from different directions (and some more radically different from others). Actors and theatre companies perhaps need to recognize the sophistication of much storytelling and the artistry of many storytellers and engage more readily with the storytelling movement, but likewise storytellers must not consider themselves the sole and true guardians of an ancient art. There are many ways to skin a cat and storytelling remains, as it has done for centuries, a primary concern of the theatre. It is interesting that recent trends in storytelling in Britain suggest that as the storytelling movement begins to gather in confidence and storytellers begin to push the boundaries of their art, then we are likely to see more storytellers creating longer shows based on a single narrative, such as have been seen recently. In shows like this the differences between storytelling and theatre become more blurred and less distinct, as storytellers readily adopt the techniques and means of performance and production of the actor, whilst theatre companies continue to produce shows that adopt the techniques and repertoire of the storyteller. If these trends continue, then theatre and storytelling will once again converge, becoming indistinguishable from each other, and the terms 'actor' and 'storyteller' will be interchangeable.

6 Closing Thoughts

The rise of the professional storyteller over the past thirty years has been one of the remarkable success stories of the performing arts in the closing decades of the twentieth century and the opening years of the twenty-first. It has, however, taken place almost unnoticed. Storytelling did not suddenly burst onto the scene, but has gradually been developing and expanding, exploring itself and establishing new territory and new audiences. The revolution has been a relatively quiet one, but none the less significant. Storytellers can now be found everywhere, because storytelling has not just arrived but, it seems with every year that passes, it is here to stay.

During their relatively brief history, the storytelling movements on both sides of the Atlantic have faced their challenges and debates, all of which have taken place (or even been avoided) against a background of increasing professionalization and commodification. In the United States there have been fierce debates surrounding owner-ship and cultural appropriation. The British and Irish storytelling movements have largely avoided those debates so far, but instead have concentrated on issues concerning the setting of professional standards within storytelling and the relationship between contem-porary tellers and tradition. The storytelling movement as a whole has still not yet fully worked out its response to interculturalism on the one hand, and globalization on the other, and those debates, which have been raging in the theatre world for some time, will no doubt surface in the years to come.

On the issue of the relationship between acting and storytelling, there is a diversity of opinion amongst storytellers and the observers of storytelling. In the interviews that I have conducted in the making of this book, most storytellers make a distinction between storytelling and acting, but also, to varying degrees recognize the importance of theatre to what they do. Daniel Morden is keen to emphasize what he sees as fundamental differences, saying, 'I had no idea how different acting was to storytelling ... the more you explore it, the more subtle you find the differences are' (interview), yet he readily acknowledges that there exist 'elements of theatre in my storytelling' and that 'theatre was the inspiration for me to start performing at all' (interview). Most interestingly, Morden sees himself, as a performer, taking the role of 'narrator':

> I don't embody a character even when I'm telling *The Odyssey,* and I tell that in the first person. That's as close as I would come to acting, but nevertheless there is a kind of distance between me and Odysseus.
>
> (Interview)

While Morden is explaining what he does in order to distance it from acting, what he says is nevertheless entirely consistent with Brecht's notion of epic acting. Indeed, when storytellers are making a distinction between storytelling and acting, they are usually making a distinction between storytelling and a particular kind of acting and a particular way of making theatre. What storytellers are keen to point out are the differences between what they do as solo performers and the business of learning the lines of a character, becoming that character and presenting that as part of a play, under stage lights, with a number of other actors, while pretending that the audience isn't there. Jack Lynch is adamant that it is his ability, as an actor, to see beyond that model that has prepared him well for his work as a storyteller, explaining that 'in naturalism there is a fourth wall and a lot of actors are afraid to go beyond that. But I never was. It's just my style of acting. So it's very easy for me to tell a story directly to the audience' (interview). Other storytellers, such as Taffy Thomas and Billy Teare, for example, are much more comfortable within a tradition of *popular* theatre, placing themselves amongst the ranks of street performers, stand-up comedians and music hall performers. For many, like for Teare, acting and storytelling, despite some perceived differences, are ultimately inseparable:

> These conversations I keep having with people, all this 'What is a story-teller?', 'What's the difference between a story and a joke?', 'What's the difference between storytelling and telling jokes/acting?' I suppose they're all sort of interlinked so you can't really say that storytelling is different from acting because storytelling can have elements of acting in it. Yet I know storytellers that don't act. But then I know storytellers that do!   (Interview)

Likewise I have come to the conclusion that theatre and storytelling are inextricably linked. I say this with conviction, fully aware that it is a statement that may be met with howls of protest from some storytellers and sanguine nods from others. I am quite happy to accept that some storytellers will never feel as if they are actors and I am certainly not suggesting that the storyteller and the actor are not often engaged in quite different activities. It is obvious that a storyteller performing to half a dozen pre-school children in a public library is doing something very different from a classically trained actor performing Shakespeare on the stage of the National Theatre. I am also not making this statement in order to denigrate storytelling in any way, to classify it as a sub-category of theatre, rather than an art form in its own right. Conversely, I think the case for storytelling is strengthened by placing it within a wider tradition. And there can be no doubt that storytelling has played a fundamental role within the tradition of theatre. Ultimately, the skills and techniques of the storyteller are, and always have been, the business of the actor, and the skills and techniques of the actor (in the broadest sense of the term) are, and always have been, the business of the storyteller.

If the impetus for the storytelling 'revival', on both sides of the Atlantic, emerged from the counter-cultural movement of the late 1960s and 1970s, then one criticism that might be levelled at it today is that, in many cases, it no longer displays the political radicalism and idealism from which it evolved. To some extent this is undoubtedly true, in the same way that many small to medium-scale touring theatre companies no longer subscribe to an oppositional politics. It is also, as Jack Zipes argues, an inevitable consequence of professionalization and commodification, as storytellers, forced to deliver according to market expectations, are less able to play the role of the subversive. Nevertheless, I would argue that the radical spirit can still be found alive and well within certain quarters of the contemporary storytelling movement.

Although Taffy Thomas admits to having 'a collection of stories that deal with peace and redistribution of wealth and so on – a little collection of stories I like to call "Red Tales in the Sunset"' (interview), most storytelling does not take, and never has taken, an overtly political stance in the same way as agit-prop, issue-based theatre or the work of practitioners such as Fo, Rame and McGrath. Certainly the repertoires of most storytellers would carry broadly 'left-of-centre' sympathies and some storytellers have deliberately developed programmes designed to give voice to the culturally under-represented or to redress imbalances seen elsewhere, and in the media in particular. Nevertheless, the radical core of contemporary storytelling lies in its purpose as a project for democratization, for altering the hierarchical relationships within bourgeois culture and empowering people by providing opportunities to articulate their own stories and their own lives. Mary Medlicott emphasizes the importance of the democratic impulse in her own work in a way that is typical of many:

> There's a democracy of participation which I've always grown up with and which I love. It's a spreading of that creative spark. That is ultimately what I want to pursue. The democratic element in my approach to storytelling is what has enabled me to be an advocate for storytelling and it's empowered a lot of the things that I've also done within storytelling. There's a whole side of storytelling which is about storytelling as listening, as mutual listening, to a variety of things, to what is important to us as human beings and I think I have acted as a person who can stand for that. I think that's been very important to me. It's an approach to storytelling which is a mutual approach.   (Interview)

Jack Lynch, who began his acting career in agit-prop, is equally adamant that his storytelling work, although less overtly political, emanates from the very same radical impulse:

> I often do storytelling as part of campaigns or benefits for this or that. In the past I've been involved in ad hoc agit-prop groups. But when I put together a new story it often comes out of something I hear. I don't want to make it explicitly political, but I would like to find ways of making it more implicitly political and it can be implicitly political in that there's maybe an anti-authoritarian or an anti-clerical thing to it, in the way that you get with Dario Fo. And that is also very strong with Eamon Kelly and it's strong with John Campbell. Because of the power of the clergy, which is, thank goodness, fast draining away in Ireland because of all sorts of things, the priest was an authority figure, so the stories put the priest down, the priest has his come-uppance, you know. ... I bed down with that noble tradition in folklore that mocks the master, the tyrant, the exploiter, the unjust, the cruel, the pompous, the greedy ... Jack the Refusnik.   (Interview)

Underpinning the very foundations of contemporary storytelling, therefore, is a core of disestablishmentarianism – a legacy of the post-1968 radicalism that rejected the political and cultural establishment and the hierarchies that supported them and articulated a wish to replace them with structures that were ultimately more egalitarian,

progressive and humane. Even nearly forty years on from the turbu-
lent days of 1968, many involved in storytelling are still driven by a
dissatisfaction with what can be offered by a cultural establishment
that is moribund, elitist, reactionary, largely white and bourgeois.
The problem is that the storytelling movement has simply dismissed
one establishment in order to replace it with another. This is certainly the case in the United States, where the endorsement of
the National Storytelling Network and an invitation to perform at the
National Storytelling Festival can make or break a career. It is fast
becoming the case in Great Britain and Ireland too. The challenge for
storytellers in the future is to be continually willing to challenge
standardization and orthodoxy, particularly when it appears within
their own ranks. That means that storytellers must not only seek to
subvert, and offer more democratic alternatives, but must also be
willing to constantly question the validity of their own work, the
work of their colleagues and even the very value of storytelling itself.

Interviews with Storytellers

Introduction

What follow are seven edited interviews conducted with contemporary storytellers during the course of writing this book. Many more interviews were conducted (some of which are cited in this book) and I hope that those that it was not possible to include here will be made available elsewhere at some time in the near future. In one way, this selection is not a representative sample of storytellers and anyone looking for gaps will certainly find them. It is arguable whether such a small sample could ever be representative, although there is a degree of diversity in that, of the storytellers included here, one is from England, one from Wales, one from Scotland, one from Northern Ireland, two from the Republic of Ireland and one from the United States. Where the sample is broadly representative, however, is in its range of storytelling practices, since here are practitioners who represent the diversity of approaches that currently exists within the contemporary storytelling movement. Additionally, they all cover some of the key issues and debates that are the concern of this book, such as character, improvisation, context/environment, stance and identity. These interviews should be seen not as a storytelling 'hall of fame', but rather as a snapshot of the range of storytelling work that is currently being undertaken, and they will, hopefully, provide some insight into that work. They are also included with the purpose of providing the reader with a supply of primary source material and the storytellers themselves with the opportunity to reflect upon the processes associated with their practice.

NUALA HAYES

Nuala Hayes trained as an actor with the Abbey Theatre and was a member of the Abbey Company for five years. During her time there, she became involved with Theatre in Education and subsequently set up TEAM, Ireland's first touring theatre for children, which specializes in theatre in education. Her favourite roles, as an actor, include Máire in *Translations* by Brian Friel, Kate in *Dancing at Lughnasa* by the same author, Winnie in *Happy Days* by Samuel Beckett and The Widow Quin in *The Playboy of the Western World* by J. M. Synge.

Her interest in storytelling began thirteen years ago when she set up Two Chairs Company with musician Ellen Cranitch. Together they have toured throughout Ireland and frequently abroad to the United States and Canada, and to many festivals in the UK and Denmark, and they have represented Ireland at a European storytelling marathon in Guadalajara in Spain. Nuala founded and was Director of Scéalta Shamhna, the Dublin Storytelling Festival, for ten years.

In 2002 she was Artist-in-Residence in Co. Laois, where she collected and recorded local stories. She produced the RTE radio series *Tales at the Cross-roads*, from material recorded during her time in Laois. She has recently adapted and direc-ted *The Confessions, the Truth and the Lies of an Old Repro-bate*, based on the writings of Joe O'Neill of Mountmellick, Co. Laois, as a touring production.

Interview with Nuala Hayes

Can you give me a bit of a narrative as to how you got involved in storytelling, and how that transition happened from your theatre work to your storytelling work?

Theatre had been my medium for as long as I knew what I wanted to do. I trained at the Abbey Theatre, which is Ireland's National Theatre. I attended the School of Acting, which at that time was very much part of the theatre and was set up to train actors in what was perceived as 'the Abbey Style' and tradition. The Abbey Company was the first subsidized theatre company in the world and had a formidable reputation. When I was there, membership of the Abbey Company meant secure employment for life and I became a member of the Company at a very young age. So my background was in conventional theatre with a strong sense of a tradition that was passed on by senior members of the Company to the younger people. There was, however – because of the mood of the sixties and the questioning of the assumptions behind most institutions – always for me a concern about the audience. I was always curious as to why this wonderful form of expression that I loved so much, theatre and drama, was not accessible to more people and seemed to be the preserve of an elite few. I felt a crusading mission to introduce theatre to everybody and thereby change the world. I mean, this was the end of the sixties, after all! So when the notion of theatre as a tool in education became part of the culture at that time, I latched onto that very much and became involved in the Young Abbey Theatre-in-Education Group with other young actors who performed in schools, but we also began to experiment with different ways of using theatre in educational contexts. Then, still as an actor, I became very interested in the fact that you couldn't perform to children in the way that you would perform to adults because children did not experience the play as a fixed entity. Children demanded that you involve yourself with them, and I became really interested in that. I took a year off and went to live in Denmark and began to look at the many children's theatre groups that were independently funded by the state. This was my first experience of Social Realism geared towards young people, where theatre was a means of bringing about social change. It was all very idealistic and utopian.

When I went back to Ireland I started a group called Team Theatre-in-Education and it was to be the first touring, independent theatre company in the country, whose brief was not to be attached to a particular theatre, but to travel around independently and develop work that related to where its audience was. The audience were young people and children. I'd actually set it up but believed it should be run collectively – very difficult to do in Ireland because collectivity and Irish people at that stage were not mutually compatible, so it was hard work. So I sort of withdrew from it and left Team to stabilize itself as it is now, an administrative structure which organizes touring theatre for children.

So there I was, fairly idealistically interested in an audience but also wanting to develop as an actor as well, so in 1980 I returned to freelance acting. I loved taking work out of a theatre building and going to places that didn't have the traditional connections with theatre. I really liked that sense of something happening to an audience that weren't trained into it. I really enjoyed the early days of touring in Ireland when there weren't these lovely arts centres or theatres, where you might go into a school hall or community centre with your play. Field Day Theatre Company, founded by the playwright Brian Friel, the writer, and Stephen Rea, the actor, was committed to that kind of touring in the 1980s. I took part in the first production of Brian Friel's wonderful play *Translations*, which opened in Derry and then toured to small venues throughout Ireland. I found that really satisfying. But then at a certain age I quite pragmatically discovered that when you're a woman and no longer in your twenties or early thirties, suddenly all these very interesting young male directors are not interested in you anymore. I had a sense that if I went on like this I was going to be very dependent on people coming to me, hiring me or firing me, and I wanted to be in charge of my life and my work.

That isn't how I found storytelling but I came to storytelling through exploring what it is to perform, and I began exploring poetry first of all, exploring words and music. I worked with a musician, Ellen Cranitch, with whom I still work very closely. We started first with new writing by Irish women and we worked on a programme around that. Then we began to look at short stories because of the great tradition of short story writing in Ireland. We began to look at short stories as perhaps a way of communicating with an audience and telling a story really. It was an exploration of being with an audience, telling a story to that audience and performing. We came across a particular story, in the anthology of new Irish women's writing, called 'Midwife to the Fairies' by Eilís Ní Dhuibhne, based upon an old folktale. We found ourselves performing this story with music and something opened in my mind about the actual folktale itself, as opposed to what the writer had done with it. I then went off to the South of France, to the Roy Hart Centre in Malérargues, to a workshop for performers exploring creativity. While I was there, in this lovely, comfortable, alternative place with lots of dancers, singers and actors moving round, the people who, I thought, were having the best fun and seemed to be most engaged in what they were doing, in the most human and enjoyable way, were a group of people doing a workshop on storytelling. I remember being with my group, being very sensitive – there was lots of movement but very little language – and I remember hearing gales of laughter from the storytelling group. In the evening they would all gather together outside around a mulberry tree. The sun had gone down and lots of people would gather round and one by one they would get up and tell the story that they were working on. I was fascinated that the audience would go from really small children up to adults and they would all be held by this one person telling the story. It was all in French, and my French would've been adequate, but I kept missing the punchline at the end, or didn't quite have the language to really appreciate where it was going. But not understanding, I was fascinated that such a simple form could be so engaging.

When I came back to Ireland, I wondered not so much about whether there were storytellers, because I knew of the great storytelling tradition here, but I wondered if there would be an audience in Dublin for this? So I set up four evenings in November in Mother Redcap's Tavern. I was terrified that no one was going to listen to the stories so I got loads of musicians as well and discovered to my amazement that there was a fantastic audience for the stories. I gathered anybody that I knew that I thought could tell a story including the famous Eamon Kelly, who was a household name in Ireland. I had worked with him numerous times as an actor and he was happy to come along. So it really grew from there.

When you first started working in theatre a lot of your development and interest was led by a desire to democratize theatre and to get theatre into places and to audiences that wouldn't otherwise have been engaged in theatre. So in a sense, the work that you were doing was politically driven, if only with a small 'p', and yet the folklore was viewed as being politically reactionary. Do you feel that the storytelling is equally driven politically or driven by the same politics?

Yes, I know what you are saying. In the early days I was very interested in theatre as an instrument for social change. I wouldn't say with a very small 'p', it would've been a very big 'P'. I would have instigated and been involved in productions that would've been quite polemical and would've really put it out. We did a production at the

Young Abbey called *Strike*, about the 1913 Lockout, which was very much driven by a belief in socialism. I think I personally have changed over the years, not that my beliefs are any different, but I actually find polemical theatre and preaching quite boring now. I think that change is carried out by action and that preaching, be it a story or a piece of theatre, is just boring. I mean, in the early days when we were working with stories I really wanted to tell stories from the point of view of a woman, but you have this huge store of folklore tradition that doesn't reflect very well on how women were treated. I stayed away from that for a long time saying, 'I can't tell those stories, they're too awful and it's terrible that they're told in this way.'

But, in fact, now I find it very interesting to take stories and look at them again in a different way.

Is your storytelling, or your involvement with storytelling, part of the same project about democratization? Is that one of the things that attracted you to storytelling?

I think that what it is, is that you don't have to get involved in the whole palaver of the politics of theatre and the politics of how to get your play on and who decides what play goes on, and who decides where it's going to be. With stories you can have them in your bag, which is in your head and in your heart, and you can take them anywhere. I was never hugely comfortable in the world of storytelling in pubs because I'm no good at that kind of stand-up comedy in pubs. For me it's that you can take the material in a very simple and a very direct way. I have often seen a good storyteller make a connection with an audience that is as powerful as any theatrical experience. I like the engagement with the audience and the fact that there is now an audience for stories.

If those traditional folk stories were viewed as being reactionary back in the late sixties, as being to do with the past and nothing to do with the progressive, logical, socially responsible society, what has changed to make those stories relevant now?

I changed. I view the experience of art in a way differently now. I think it's very often something personal and that everybody sees a story, or sees a play or sees a painting, or film, in a different way. Of course it's a collective thing, but I'm more interested now in the individual response. I think that there's something about what happens in the imagination when you hear a story and it changes as time changes. I'm more interested in the imaginative way that people respond to listening and also just the experience of actually being there with someone else telling a story. Storytelling has a very good way of handing over – very often a storyteller will step back and listen to somebody else telling a story. There is a kind of give and take in it that your theatre production doesn't allow. The most you get is a discussion after the performance.

Is the storytelling experience different from the theatrical experience?

One is not better than the other, they're just different. I often liken storytelling to being alone in a small boat, rowing away on your own, trying to survive the wind and waves and the currents, always having to be alert, but being in charge of your own destiny in a sense. Being in a play is like being in a great comfortable ship, where everything is organized. There's a place for everything and you know what you have to do. You've got the same feeling of being on the sea, whether you like it or not, but you're well supported and feel very, very safe. Storytelling is more scary and dangerous and risky and you're on your own. To me storytelling is quite challenging and difficult and you have to be really free and open, and experience has just taught me that the more relaxed and unworried you are about it, the less you rigidly plan what it is you are going to do, the more effective it's going to be. In theatre the better one is prepared, the clearer the cast and the director and all the crew are about their collective vision, the stronger the impact will be.

Do you think that when you are telling stories you differentiate that with what you do as an actor or is it simply a different facet of the same?

Yes, I think it's a different facet of the same thing ...

Because you are using similar kinds of learned techniques and skills?

Yeah, I think so. I know that I could go on about the debate that storytelling isn't acting, storytelling is not theatre. There has been a dismissal of some storytellers saying 'Oh, they're performers, they're actors – it's different.' I don't think it really matters, it's ultimately about communication and a storyteller is good and effective if they can tell the story and the audience receives the story. Ok, so what if they come at it theatrically or if they simply sit there? I think the ability to hold an audience is innate to an actor. I think that probably my acting experience is what makes me the kind of storyteller I am.

As an actor of course you're aware of the audience, but your total concentration is on helping the play tell the story. I think it's two aspects of the same thing. The big difference for me is when you're telling a story I desperately need the audience, because it's no good if the audience doesn't want to be with the story. You can do your play and, if the audience isn't into it, you are still going to do exactly the same thing and try and make the connection with your fellow actors. In stories, if you don't make the connection, everybody feels pretty let down. As a performer you feel pretty let down also.

Is that notion of audience so important? Does that mean that perhaps stage acting and storytelling are actually closer to each other than stage acting and television or film acting?

Oh yeah, definitely . . .

So, in fact, it's not really a distinction that needs to be made between acting and storytelling but actually live performance and recorded performance?

Yeah, that could be true. With live performance you have that sense that you're with the audience and the audience is with you and actors will always say, 'Well of course, there's nothing like that energy that you get with an audience when the audience is there.' The style of acting that's required for television is much more quiet and introverted than a physical form. The stage actor has to be so concerned with the physical, just as a storyteller has to be concerned with the physical. Certainly the storytelling that I do is performance storytelling, because it's necessary – you are faced with a group of strangers sometimes and you can't just chat and be intimate with them because you just don't know them.

Then there is this other aspect of it all, the persona. The late Eamon Kelly had a persona, a storytelling persona. But Eamon would put his hat on and he thickened his accent and everybody would go 'Ahhh, it's Eamon Kelly, the *seanacaí*', but there was also Eamon Kelly the superb actor, one and the same. Interestingly, he was remembered when he died as the *seanacaí* and only people in the theatre knew that he was also Eamon Kelly the brilliantly focused and concentrated actor. I worked with him as an actor and he applied the same concentration when he was telling stories. He loved his audience and his storytelling evolved from his ability to become the *seanacaí*.

I think that what makes a storyteller is the fact that we actually really do like standing up with our material and telling the story. So every storyteller is a performer. They have to be, how could they not be? The very act of telling the story is that they're telling it to people. So I just don't buy it or get it that it's a shamanistic thing, I don't go with that at all. As a storyteller, your job is to tell the story. That's what matters and I really believe it's more important to tell the story than show yourself and how brilliant you are. If ever I'm more impressed by a performance of the storyteller and I can't remember the story, I get annoyed. Very often it happens, that you're so enthralled by the way the story is being told that you don't get the story. To me, really effective storytelling is like really effective theatre, it stays with you afterwards, you remember it, you can pass it on.

Do you think about costuming when you are telling a story?

I have to say I used to and I had a storytelling outfit, a couple of storytelling outfits, and I do it less now. I suppose I have more confidence that I can tell the story no matter what I'm wearing. In the early days it was difficult because I had been used to not having face-to-face contact with audiences, so if you had a persona it was easier, it was closer to the theatre experience. I liked it if you didn't have to take in all the eyes of the audience, if I could just deal with the front row and I couldn't see them at the back, whereas now I dislike intensely not seeing the audience because you don't get the feedback.

What about the way that space is arranged? Do you think space needs to be carefully arranged and managed or can storytelling occur anywhere?

Yes, I would always want to go into the room to check it out in advance. I would always arrange the performance space to the way that I want it.

What would inform those decisions about space?

Contact with the audience and not having a 'them and us' feeling. So I would get off the stage unless it was necessary to be up on the stage in order to be seen. But the rigid lines that are usually the audience I would always, if possible, break.

What about decorating the space? Do you think about what goes into that space?

I love the idea of maybe having something nice in the background or something to look at. I love the idea, but sometimes it's just too complicated to organize. I certainly don't come travelling with drapes and things like that. It's just not appropriate to Ireland or Irish storytelling. I like candles a lot and if I would do anything consciously, particularly in the evening, or very often with children, I would have a candle and I would light a candle at the beginning of a story and blow it out at the end and sometimes I would use a candle in a story. So light, I think, is probably more interesting. I'd be more interested in lighting than I would in décor. I hate what these bright strip lights do. I think that matters. I think atmosphere matters.

What about movement in the space and storytelling? Is that important, the way that you use your body? Do you use a gestural language or more of a mimical one? To what extent would your physicality be about 'acting out' the story or be based on your natural gestures?

No, I wouldn't mime, but I probably would use my body. I probably would use my body because I prefer standing up to sitting down generally and I would use my body to either create an atmosphere or illustrate an action using my own natural gestures. I think I use my whole body instinctively. I do like big gestures and movements sometimes.

Can I just ask about this particular project, this residency you've been working on because that, for you, doesn't involve performance. Do you still see that as you being the storyteller? Are you in a different role there?

The residency with the Arts Office of Laois County Council involved unearthing the storytelling tradition of this part of the Midlands of Ireland, which at one time was very strong. I see myself as having a slightly different role in that I'm exercised in listening and drawing out stories from other people, but it's very active listening. It's discriminating listening as well. It's the storyteller in me that is drawing them out. The emphasis I put on the oral experience, the live retelling, rather than the writing down of the stories, is because I am an oral storyteller. I recorded the stories on tape and then made a video of some of the storytellers so there would be a visual record of the project also.

And you are able to do this because you are a storyteller?

Yeah, I think so and I'm not a folklorist. I'm not a folklorist, it's a storyteller working.

JACK LYNCH

Jack Lynch, a member of the Dublin Yarnspinners, has told stories throughout Ireland and has toured to the UK, the USA and the West Indies. He leads storytelling sessions at the National Museum for school children and with teachers, and also performs in prisons, retirement homes and mental institutions. He is also an actor, who began work in the radical counter-cultural climate of the early 1970s, performing street theatre, Theatre in Education, and in support of the anti-nuclear movement. His one-man show, *The Humours of Breffini*, is a character-based extravaganza of tall tales, music and lies.

Interview with Jack Lynch

Well, let me see, I'm fifty now and I was late to acting, I was in my mid-twenties. I'd go to loads of plays in the university drama soc. and there was a very interesting wave happening there at the time with Jim Sheridan and Neil Jordan and others, but it never occurred to me to act. From 1979 I was involved in the protest movement against nuclear power stations in Wexford. We were planning a roadshow that involved musicians like Christy Moore and Donal Lunny and an agit-prop playlet. This coincided with the Dublin Theatre Festival, and the Living Theatre of America were over. There was audience participation and I found myself going every night and playing a different character in this amazing play, *Metamorphosis*. I had organized the tour in the sense that I arranged where people were staying and all that – and they said, 'Oh Jack wants to act' – they realized it before I did. So they wrote me a part in the playlet. So my first time on stage was with professional actors and I got the buzz and found it was something that I loved to do and have been doing it and starving ever since. (*laughter*) One small independent company I was involved with was funded by a government training scheme. It meant we could take six months to learn juggling and fire-eating and this, that and the other and we started telling stories in gobbledygook, trying to get the meaning of it across through the tone and the phraseology.

So like a kind of grammelot?

Exactly like *grammelot* – though we didn't know it at the time. It was round that time when I came across Dario Fo. We weren't doing that much mime and that, but there were six in the group, it was a street group, and we took on different characters. One guy told a traditional Chinese folktale, I made up a story that was anti-religion, about a priest character. It was very simple, but we went out on the street during the Dublin Theatre Festival, spoke no English, and were taken as being foreign clowns and told these stories to people and people began to follow it. So I look back on that now and see that it was elemental in some way towards a training in storytelling. The gobbledygook was like wearing a half-mask. And in different ways I fell into the storytelling thing. There was a friend, Art o'Briain, who was doing a telly programme, *Ten Minute Tales*. He asked me to perform, he gave me a couple of stories from writers that had been commissioned and one of the stories, I didn't think, worked that well, so he said, 'Can you come up with one?' And I thought of mixing two stories, one from *The Arabian Nights* and another story I'd come across a fragment of. And so I wrote the tale, learned it and told it to camera, which is not the way I would work now. But anyway, I started doing solo acting things, comedy things, they weren't stand-up but theatrical comedy. At other times we were with a troupe of actors and we would do a show three nights a week in different parts of Dublin and then we'd write the next week's thing – topical, comical social commentary. And through that I had come up with a character. So I began collecting stories and I just developed that. And I would hear stories and I developed lots of characters. And after a while somebody pointed out to me that the main character in it – PJ – he's like the trickster character and so you find yourself using these stock characters (Quighie, another character, is the Holy Fool), because those stories are sort of picaresque. So I always resisted doing stand-up venues, because it's not stand-up, it's narrative, it's character-based, and you're not having to deal with hecklers because they're going to break the narrative.

So I then found myself on the edge of what was becoming the revival of the storytelling scene here. Liz Weir had been a dynamo in the North with the Cultra, Omagh and Derry Festivals and then Nuala Hayes started organizing things down here. So then I began to hear a lot of other storytellers and of course I'd grown up listening to Eamon Kelly and I would have heard him on the radio when I was growing up and would have seen him on the telly. And for a lot of people he would be their image of the *seanacaí*, the traditional Irish storyteller. And Eamon, of course, was coming from an acting tradition too – he was an actor. A lot of his stories were highly crafted, very like John Campbell's style in that way, a lot of work goes into putting them together.

As time has gone by, the acting and the storytelling have gone hand in hand. It means that I'm not sitting and waiting on the phone. I love the wealth of the storytelling tradition in Gaelic and English, and I know for the rest of my life I'll be delving into it and I won't exhaust it.

So do you separate those activities of acting and storytelling?

You can't help but separate them. If I'm in a play, if the script is written by Ibsen or Shakespeare or whoever, I have to stick to that script. I know I'm telling a story, but as part of a company and involving all the effects and the lights and having been directed and all that. And I love acting, you know, it's something I enjoy doing and I enjoy stage work much more than film or television work. Being a storyteller means that I have a live audience. I would very rarely write out the story. If I write it out I'm not going to learn it, like a script, but I'll tell it conversationally, so it's different every time.

Do you find that it does eventually become fixed, that the actual variation in how you tell it becomes limited after a while, so it becomes fixed through doing, rather than sitting down and learning? Or is it constantly fluid?

I wouldn't say constantly, but it does tend towards getting fixed. I wouldn't use the word 'limited', but it never does get fixed, and the reason is because of the audience, because of the listeners.

But is that not to do with the fact that it's a live performance rather than the fact that it's storytelling rather than theatre? You get some variation as a stage actor because you're still responding to the audience, aren't you?

Yes, you are, although they are not visible. They are there and one half of your brain is judging their response and the other half is judging how the actor opposite you is responding to you. A third half is portraying your character! So if I'm telling a story as a storyteller to an audience, the story will change for a number of reasons. What I'm saying is, you tell the story differently depending on your audience, but also sometimes depending on a new thing you see in the story. I'm always doing 'maintenance' on stories. Collecting and adding details, strengthening effects. Sometimes, now, you can find yourself in a disastrous situation – say, in a pub venue at a local arts festival, the *wrong* pub. I did one where the entire audience had been ensconced since midday when they'd returned from a tragic funeral. If you're trying to muster a listening quota in a damage-limitation situation like that, you find yourself playing to the few responsive faces and paring the stories back down to the bone in an effort to retain your dignity. On other occasions a story can bloom. If you get an audience onto your wavelength you can really relax, coax them into the palm of your hand and begin to tickle them under the chin. When you're that relaxed, you find new riffs coming out. I usually discreetly tape my performances to catch new flourishes that might emerge. So the story will change and I think the main thing that changes, that keeps the story changing, is the audience – the importance of the act of listening. It's the gift of the audience, and people have said that to be a good storyteller, you need to be a good listener.

Is the difference then more the process that goes behind the storytelling? On the one hand storytelling is an extension of what you do as an actor anyway, but if you're preparing story material then you go about that in a different way than if you were working on a play, because you're working on your own for a start? And it's not that theatre can't be made in that way – theatre can be improvisational, it can be a solo performance – but it usually isn't. Is that where the difference is for you then?

Yeah, you're right. I don't think it is intrinsically a different activity, although if you're doing, say, a Beckett play, there's a precision to the language that can be quite far away from telling a comic story or even one of the old stories that I've refashioned myself. It keeps occurring to me that it's very much like jazz really. Before going on stage it's very hard to say, 'I'm going to tell this one, this one and that one, depending on the time that I have', because once you get up there, something else will probably occur to you.

Sometimes I forget. I get lost in a story, so I have to improvise in the way that an actor who gets lost on stage will improvise and try and not let the audience know that the plot has gone awry. I've been in plays when you're in the first act and an actor will jump to the third act and how do you get out of that? But I think maybe my writing experience and the fact that I'm a talker, if I get lost in a story, I can pull myself back onto the rails, because I can think grammatically. I'm not going to get stuck in a cul-de-sac of words.

You didn't have a formal actor training?

No, but working in Theatre-in-Education, there was a kind of training there. And then over the years, being in certain productions meant receiving training from this director or ... Cicely Berry, the voice coach, co-directed a show and I spent some time in the Stanislavski Studio in Dublin, but not long – Brecht was closer to my sensibility. But you're learning all the time. You find yourself soaking up things from other actors. We were talking about jazz musicians, but I could also say a singer, because I tell a story in the way a singer would sing a song. You can sing a song differently or arrange a song differently, you know what I mean? Also some actors are fearful of a style where you address the audience directly, and in a lot of plays I've been involved in, you get that, but in naturalism there is the fourth wall and a lot of actors are afraid to go beyond that. But I never was. It's just my style of acting. So it's very easy for me to tell a story directly to the audience. If I'm doing support for musicians I sometimes go up on stage. I often forget to ask them to bring down the stage lights or bring up the house lights, because it's important in telling stories to see people's eyes, because you're making contact. You know they're following the thread of the story and I think you need to see people's faces, whereas some storytellers who've come through acting, they'll want to be lit, they'll want to be seen and, therefore, also want to be playing into the darkness. They don't want to see the listeners' faces. It is quite a definite point of difference between some storytellers. And, of course, many actors make lousy storytellers. They can succumb to the rhetorical or the twee. There can be an issue about character. A script can handcuff a story. Some can't see the direct, immediate, and interactive nature of storytelling where, for once, you're not *showing* – you're *telling*.

You said something quite interesting, that you didn't spend long at the Stanislavski Studio because you're more of a Brecht man. Unlike a Stanislavskian actor, who inhabits a character, a Brechtian actor shows character whilst still showing themselves as the actor, and the storyteller also likes to be themselves.

Yeah. I've done the character PJ on the radio a few times and the presenter will often introduce me as PJ, but I'm not PJ. I'm the feller that tells about what the character PJ gets up to. So my persona is different again. It's very close to Jack, although I am using an accent. The sense of humour in the telling is mine. They're laughing at PJ, but they're laughing at my telling the story. So I haven't really a character, I'm just telling the story. There is an amount of artifice and I'm using actorly techniques, like projection, and writing techniques in how I put the story together and how, if inspiration tickles me, I can leave a story, improvise, go off on a tangent and then bring them all back at the end. Billy Connolly was saying recently how he has a name for doing that, but sometimes, he says, he never comes back!

But that approach to character is, wouldn't you say, much closer to what Dario Fo was doing in Mistero Buffo? *He's showing that character, but he's not inhabiting their psyche and we're kind of laughing at Fo showing us Boniface by being Boniface. It's a different kind of relationship that the actor has to character, or it's a differ-ent relationship between audience, actor and character.*

Yeah, sure. I was always interested in Dario Fo. I was never in any of his plays, but I got to see as many as I could. And then I did see Franca Rame do *Female Parts* and it was after that and after I'd started storytelling and after I'd started that grammelot exercise with the other actors, it was only then that *Mistero Buffo* was translated and published. But sure, a lot of what I do is closer to Dario Fo, but not consciously. Now I was thinking of going back to the *grammelot* stuff, and some of Fo's writing and the techniques he's used that are in *The Tricks of the Trade*, for a scurrilous story. I would need a director, but it's a very short, simple piece, but to try and get the audience to understand just by the rhythm of the words and the tone. And, of course, I would also have an affinity with Fo's politics as well.

Even now, when you're doing the storytelling, do you see that work as implicitly, if not explicitly, political? Would you do it as part of the same project?

It's a hard question. I often do storytelling as part of campaigns or benefits for this or that. In the past I've been involved in ad hoc agit-prop groups. But when I put together a new story it often comes out of something I hear. I don't want to make it explicitly political, but I would like to find ways of making it more implicitly political and it can be implicitly political in that there's maybe an anti-authoritarian or an anti-clerical thing to it, in the way that you get with Dario Fo. And that is also very strong with Eamon Kelly and it's strong with John Campbell. Because of the power of the clergy, which is, thank goodness, fast draining away in Ireland because of all sorts of things, the priest was an authority figure, so the stories put the priest down, the priest has his come-uppance, you know.

So for you there's a political agenda that's implicit throughout?

Yes. And even not taking a stance is taking one. The Dario Fo connection wouldn't be uppermost in my mind, but it's very true what you say. I bed down with that noble tradition in folklore that mocks the master, the tyrant, the exploiter, the unjust, the cruel, the pompous, the greedy ... Jack the Refusnik.

DANIEL MORDEN

Daniel Morden grew up in South Wales and studied drama in London. This was followed by a brief career in community theatre before encountering the London storytelling scene. Since then he has worked all over the world, telling and collecting stories. In 1992 he was resident storyteller at the National Garden Festival in Ebbw Vale and he has worked extensively in radio and television. He regularly collaborates with other artists, including India Dance Wales, musician Oliver Wilson-Dickson and storyteller Hugh Lupton, with whom he has performed *The Odyssey*, *The Iliad*, and *Metamorphoses*. He currently lives in Abergavenny, South Wales.

Interview with Daniel Morden

So, what was your own route into storytelling?

I grew up in Cwmbran and I was a bookish kid. I would walk to school by myself and I'd be telling myself stories all the way, stories that I was making up. At the same time I was reading a lot of mythology, particularly Norse mythology for some reason, and comics like *Batman* and *Spiderman*. My father suggested I go to the local youth theatre that is run here in Abergavenny. It was run by a community TIE [Theatre in Education] group, Gwent Theatre. So I was making up stories myself and going to see theatre whenever I could. I went to university to do Drama and English at Goldsmiths College in London. Again, there was a blend of bookishness, the fascination with plot, of story structure, combined with performing. The course was about drama as an art form rather than learning how to be an actor but I was in as many plays as I possibly could.

When I left university, I started a theatre company with friends in Lewisham. It was very closely modelled on what I'd seen at Gwent Theatre. We performed in places that the community would visit anyway, libraries, shopping centres, parks, schools. We hoped to make that everyday place different and startling for the hour while we were there. It was devised work. I began to find devised work frustrating. I often felt as though the finished piece was a compromise. It seemed to consist of the elements that we all found inoffensive, rather than the elements that were exciting. Also the whole business of the set and the lighting and so on … if we were trying to visit libraries and parks and schools, then the theatrical paraphernalia became an unwieldy encumbrance.

At that point I went to City Lit. and I took part in a storytelling course which was being run by Pomme Clayton. I remember thinking, storytelling manages to combine the elements of story that I loved as a child with the performing that I loved as a teenager and while going through university. I can arrive at my venue on the bus and, provided that there's silence and the audience are willing, something extraordinary might happen.

Did you think about it as being a departure from what you were doing, or were you thinking: This is the direction I want to take my theatre work?

At the time, I was doing schools and the odd library. I thought storytelling was more performing. My attitude was 'I can do the things that I enjoy doing without having to do quite so many of the things that I don't.' I had no idea how different acting was to storytelling. It was a slow process of discovery, which still continues. At that point I thought storytelling was close to what I was already doing. In fact, the more you explore it, the more subtle you find the differences are.

What are the essences of that difference then, for you?

Well, I think every storyteller would have a different answer, but for me the ideal comes from seeing the Scots traveller storyteller Sheila Stewart. When I first heard her tell, she told a ghost story. She spoke in the tone of a conversation. The hairs stood up on the back of my neck. The story was so directly communicated that the performance element seemed to have vanished. Hugh and I feel when the story is really working, when the evening is very successful, we disappear. There's something about the economy of being a storyteller, something about just standing or sitting and speaking, that appeals to me.

When you say that you become invisible, is that you or your artistry that becomes invisible?

Certainly the artistry becomes invisible ...

What always impresses me, when I watch videos of people like Dario Fo doing Mistero Buffo, *or even somebody like Billy Connolly, is the ease with which they do it. They make something that on the one hand is incredibly complex and skilful look as if it's second nature to them, as if they're making no effort at all. Is that what you meant or do you mean something else?*

I think a step further: the audience almost forget that we're there. With Billy Connolly you're always aware, in the convivial presence of Billy Connolly. His personality is a big aspect of the experience. You feel at the end of the show as if you know him. We tell *The Iliad* and *The Odyssey*, and a version of *Metamorphoses*. We dress very neutrally and we try – some circumstances in which we perform prevent this from happening – we try all the time to be neutral, to appear to be as neutral as possible, so neither the artistry nor our personalities are prominent. We hope the audience is left with the images from the story, which of course take place in the mind's eye rather than on the stage.

So you become simply a vehicle for that story and nothing else? When the audience is watching you on stage, who are they seeing? Are they seeing 'Daniel the storyteller', are they seeing 'Daniel being a storyteller', are they seeing the characters within the story, or are they seeing a kind of neutral mask?

Out of the list that you've just given me, 'Daniel being the storyteller' and the neutral mask are the two possibilities that chime with me. When I'm performing with children I'm an exaggerated form of myself, much more myself than I am when we're telling the Homeric material. 'Daniel being the storyteller' is 'Daniel wearing a neutral mask', presenting as neutral an image as possible. The technique is about trying to eradicate any physical and vocal mannerisms that might pull the audience back to me. Anything that I do has to be in order to make the story more apparent for the audience. The introductions are simple, the clothes we wear are simple and neutral. The presentation style is quite formal. We have some of the trappings of theatre, which establishes a certain kind of relationship with the audience, such as a darkened auditorium and stage lighting and seating in ranks rather than around tables. These elements contribute to a formality which means that the story is being served by its presentation. It's more heightened than one might have in a pub, for example.

What's always interested me is the range of work that you do. You've mentioned the children's stuff. You've got the formality of The Iliad *and the work that you've done with Hugh and there's the work that you've done with India Dance Wales, where you are very, very visible with all the costume and everything. And then there's the work that you did on* Double Yellow *for the TV. That was really interesting work and all the time you are having to invent and control different identities of yourself as a performer and present different identities.*

That's true. I've just been talking with Cat Weatherill about taking a show that we've been doing for some years round village halls. She's adamant that we would need a set, because this group of people that come a relatively short distance want their village hall to be transformed. They want lights, they want all those things. So every one of the different kinds of work presents a different kind of challenge. The *Double Yellow* work was a process of discovery because the project changed as I was doing it. Originally I was to hand the stories to other people, members of the community with whom I'd work. Then they'd tell the stories direct to camera in the context in which they lived and worked. Eventually the project shifted and I had to tell them all. I felt that some of the films worked and some of them I'd like to do all over again. If I'm going to tell stories in another medium I want to play to the strengths of that medium. In the case of *Double Yellow*, the strengths of the medium at times, I felt, overwhelmed the story. The question is, how can I utilize the strengths of the medium in order to help the story?

That's interesting because one thing you've never been afraid to do is actually experiment with a traditional art form. You're very strong on tradition, you give great value to the sense of tradition, and yet you've always been pushing those boundaries.

Traditions change all the time! So the question is, how can I present the story in an interesting way and make what is essential to that story fresh again?

You used the word 'presenting' stories rather than telling stories. I find the word 'presentation' very interesting in terms of storytelling because it seems to suggest not simply the verbal language but actually conveying the story without actually turning into characters.

The nature of my presentation changes according to the different kinds of story. My approach would be different for different stories and different projects. On the most obvious level, if I'm at a noisy location, I will be physical in my telling of the story. There will be moments where I will be enacting what is happening. But my ideal is to return to standing or sitting and speaking in the tone of conversation. I suppose what I am is a narrator. I don't embody a character even when I'm telling *The Odyssey*, and I tell that in the first person. That's as close as I would come to acting, but nevertheless there is a kind of distance between me and Odysseus. There are, I've already said, elements of theatre in my storytelling. A style of theatre was the inspiration for me to start performing at all. And Peter Brook's work is still a touchstone for many storytellers in Britain. I find Kneehigh Theatre tremendously inspiring. I get very excited about the prospect of doing so, in the way that I do about seeing Abbi Patrix tell stories. Both of them feed me in some very basic way. I find no connection with much touring theatre. Four actors doing their best in an adaptation of a Jane Austen novel holds no appeal for me.

Do you feel perhaps that the need that storytelling fills for us is the same kind of need that the theatre fills, or is it different do you think?

The poet Gillian Clarke described poetry as 'private company'. You have to have a conversation with a poem, bring yourself to it in an intimate way. I think the same applies to a storytelling audience. Because of the neutrality of the storyteller, it is more the case with storytelling than it is with theatre. The teller relates the story very simply and the listener makes the picture in his or her mind's eye. The story is private company. It happens inside you as much as on stage. Everyone has their own version of the story.

CLAIRE MULHOLLAND

Claire Mulholland was born in County Antrim, Northern Ireland, and now lives in Edinburgh, both places which are strongly represented in her repertoire. A social worker by training, Claire's work as a facilitator of storytelling with young people, families and across the community has earned her a reputation as a pioneer in contemporary urban storytelling. She has worked extensively as a trainer and workshop leader with the Scottish Storytelling Centre and has appeared at festivals both in the UK and abroad.

Interview with Claire Mulholland

I suppose an obvious way to start is to tell me a little about how you came to be involved in storytelling, what drew you to it.

I studied in Bath for four years and whilst I was there I was really into triathlon and there was a massage therapist working there, a guy called Brook. So anyway I ended up marshalling a race with him the day before I left Bath and he said to me, 'Oh you know, you're moving to Edinburgh. Listen, I've a friend that just moved there, you must get her contact details from me.' She was actually working as an administrator for the Scottish Storytellers and we really got on. She introduced me to David Campbell and I was invited to a lot of ceilidhs at David's house and I just got completely blown away. I had never thought that storytelling was what people did for a living, as grown adults. I began by singing a few songs and things like that and over time it progressed from that. Initially I just listened, probably for a good couple of years, just completely open-mouthed at these stories. And I began to realize that so many of the stories carried these metaphors that were really powerful, and I began to see how these stories were interconnected with the children and families I was working with in a social work context.

Was your training in social work?

Yeah, that's what I trained to do in Bath. When I first moved to Scotland I was working with children who were in foster care and were adopted and my role was to support the adults who cared for them. So initially a bit of funding from Children in Need brought in some storytellers to hold workshops with the foster carers so that they could tell stories to the kids that they were looking after, and also a wee bit of direct work with the kids and that was really, really successful. I suppose that gave me such a tremendous sense of satisfaction. I remember thinking, I need to do something with this job that's going to be a bit more creative, so that was my first step into the creative world, if you like. And then I applied for a job in quite a deprived estate in Edinburgh and in the job interview I was speaking about storytelling and they said, 'If we give you this job will you try storytelling with the children?' So I got the job and off I went to do my first storytelling session and I was just absolutely petrified. I really, really thought they'd be able to hear my heart beating, it was just beating so loudly, and I started off and got a couple of sentences out and I knew I had them completely agog, and I'll never forget their faces with the big saucer eyes. It just marked a whole transition into a completely new, different life. It's so strange now to imagine not being a storyteller and not kind of having that in my life because it seems really core to my whole life now.

So what happened very quickly was I did more and more storytelling across the whole community, and I just began to think it would be so nice if these children had an opportunity to become storytellers themselves. I ran the session in a kind of ceilidh format then, where I was inviting them up to share a rhyme, a riddle, a joke or a song and you would see kids who were so able to contribute. What really excited me was that these children who were contributing were often not succeeding in any other way in school and there was often a correlation between children with some sort of learning disabilities or behaviour or emotional difficulties and the ability to express themselves orally. That really excited me so I set up a group with some colleagues. We ended up working with that group over a period of about four years, on and off. We did some fantastic work with that group but I really think that we created experiences with those children that will be with them for the rest of their lives; we gave them skills that they will draw on for the rest of their lives, and we watched them grow in confidence. They'd be going to the library more often getting books out, and not just for themselves – they'd be getting books for the wee ones of the family and reading stories to them as well and we were finding that these stories we were doing as a group were like little seedlings that rippled right across the community. I worked there for five years and the project was ongoing for twelve years in total, and I've got a great sense of satisfaction that the storytelling survived and still thrives. The adults that we worked alongside there, the parents in the community, still run storytelling groups in the area, in the church, the school. So that, I think is fantastic.

So, was the driving motivation one of educational improvement or social, behavioural improvement?

It was really both, probably tilted a bit more to the education, I would say. It's quite interesting you ask that because I think, although I'm social work trained, a lot of my work has been tilted towards the educational rather than the healing aspects. I think now I'm beginning to move more to explore feelings. The storytelling deals very directly with people's emotional welfare.

Have those transitions been because of your own choosing or are they determined by the kind of work that you are asked to do?

It feels a bit like it's a creative journey. I've always thought I'd like to explore this kind of healing aspect of stories a bit more because I've always seen stories as emotional maps and I've seen people respond to them emotionally.

Is it perhaps easier for you to do that because of your training? I'm just wondering whether there's a danger for storytellers, who aren't trained in the way that you are, in presenting themselves as therapists?

It is interesting, as even trained therapists such as Pat Williams take the view that the stories do the healing work without requiring analysis. I think it's better to let the stories just work themselves. My position has always been to not analyse stories too much; it's a bit like pulling the wings off a butterfly and I still think, to a large degree, that stories do their own work without your doing much more beyond that. I'm beginning to think there's probably some benefit in, at least in your own head, being aware exactly of what the metaphors are and what exactly they might be doing.

Does the therapeutic value of storytelling reside in the stories themselves or is the kind of human interaction that comes with telling stories more important?

I think really that the intimacy that you create is therapy in itself, definitely.

So is that kind of extended work the most important work?

I think so.

You're presumably still doing the one-off Book Week school visits as well. Do you see that as bread-and-butter work, or is there a relationship between that work and the other work?

I think the work that is the most fulfilling and satisfying is the extended work, that's the work where you can see creativity flowering in other people and that's definitely the thing that I find most satisfying. But the one-off work feeds back because you're developing yourself and exploring new creative avenues. So I've had my opportunity to work alongside other artists, such as I've developed a really interesting relationship with a model maker and I've taken that back into my other work. We did it first of all down in Lanarkshire as part of a festival where I was the resident storyteller a few years ago. With that group we created a story using a series of mind maps and then the kids took the character that they had contributed to the story and they made their own model of it. The day ended up with them telling the story, moving the models around and telling the story to their families and friends. It was hugely successful. So I took that model that was developed with my freelance hat on and brought it into the social work context. What was really interesting was when I was working with those children who were vulnerable and children who I knew what the issues were and their background, when they were making their characters, I could see that it resonated with their own life experience. It was just absolutely fascinating to watch and with each and every child there was some kind of issue that was being played out in the story and in the model that they were making. So it was very interesting.

Do you think about those different identities that you have to have? How do you think about those transitions that you have to make between being performer and facilitator?

I try and keep it as fluid as possible. I try and not keep it separate because I think it's a lot more healthy to let it flow, because then you can allow the experience from one field to then float back into the other. I mean if I've been asked to run a children's workshop, I'm not just doing that with storytelling skills. If you're moving beyond performance to facilitating children's storytelling or adults' story-telling you need to have more than just performance skills.

What about yourself as a performer, where did that acquisition of skills come from?

It's funny to watch the sort of journey that you take. I have a tape of myself as a four-year-old child telling a story. It's fantastic; the story has a beginning, a middle and an end. There's even me asking my father to participate in it, so it's got all the elements of good storytelling. My secondary school was really academic and I can remember feeling completely frustrated. Then I left school and went to America for a year and worked as an au pair and was given the opportunity to do some kind of course that our family would pay for, and I thought, I'm going to do a clown course. So I went to a wee evening class and became a clown and performed quite a lot for the kids that I worked for and all their wee friends and I loved it. I'm aware that skills that I learned on that clown course definitely transfer into storytelling.

Such as what, specifically?

Well, just that bit about engaging the group and introducing yourself. It's different in that as a clown you are introducing your persona as Clover the Clown, but I used to dance in and sing a wee song to introduce myself. Now I don't have the persona of Clover the Clown and I'm introducing myself as Claire the Storyteller. You're doing the same thing but you're tweaking it slightly.

So it's still a specific identity even though you're there as Claire and that's just you, you're not adopting a separate character. In a way it is a separate character because it's storyteller Claire not another kind of Claire and there's a very specific identity you adopt.

Yeah, that's right. What you have to be aware of is that the children who are watching you are taking in your costume as a storyteller, so even though you're not putting on a costume as such, what you wear is important to them. If you get letters from children they will comment on what you've worn or comment on your jewellery, so I think it's really nice to pay some sort of attention to that.

So what kind of things informs those choices then? Because you're specifically presenting an identity . . .

I tend to dress quite colourfully anyway, but I do tend to wear certain things. If I'm working in a school it tends to be a wee bit more low key but, you know, definitely it would be colourful and quite often I like to be a bit Celtic looking, you know.

It's quite interesting the way some storytellers approach dress and costume, though they probably wouldn't call it costume. Some people deliberately dress down, some people try as much as possible to give a rural folksy kind of look and other people will take a particular ethnic look and develop that.

Yeah, absolutely. I definitely think it's good to make an effort. Just turning up in any old outfit is a let-down actually for your audience.

It's as much about making the event. It's contributing to part of the event itself, so there's a specialness to what you are doing?

Yeah, absolutely. I went on this course recently with Nancy Mellon, about healing stories. She talked a lot about creating the environment and it's something that I've always been aware of, that the environment that you are storytelling in is your beginning point. Any sort of learning or absorption has to be done in a pleasant environment. Since I've done that course, I do take more time about that. We invested in these colourful nets that are every colour of the rainbow and we take those with us now, we drape them around the room, we're more conscious about bringing a candle or bringing some flowers and a wee table cloth and definitely the group appreciates that, whether it be adults or whether it be kids, they definitely do.

Are those a particularly decorative use or do they have a practical application for you?

I think they're both. You're creating a space and if you're working with a vulnerable group you'd be creating quite a safe space, and if you put a rug down on the floor and you sit around that and have a candle on the rug it is a focal point. It takes it beyond just an everyday event into more of a ritual. It's lovely and for these children that have so little calm and serenity, it's crucial.

When you started storytelling did you think of yourself as being a performer at that point?

No, no, because I started off with the kids really. I thought of myself more as a channel. I felt this desire to pass on something to these children that I really felt would get something from it. I remember making the transition into more formal performing was quite frightening. My first formal performance was with adults, so it was the transition to formal performing and it was the transition into adults.

Do you feel as a storyteller you are improvising in performance to a large extent in a way that you might have done as a clown, or do you find that there's not much improvisation in storytelling?

It depends a bit on the context. I think when I'm at my best there's definitely a degree of improvisation. When I'm at my best and I'm relaxed within any story, I'll improvise within it and it definitely does connect it more to that time and that place and that moment, and that's when you are at your best.

Is it quite minor things? The actual story itself is the same. You don't sit down and learn a story by heart but as you tell it, it becomes a bit more fixed. So if I were to see two performances, a month apart, of the same story, it would be unlikely to have a huge amount of variation between those tellings? Improvisation is all to do with working the audience and being in the 'now' rather than the text itself.

Yeah, that's right. I would say my view is, the traditional story is relatively fixed and you're going to maybe add different colours to it.

Some of the description, different scenes, might be different, but in essence it's mainly the same core. I think the context that you create is as important as the story, so this bit that I'm talking about, creating the environment, creating the ritual, that's important because that enables your audience to relax and be ready and open, and if you do that you are creating a pathway for the story to go directly to the listener.

It was interesting watching at Draperstown when you were performing next to Michael Parent, who takes a very particular approach to character. He will actually not become the character, but he will at least show the character, whereas British storytellers tend to just present the character to you and it's far more reported than direct. What happens to you in relation to those other characters?

It does depend a wee bit on the story. Sometimes I will get right into the whole voice bit and everything. There are some stories that you want to let the characters just appear for themselves and the advantage of doing that, I guess, is that you're allowing the listener space to create the character in their own head and make pictures a wee bit, whereas if you get into a lot of animation, you probably aren't allowing your listeners the space to do that. For some stories I think it's important that they are given space to visualize.

In traditional stories, characters aren't developed, certainly not psychologically developed. They exist to serve the narrative, to serve the story rather than be fascinating character studies. The narrative is the central character in it, I suppose. Does that ring true for what you do with character?

It does, I would say. I think it does. I'm trying to think, because there are different kinds of stories out there. The Celtic stories are interesting because a lot of them do have quite a lot of detailed physical description, and that's different from the traveller stories where the description is quite minimal. I think for the most part I don't really animate or inhabit characters; I tell the story and let the listener paint the picture themselves.

You mentioned a couple of times, in relation to costuming and stories, the idea of Celticness. How important is that to your identity as a storyteller, or is it just coincidental?

It's funny how you can have a certain identity and then other people can put an identity onto you as well. So I think what's probably happened over a period of time is that a lot of people have seen me as a Celtic storyteller. There's a whole bit in Scotland here about being Irish and there's a whole set of expectations that comes with that. In some ways it's an asset.

When you're talking about Celticism, it carries with it certain connotations in terms of tradition and a sense of the ancient and those kinds of things, which often is what people's perceptions about storytelling are – that it's about something that primarily inhabits a time long ago, even though it's happening now. We're doing it now in order to inhabit that old world.

Umm, yeah, I don't think that's really what I think about storytelling.

MICHAEL PARENT

A native Mainer of French-Canadian descent, Michael has performed as a storyteller and singer, in both English and French, throughout the United States, and beyond, since 1977. He has been featured at many events, including the National Storytelling Festival in Jonesborough, Tennessee (1981, 1989, 1998, 2002), the International Storytelling Colloquium in Paris (1989), the Glistening Waters Festival in New Zealand (1998), the Sperrins Autumn Storytelling Festival in Northern Ireland and the *Scealta Shamhna* Festival in Dublin (2002), as well as the Multi-Cultural Storytelling Festival in Eugene, Oregon (2004). In addition to his

performances for a wide range of audiences, including schools, libraries, theatres, and festivals, Michael also leads storytelling, story-writing, and performance workshops.

After living in Virginia for many years, where he was a co-founder of, and frequent performer at, Live Arts, a thriving alternative theatre in Charlottesville, Michael returned to his home state of Maine in July 1998, and now lives in Portland. He received the National Storytelling Network's 'Circle of Excellence' Award in 1999, and was a keynote speaker at the 2001 National Storytelling Conference in Providence, RI.

Interview with Michael Parent

I'm interested in the identities that a storyteller presents within a performance, so that at one minute you are being yourself and one minute you might be yourself being the storyteller. And then there's the self being the storyteller presenting the character. You're using accents and physicality to present character in ways that very often British tellers don't. They would probably be more distant, wouldn't you say? The distance between performer and character is greater, I suppose, amongst British tellers.

That's interesting. I hadn't thought about that, but I think it's true.

With a lot of storytelling in the UK you are always aware that this is the storyteller on stage. What you seem to do at times is shift slightly further along the continuum where the character becomes more visible and the storyteller more invisible, but then there are other times when you bring that right back.

Well for me, what it boils down to is this: Does whatever you are doing move the story along or does it not? So there are people who move a lot during their stories, but it seems to move the story along. And there are other people who do movement because they think that's the trend, or for whatever reason they've come up with, and it doesn't move the story along, because you, the listener, are more conscious of the movement than you are of the story.

So if I was doing a character ... let's use a specific example ... the story about my grandfather and my grandmother. I feel that it works better told in the first person and I feel I can do the character of my grandfather. I'm not a trained actor, I've never done any method acting or any of that, but I feel I'm a fairly good mimic, which is not necessarily acting. I have had some informal training, but if I have the sense that the story is best told from that character's point of view, I do it and I make an effort to imitate his voice. If I consistently got some feedback like, 'All I could think of during that story was how well or how badly you were playing your grandfather', I would drop it like a hot potato because I really want the audience to get a sense of the relationship between these two people. I want them to get a sense of how much power she had, in a time where women had no power at all. I also want to honour that part of us that keeps people alive by just talking about them. One of the other things I love about storytelling is when somebody comes up to you and says, 'You know, that granddad (or that grandmother) of yours reminds me so much of my own grandfather (or grandmother) and I want to tell you a story about that.' Or they might just say thank you, because it revived some sort of memory, and you feel that in their next conversation, they are going to tell that story.

So I make a conscious decision to play my grandfather. Sometimes I'll put on my wire-rimmed, grandpa-type reading glasses, but sometimes I feel props and all don't matter. If I enjoy being my grand-father for those five minutes ... I mean if I can see my grandfather in that moment especially, then it works.

You said something really interesting there about storytelling being not so much acting, but mimicking. When I was watching you do your grandfather I was very aware that I was watching it in a different way than if I had been watching a method actor portray your grandfather. I could see your grandfather, but you were still very visible.

I understand what you mean. There was a time when I wrote a play, a one-man show called *Grandpa's Birthday* and it was basically some family stories that fitted together into one story about three generations of men in a family. It came down to my grandfather, my father and me. It was autobiographical to anyone who knew me but what I did then is – since I knew that I was going to be this character for an hour and fifteen minutes, I gave myself some support for maintaining the character. I set up on the stage a rocking chair and one of those cathode ray radios and a tobacco pipe and I wore a watch on a gold chain. Part of the reason for doing that was to create an atmosphere for the audience, because we're trying to create it not for four or five minutes but for an hour and a quarter. So this was to help me stay in character. I wore a little hat, the glasses and a vest. To sustain a character for an hour and fifteen minutes, I felt like I needed that help to get out of the story's way.

But you could say, if you were a storytelling purist, that's not storytelling – because you shouldn't be using props, you don't put a rug on the floor, you don't use a particular chair or radio, you don't use scenery or all that sort of stuff. But to me that wasn't the argument. It goes back to what I was talking about before – does it help move the story along? Whatever it is you do, the props, the voices, the impersonations. And there were times, there were some evenings, I felt that I nailed it, that I really sustained that character, that I sustained his physical voice and the story absolutely worked. There were other times that, for whatever reason, I was conscious of the fact that I had gone into my own physical voice for three or four sentences and I had to pull myself back. But I found the more I enjoyed it, the more I enjoyed reliving the images, the more I enjoyed listening to the story as I was telling it, the less self-conscious I was. And the less self conscious you are, the more you focus on the story, your enjoyment of it and your connection with the audience, the better it works. You see what I mean? You are not questioning yourself half way through the story as to whether or not you should be telling this story. Self-consciousness, I think, is the death of storytelling.

Talking about what you said earlier, about character, or whatever you do having to move the story along, having to work for the story. So that means that between story and character, the story always has the upper hand? The idea is that we are always listening to the story, rather than looking at the character?

I think so, absolutely. I think the story always has to have the upper hand.

I was wondering if there's a nervousness that if you go into character too much then there's a danger of losing the story? Within the stories that you were telling yesterday, we had maybe two or three characters that had to be maintained and there were also times when you were leaving those characters behind and deliberately coming back in as yourself, as the storyteller. How do you manage those transitions?

For instance in the Garbage Hero story I feel that the transitions are fairly simple. Partly I don't often do characters I don't feel I know. But the character of Richard, the garbage guy, I felt like I know him. I grew up with guys like him who had areas of talent. It was mostly hockey players in our town. There were guys walking all round the streets who had been offered scholarships to places like Brown University, which was an Ivy League college, just one notch down from Harvard. These guys, based on their athletic skills, would be offered scholarships to these places and then the college would look at their grades and that was the end of it. These guys would spend their life working in the mills, or gas stations, and they would wear their championship hockey jacket for the rest of their lives, all faded and the sleeves all coming apart. They might still be playing hockey in some sort of a league or whatever but they always had this mantle of disappointment. But some of them, the guys that I was most attracted to, were the guys that were in that situation but somehow rose above it. They could say to you 'I blew my chance; if I'd've had any brains at all I would have studied and done things differently. Here I am now and I'm going to make the best of it.' So that character, that guy Richard, I know him. So the transition isn't very difficult but what I do to try to help myself, I have him stand a certain way. And when there is a dialogue between the kid and Richard, I always do it sitting down. I always have Richard looking at the kid in a certain way and the kid looking up. I mean this isn't Laurence Olivier in any way, but I'm very aware of that.

The way that that character might stand or sit or whatever is very simple, right: two or three different things that will help you present that character to the audience? Are they there to also add some kind of comment, or social aspect to that character? Do you make the choice for the Richard character to have physical characteristics that tell us something about Richard in relation to the story?

Yes, absolutely. I feel like I want to convey that this is a guy that's kind of rough hewed. I mean, he's a garbage collector so he's not going to be sophisticated in the way he talks. He's a working guy and he talks like a working guy, and I don't want there to be a dissonance between the character and what he is saying or between the character and his job.

As a key way of altering the quality of the voice between characters, you would see yourself using accent more than pitch, or pace, or rhythm?

It seems like a mixture of things but let's say that one cues the other. If I slip into Richard, then the pace might change or the intonation of voice might change because I've taken on his accents. Or perhaps one of the first things that will change is the physical presence, and somehow there's some sort of kinetic memory. If you do it enough times in the presence, of the character then those things come along, the accent and the pace and all.

Those characterizations ... and also the way that you present yourself within the story ... there's a series of attitudes towards the material that comes through. There's your attitude, what your relationship to the story is. There's Richard's attitude. There are the different characters' attitudes towards what is happening. Are those attitudes enhanced in some way by the physicality of the characters? You were talking about the total disappointment in what he does and that is his key attitude towards the story or towards what is happening. What you do with your body when you physically become that character,

*does that disappointment inform the way that you think about pre-
senting the character physically, or is that something which just
naturally occurs?*

In acting there's this whole idea that you should write the biography
of a character, all the things that are not in the script or are not
revealed in the script. Well, let's stay with Richard for a while.
I haven't sat down and written a whole biography about Richard but
if you asked me questions about what his life had been like before he
got into this kind of work, or what his life was like at the moment of
the story, I could come up with something. It might not be the same
something each time, but I feel like he is OK with his life. That
moment when the kid tells him that he wants to be a garbage man
when he grows up, I can feel Richard is thinking, 'Why would you
want to do that?' I allow myself to feel what Richard might be feeling
at that moment and it feels like the story works better. There's a way
in which, if I feel it in my body, I don't really have to worry about
how the words come out. It's not as if I have to practise those lines
and it's not as if I have to say the words exactly the same every time.
But the more invested I am in each moment of the story, if I allow
myself to just be in the moment, to be present, I think that's the key to
acting and storytelling. That's one of the ways in which they touch.
But in theatre you have to really concentrate on the people you are on
stage with and stay in that world, and you hardly ever look at the
audience. There are some that break the fourth wall, but for the most
part you would only be secondarily aware of the audience. To me
that's the biggest difference. The pay-off in theatre comes from that
energy of having other people on stage with you and having it work.
In storytelling I feel like it's a completely different pay-off. There's
a connection with the audience that I haven't felt in theatre in the
same way.

*Just going back to what you were saying about not writing a lot
of biographical stuff about the character. That's quite interesting
because I suppose that means that the character primarily exists for
the story. Richard's function is to play the particular role in the story
and to have that particular attitude and to say those particular things.
Ultimately we are not necessarily interested in what he had for dinner
yesterday, or how many brothers and sisters he's got.*

Or how did he lose that finger?

Absolutely. What we are interested in, what makes the character of Richard worthwhile, is his function within the story and how he moves that story along.

Yeah, I would say so, because at some point. ... Let's use the finger as an example. I threw that in because it came to me. It seemed quite natural that someone like him would have lost a finger. I don't know where he lost it. He might have lost it in a rare moment of uncoordination, his finger got caught in the compression mechanism, or whatever, but I decided that I didn't want to tell the audience any more about Richard's life. I didn't want him to talk about his childhood; I didn't want him to talk about his finger or anything like that, because the story is not about Richard.

As you were saying, the method actor would spend weeks and months composing the biography for this character, which would then inform that performance. We, as an audience, might not know about that but they would have used that biography to inform their development of character. For you, that's not important because that's not part of the story. All that's important really is Richard, or any other character in the story and what their function in that story really is.

Yeah, and the other minor characters, Polly and Butch, the other two drivers, have a different function, but we don't need to know anything about them except how they perceive Richard. To me it's something about the nature of heroism. The fact is that I'm clear that the telling of that story has some impact on me.

Yes, and you need to know that that story is worth telling.

Oh yeah, I think so. And sometimes you can only determine that by telling it a few times.

Going back to talking about audience, because one of the things that drew me to storytelling was precisely that relationship that you have with an audience, and it seemed very democratic, that it actually dismantled the hierarchy. Theatre is a very hierarchal system. The whole auditorium is laid out hierarchically and you shut off any vision for the actor to see the audience. The actor is on stage to be watched and observed, which suggests another kind of hierarchy, and storytelling seemed to dismantle those hierarchies. I was just wondering

*what you thought, because you keep coming back to audience and the
importance of that relationship.*

Yeah, I had forgotten about footlights and everything blinding you,
even if you wanted to make some sort of contact with the audience.
Sometimes people will set it up that way, and I will say I need the
house lights, and if people are familiar with storytelling they'll usually
have it that way. I find it very disconcerting not to see the audience.
And the fact is that sometimes when you can see them it can throw
you off, but you can react to that.

*Does it not invite a response from the audience, if the audience knows
that you can see them? It kind of opens up the stage for them to
comment, in a way that theatre audiences won't. They'll sit there, very
well behaved, generally, where storytelling audiences will interrupt if
they want to.*

There's a different etiquette. Well for instance, last night. Liz (Weir)
said something and somebody kind of shouted something back. They
felt comfortable enough because Liz created an atmosphere of
connection rather than an atmosphere of hierarchy. I find that to be
a completely indispensable part of the form.

*It also, does it not, invites the audience to play a more active part in
that process? You are also inviting them, therefore, to be part of
making the meaning of that story.*

Yeah, because you are not showing them as much. I could tell the
Garbage Hero story without slipping into the character of Richard.
Other than his hands and his physical movements I don't describe him
at all. I don't tell you he was tall, had dark hair, he was short or had
... they can look at me being Richard and they can imagine a thirty-
eight-year-old guy even though I don't look thirty-eight. I don't
describe the little boy. He could be lanky, he could be a bit stocky, it
doesn't really matter. You invite them to make their own visuals,
to make their own meaning. Absolutely. I think that's the fun of being
in the audience. I like being in the audience as much as I like being
on stage.

TAFFY THOMAS

Born in Somerset, but now resident in the Lake District, Taffy Thomas is one of the most established performers on the English storytelling scene. His background is as a street performer and community artist with Welfare State International, Magic Lantern and The Fabulous Salami Brothers. He also worked on the major folk operas *The Shipbuilder* and *The Transports*.  In 1984 he suffered a debilitating stroke while performing, which left him without speech and partially paralysed down one side, and he developed his storytelling skills as a means of helping his convalescence. He was resident storyteller in the North Pennines and also in South Lakeland and is co-director of the Lakeland Storytelling Festival. He also works with his wife Chrissie, as part of Dancetales, exploring storytelling and narrative dance. In 2002 he was awarded the MBE for his services to charity and storytelling.

Interview with Taffy Thomas

The thing that's interesting about you and your storytelling is that before you were working as a storyteller you had this career that was still performance-based, but was more to do with theatre. How much do you think that career informs what you do now?

One of the ways in which it informs my work now is that I am prepared to tell stories in almost any situation, so I will tell stories in the street, in a pub, in a field or on a walk, whereas many of the storytellers in the revival are slightly more precious about the circumstances they perform in. You would have thought it would make me more physical as a performer, but it hasn't because I am also disabled, and I would not have chosen to be more physical even if I was fully able-bodied because I think it's about the power of language. It's very much language-based.

Do you, then, see the storytelling that you do as literature or theatre, or is that a false distinction?

I probably see it as visual art actually, except that the piece of visual art is conceptual rather than physical, in so far as it's about making pictures with words and transferring those pictures from the storyteller's mind to the mind of the listener.

It's interesting that you say the sort of storytelling you do isn't particularly physical.

Let me just tell you a little story. I was doing a workshop in Manchester and the way that I do a workshop is, after doing a skilling session, I get people to choose a partner and one half of each pair leaves the room and I tell the remaining half a story. Then the others come back and they retell this story to their partners. Then we swap over and at that point everyone has told a story. But this workshop was working with the writers' group who write for theatre, and the story I very often use is 'The Tailor and the Button'. I always begin with, 'There was this little tailor. He was the finest tailor in the land; no he wasn't ... he was the finest tailor in the *world*.' I did this in the morning and, sure enough, everyone who was passing the story on to their partners started with, 'There was this little tailor.' But in the afternoon I did it with the acting group and I shuffled over to the first pair who were passing the story on, and this chap immediately started, 'I was a tailor,' and I thought, 'No, this is not what storytelling is about, or at least the type that I do.' It's a reported art form in the way that you report the story, a couple of paces away from it. In that way, you almost declaim it in the way the old ballad singers, like Harry Cox, used to declaim the ballads.

I would always describe everything I have ever done as small-scale, self-made entertainment. That's the phrase I use. I suppose the smallest-scale entertainment you can have is a person sitting or standing with one or a few people around them telling them a story.

But there still is something very theatrical, I suppose, about what you do, in the way that you show quite a sophisticated sense of theatricality and occasion in what you do.

I would call that showmanship rather than theatricality. As a street performer my roots were in circus and fairground arts, so perhaps that is what informs what I do. For me it's showmanship rather than theatre, because I try to deliver. I'm also not ashamed to be an entertainer. It doesn't mean anything I do is of any less importance or value or seriousness. I think that it operates on all sorts of levels but if you don't entertain, you can't achieve any of the other goals.

So what's your relationship to material that you choose?

Two decisions I made at a very early stage in my career was: one, that I would, wherever possible, get my material from oral sources, from people rather than print, so that is the main feature of my material. I spent a lot of time with people like Betsy White, Duncan William-son, John Campbell. I also would argue that it isn't actually the storytelling revival because it's never actually died. It's a revival in so far as it's had a sudden impetus of interest. I sometimes feel that I occupy the space between storytelling and stand-up. I learned from watching the better of the stand-up comedians, and, of course, there has been a massive revival of interest in that.

Who are the influences there?

Probably Dave Allen, Billy Connolly.

Do you consciously set time aside now for learning new material?

No, I don't. What I have consciously done lately is to look to ways of taking advantage of the fact that a lot of people come to the area where I live, as tourists and so on. We have set up this little story-telling centre in Grasmere and the garden is the storytellers' garden. It's the most unique open-air venue in the North, I should think, for the performing arts. Because it's a garden it really influences my repertoire in terms of making it seasonal. I have stories I only tell seasonally so I don't get fed up with them, because they lie fallow until the next time that Christmas or Autumn comes around. I like being in the open air where I can. The experiences any storyteller has in their lives inform the story. So the fact that for two periods in my life I have been a fisherman has increased my repertoire of sea and fishing stories, but even within the other stories it has informed them with little references. If I talk about whistling, I might add within the story the fact that when I was a fisherman, one day I was stood before the mast whistling, twenty miles out into the Atlantic ocean, and the skipper popped his head out and said, 'Taffy, if you whistle again you can walk back!' Had I not had that fishing experience then that reference wouldn't be there in the story.

Do you see your work as a storyteller having a kind of political impetus behind it?

For me the politics is that you actually stand in front of people and entertain them just by telling them a story – that is a political statement in itself in an era which is completely dominated by commercial mass media. Also I have a collection of stories that deal with peace, and redistribution of wealth, and so on – a little collection of stories I like to call 'Red Tales in the Sunset'.

Do you see tradition as a liberating force rather than as a conservative force?

Yes, I think that the tradition exists, and the stories and the songs mean different things to different generations. But love, war, food – these are things that are there for all of us and always have been. Hugh Lupton once was asked if he told any stories about contemporary issues, and he said, 'I can't think of any issue, any contemporary issue that hasn't been an issue in the past.' Of course he went for the nuclear debate, and you could go back to pollution of another kind and get into 'Pandora's Box' sooner or later.

'Tradition' is a word that is used incredibly loosely in association with storytelling, and people will often use it as a merit of quality.

For me it's a description of a process where I see myself as being a link in a chain. So somebody tells me a story, and I tell it to somebody else, and eventually it comes back to me. If you throw a dart hard enough, it goes all the way around the world and lands in the back of your head!

So for you a traditional storyteller is someone who engages in a process, rather than the material that they necessarily tell, or even their ethnicity?

And that process is social. Of all the art forms I think it's the most social, because you immediately enter into a communication or a debate with your audience. If you shuffle close to an audience, if there are two people talking quietly, try to hear what they are saying. The chances are that they're talking about what you're doing and it's an expression of enjoyment of what you're doing. I think about giving people a good night out. They've got to feel comfortable. But part of feeling comfortable is in some cultures that they could speak to you if they wanted. There isn't a great barrier. If there's a stage, the chances are that you'll stand or sit in front of it, rather than on it.

That's something I always used to do – for me it was about democratization of the art, breaking down the hierarchies that are inherent as soon as you have a proscenium stage.

Having said that, in our festival this weekend you get a show in the school, a show in the pub, shows in the street, but there are also some shows in the village hall in more or less a theatrical set-up with a backdrop. We borrow from the world of theatre and performance the things that are useful to us and dispense with the ones that aren't. There are some quite elderly people in the village that feel safer if you're on a stage and they're out front, but then in the school with the youngsters they're more comfortable if they're so close they can smell you!

Have you ever worked with other storytellers beyond simply sharing a stage with them, or do you see storytelling as primarily a solo performance activity?

I work quite often with musicians and link music and stories, but I also enjoy the link with dance. My wish to do something with dance came about as a result of doing a tour for disabled groups. I was working with a sign interpreter and it just felt like working with a dancer. I like breaking down barriers between all art forms.

When you are performing to what degree do you think what you're doing is improvised? Are you working eventually from a fixed text?

No, I consciously work against that. What happens when you get a new story is that the first twenty times it's in a glorious floating state where it can alter quite radically. But after about twenty tellings it tends to settle and probably doesn't alter much. But still the form is loose or generous enough, so that if you hear of a new idea while you're working, you can slide it in.

Is that partly possible because you're working on your own?

Yes, it's possible because you are the author, director and effectively the sole voice. The exception that I had to that was last year. I did a major commission, which was to create a legend to be performed as part of the Proms at the Albert Hall with an orchestra, effectively looking for a new *Peter and the Wolf*. I created a story with lots of traditional references within it, and then it went to a contemporary composer, who made a piece of music. We performed in the Albert Hall with five thousand people and a quarter of a million people listening on the radio. What was terrifying about that was it was the first time ever in my life I had a semi-circle of one hundred and twenty professional musicians around me, who were waiting for a word cue within that twelve-minute piece. I think there was something like eighteen music cues which I had to hit.

Did that significantly alter what you normally do?

Yes, but I fought to maintain my style and identity, so they were actually getting a sense of traditional storytelling. Probably I gave the conductor and musicians a white knuckle ride and then shrugged and went, 'Well, that's storytelling!' They were certainly aware it wasn't the same twice.

I'm interested in that because a lot of storytellers will say, 'Oh no, every telling is a completely new telling and words will come out as they come out and it's purely improvised.'

It's either hype or there are storytellers who are remarkably inconsistent. I'm aware you have a responsibility as a professional entertainer. Your responsibility as an artist is to be creative and exciting. As a professional entertainer you have to be consistent and that's the hardest thing to deliver.

Perhaps it isn't half as improvised as we would like to think it is?

Yes, I think that people like to say it is. I would rather say it's not improvised, but it's possible for it to change in performance, if the performer is feeling especially creative.

I'd always found myself drawing less on any skills of improvisation and more on skills as a performer, and the sorts of things you instinctively know to be right and that are going to work. That can lead to fresh ways of doing things.

Yes, I feel a lot of what I do is instinctive.

If you hadn't had the stroke, would you be a storyteller?

If I hadn't had the stroke I might just be thinking about getting more into it now due to my advancing years. Up to my early fifties I would have happily continued to eat fire, danced on broken glass, have paving stones smashed on my body. I needed storytelling after the stroke because it was a kind of speech therapy I could identify with. It's damned hard work unless you've got a point of contact.

LIZ WEIR

A children's librarian by training, Liz Weir is arguably the single person most responsible for nurturing the storytelling revival in Ireland, although she regularly works all over the UK as well. She travels the world telling

stories to adults and children, organizing workshops on storytelling, and speaking at courses for teachers, parents and librarians. Overseas she has told stories in Israel, Canada, Australia and the United States. She has been a featured teller at the National Storytelling Festival, Jonesborough, Tennessee, the St Louis Festival, Texas Festival, Northern Appalachian Festival, Bay Area Festival and the 2001 Toronto Storytelling Festival. She is also the organizer of the highly successful annual Ulster Storytelling Festival and is in the process of converting her house in the Glens of Antrim into a centre for storytelling activities.

Interview with Liz Weir

Tell me a bit about how you became a storyteller.

I grew up in a family where you had to perform in some shape or form. My job was to sing songs on stage. I was very shy, I hated it. Then I went on to train as a children's librarian. The first thing I was given was a picture book and told to tell a story to everybody and, although I loved books and being told stories, I never saw myself as a storyteller. I learned the techniques, influenced by people like Grace Hallworth and Eileen Colwell. Then as I told stories, through 1973 to 1990, I noticed that adults loved stories as well. I met my first American storyteller in about 1978 and he told me that in America people had guilds where they get together to tell stories. I thought,

'This is Ireland where jobs are hard to find and everybody has stories. This is something we should be doing.' I started with a one-day course in 1984, which attracted over one hundred people. From that we formed the Yarnspinners, which met in Belfast from 1985 to 2002, of which there were offshoots. I had a dream that there would be storytelling groups all over Ireland. In the meantime I was working as a librarian and taking the odd job here and there. I started to travel a wee bit, won awards and did a bit of storytelling in Australia. I eventually took a career break in 1990 and have been telling stories professionally ever since. That's how I got to where I'm at.

Did it feel like a break or more of an extension of what you were doing?

No, it was quite different. I was still doing a lot of training – library consultancy work – but storytelling was my main focus.

Are there particular skills you learned as a librarian that have direct applications to your storytelling?

Definitely, they've been of tremendous benefit. Organizational skills would be the strength. I've organized my own career, library events, storytelling events, festivals, work for other people. From 1974 to 1990 I organized a summer storytelling programme where we were doing eighty sessions a week.

What about the other skills you have as a performer?

I've learned them on the hoof. As a librarian I did my share of going to talks, and how to give talks to people. I had to learn how to hold an audience, in particular in Belfast, where you might have an army foot patrol going past or a swimming pool with screaming kids in the background. Anybody who works in the community, not in nice comfortable arts centres, not in a school context, but right out there, learns a lot from that and I've developed a lot myself.

You put an awful lot of time, energy and investment into things like festivals and all kinds of initiatives and projects that don't necessarily directly benefit or promote you. Being behind the scenes, setting things up for other people seems to be a philosophy that's running through everything.

The one thing I get extremely irritated about is ego. The best storytellers I've ever met are not the big-name stars you see earning huge amounts of money. The best storytellers I've ever met are the older people, the quiet people who'd never say they were storytellers and yet have taught me so much. Like everybody else, I earn a living, and I like the high-profile stuff and do my fair share of it. The other work is more important for me, I think. I would rather be sitting with a group of twelve people who don't consider they've got anything to say but who have got the most amazing stories. I love that part of it. From what I see in a lot of storytelling, there's an awful lot of ego involved. I'd rather not be in that circle; I'd rather walk away from it and so I think I'm very lucky. I have the best of both worlds. I still get to perform internationally, go to festivals and do the big stuff, and I love the small stuff. It's more important for the culture of storytelling, I think.

What informs the choices you make as a performer, in terms of what stories you're going to learn and what stories you're going to tell?

My main philosophy is only to tell stories that I like. I can hear people do really fabulous stories, but if I don't like them there's no point in telling them. Also, coming from an Irish background, and very much a Northern Irish Protestant background, I didn't learn the big Irish stories because we were never taught them. I've obviously done my work on learning the epic Irish stories because it's part of where I come from, but that part was denied to me as part of growing up. So I tend to tell mostly folktales. I love stories that promote a consideration of the other person's point of view. I started work in Belfast in the height of the Troubles and I think that part of it is getting stories to create empathy. That sounds very schmaltzy now, but I do think that stories can inform you about other people, whether they're Protestant, Catholic, black, white ... whatever. So that informs me in my choice of stories.

Do you tell stories, then, in order to try and make links with a less complicated past, or to say what we need to deal with what is happening in the present?

A combination of both. I truly believe that people have more in common than they have apart. I have this missionary zeal, to help people realize that, but I think we can also learn a lot from the past.

I have worked, for example, with prisoners in jails, people who have been right there on the front line. Politicians can talk, but you really need to talk to the people involved where there's violence. I think that in meeting these people and hearing where they are coming from has helped me understand where we are going. I know that we're not all going to live happily ever after and love each other, but at the same time we can understand a lot more about each other. As for dealing with reality, children always say, 'Tell me a horror story', and I sit and talk with them and say, 'There's so much horror going on in the world, I don't need to tell you.' I tell ghost stories, but I don't tell stories with blood and guts, but I know a lot of storytellers that do. Maybe I'm squeamish but I've seen people lying dead with a bullet through their head. I don't choose to tell stories about that. It's not ignoring what goes on, but let's learn from that and move on.

Changing tack, we were talking about the use of non-storytelling spaces.

Buses, trains, fast ferries, you name it.

On the other hand, the festival at Cultra uses these nice beautiful buildings and cottages and puts storytellers in there, which seems to be a different kind of way of creating an event. It's more of a celebration of the artifice of performance.

I see anywhere as a storytelling space. I'm very clear about that. I've heard people criticize the festival by saying it's perpetuating the myth of the old people sitting by the fire telling a story and this isn't part of the modern world. To me it's every bit as valid doing that. If I were only doing that, I would take criticism of it. If you take the tourist industry in Northern Ireland, a lot of our industry is involved with bringing tourists in to use the facilities we have. It's very much about trying to recreate the atmosphere. But that's only one way. If you like, it's 'staged'. We have a hall with lights and a microphone, but for every two of those a year there are hundreds and hundreds of storytelling events at playschemes or wherever. I honestly do think that stories can be told anywhere. I have heard people say, 'Only if the ambience is right – with the wall hangings – only if you've got the lights angled properly.' I know people who freak out if the lighting or sound system isn't right, but you can't always be so choosy. If I was sitting in the community hall with one bare bulb and people there, you can create a space for storytelling by your voice, how you treat people. You can build up a storytelling audience. We could be elite storytellers, telling stories in arts centres, but you are excluding a lot of people. I like to include rather than exclude people.

You don't generally go in and dress a space?

No, not me.

You make some transformation, though?

Seating maybe, the usual – what you have to do to be a storyteller. You must have an eye for the space and see what works best in terms of seating. You have to create a comfortable space. I always like to define a space, even if I've got a group of children coming into a library. I define my space by setting out two chairs for the teachers at the side to make them a part of it.

So you would create your space defined primarily in relation to the audience, whereas a storyteller who comes in with their drapes and curtains, what they will try to do is transform their space rather than the audience's. You both create a performative space, but you are approaching it from a different perspective.

Yes, absolutely the truth. But even if I'm performing in an arts centre I differ from other people in terms of not wanting the audience in the dark. I want to be able to see my audience. Storytelling to me is the interaction between the storyteller and the audience. It's almost a personal interaction because you are speaking to each person in the audience and I like to see who I'm speaking to.

What about stages? Do you prefer not to work on stage?

I don't mind. It depends entirely on the situation. If you've got a job in Tennessee and there are one thousand people in the audience, you have to be on stage for them to see you and the sound system has to be really good. It varies greatly and it depends on the physical arrangements. In your average church hall I'll sit on the edge of the stage or just pull a chair in front of the stage. You can't generalize. Sometimes it's very much a stage thing and there's a big gulf between you and the audience and that's just the way it has to be. It depends what you're doing and whom you're performing to. I've told stories in the pulpit of the church, and it's the only way they can see you.

When you're actually performing, to what extent is there a different Liz who becomes a performer?

There has to be. You owe that to your audience. I try to be natural – what you see is what you get, and yet I'm not as naive as to think I'm always on and up. You have to go into performance mode and I think that you owe that. If people have paid money to come and see you, you have to step up a gear. My favourite performers would be those who are as relaxed as possible, not the people that are so hyper they set the audience on edge. I've been in situations where the audience are embarrassed, either because the performer is so hyper, or superior, or whatever. I'd rather be more natural, except it's natural with a layer, a varnish on it. I think all of us in our lives as storytellers have to find what works for ourselves. A lot of people, when they start off, try to be like somebody else, the person who has influenced them the most, whoever it's been. They try to be as like them as possible, learning the repertoire off by heart, learning the information by heart, learning everything by heart. And that's a phase people go through, but you then have to do the work and find yourself. You have to find what works for you and I can only tell you what works for me. But there's not a day goes by when I'm not prepared to learn something else or find something else. That's how you never get tired, never get bored, because every day is different, every audience is different, and you are different, depending on the situation.

Notes

Note to the Foreword

1. E. Verne, 'Literacy and Industrialization – the Dispossession of Speech', in *Literacy and Social Development in the West*, ed. Harvey Graff (Cambridge: Cambridge University Press, 1981) pp. 302–3.

Notes to Chapter 1: History and Context

1. An interview with Brook was included in the programme for the 1989 International Storytelling Festival in London. Also, the French storyteller Abbi Patrix worked with Brook at his Centre for International Theatre Research in Paris.
2. This is not strictly true. Theatre producers could still be tried for obscenity, as happened in 1981 in the wake of the National Theatre's production of Howard Brenton's *Romans in Britain*, which contained a scene of simulated male rape.
3. Actually, not a college at all, but more of a loose association of enthusiasts (see Heywood, 1998, pp. 24–5).
4. 'Jack Tales' is the commonly used term to refer to the corpus of European and Armenian folktales, which feature Jack as a central character. Jack is a social under-dog, an everyman figure, often poor and uneducated, who usually through a combination of honesty, courage, wit and kindness, wins the day and transforms his own social status.
5. Perhaps the nearest thing that any British university has to a dedicated folklore department, with the exception of NATCECT (The National Centre for English Cultural Tradition) at the University of Sheffield.
6. For a full discussion of these matters and of other TV film fairy-tale adaptations, see Zipes, 1997.
7. This initiative has been so successful that it has subsequently been adopted by many other BBC regions.

Notes to Chapter 2: Acting and Storytelling

1. It is perhaps useful to distinguish between the current situation in schools in Britain (and indeed Ireland), where storytellers can be used in a variety of ways to support the curriculum, and what happens in American schools, where there is even less public funding for storytelling and children's theatre. Each school has its own budget, which it spends as it sees fit, more readily supporting trips to the theatre or bringing in 'platform' storytellers performing to the entire school, than more small-scale or developmental work, such as some of the educational work described in the chapter on 'Applied Storytelling'. In recent years, following budget cuts imposed on education and the arts by the current administration, the money has all but dried up.

2. *Grammelot* is an onomatopoeic theatrical language created by actors in the 16th-century *Commedia dell'arte*. Tony Mitchell describes it as 'a phonic, abstract sound-system in which few recognizable words of any language occur, and which relies on suggestion' (Mitchell, 1984, p. 12). More contemporary exponents might include Charlie Chaplin in *The Great Dictator* (1940) or even the British comedian Stanley Unwin (1911– 2002) who invented his own gobbledygook language, 'Unwinese'. Paul Whitehouse also employed a form of *grammelot* in his creation of the character of Rowley Birkin, QC, for the BBC comedy series *The Fast Show* (1994–2000). For further discusison see Mitchell, 1984, pp. 12–14.

3. 'in jeder neuen Lage neu nachzudenken'. My translation.

4. It is also as a theoretician that Brecht has suffered most at the hands of post-war Western critics, who found it almost impossible to reconcile artistic genius with political commitment, especially when that commitment was of a socialist nature. Uncomfortable with Brecht's unswerving commitment to Marxism, a range of Western critics such as Ronald Gray and Martin Esslin (see Needle and Thomson, 1981, pp. 51–5) have resorted to one of two strategies in dealing with Brechtian theory. The first is to attempt to deny his political commitment, or at least to underplay its significance. This is a tricky thing to do, as Brecht's politics are so fore-grounded in both his plays and his writings. To deny his politics is to deny all meaning contained within his work. The second strategy is to declare that Brecht's artistic achievements were significantly compromised by an attachment to dogma.

5. My emphasis.

6. Benjamin was, of course, writing in the 1930s. It took folklorists another thirty years or more to realize the importance of performance to the study of oral tradition.

Notes to Chapter 3: Platform Storytelling

1. One might here even make a useful distinction within the ranks of plat-form storytellers between 'pedestal storytellers', who present themselves

and their skills for admiration, and 'rostrum storytellers', who may give a formal 'cultural' performance, but do so with the intention of creating a more democratic and subversive engagement with the audience.

2. Some years ago I saw a performance by Will Coleman, a storyteller and actor with Kneehigh Theatre. As he was setting up he placed on the ground a rug which, I seem to remember, portrayed various celestial and astrological symbols. He was, he claimed, not trying to suggest a mystical or mythological aspect to his storytelling, although this was an inevitable consequence of his choosing this particular rug. Nor was he trying to emphasize the division between performer and audience, although this would naturally result from such a decision. He told me that, as an actor, used to performing on a stage or in some other defined space, placing the rug on the floor provided him with a spatial focus for his performance without which he would have felt exposed.

3. Michael Harvey even turned to storytelling following a back injury, recognizing that this was a way of continuing working as a performer without jeopardizing his health, and, of course, it also enabled Taffy Thomas to continue his performance career after his stroke affected his physical mobility.

4. Ironically perhaps, in a world where storytelling has been professionalized and commodified, storytellers need to be highly visible in order to market themselves effectively. Platform storytelling events do not advertise themselves primarily around the stories that are being told, but around the performers themselves. It is the names and photographs of the storytellers that adorn the festival posters and programmes and it is largely the individual performers that the audiences seek out, not the stories.

5. Medlicott draws extensively on her own childhood in west Wales, as well as her experiences of living in Kenya and travelling extensively throughout the world, for her repertoire. She is also the editor of a number of volumes of international folktales.

Notes to Chapter 4: Applied Storytelling

1. Often, and mistakenly, 'community theatre' is used as a synonym for 'amateur theatre' (or amateur drama). Amateur drama, however, is often conservative in outlook, a pale imitation of the establishment theatre and often avoiding dealing with anything controversial or outspokenly political. Community theatre is often very much the opposite.

2. See Zipes, 2004, pp. 239–41, for a fuller description of the work of Grips Theater.

3. The professional name of British-Guyanese storyteller Godfrey Duncan. TUUP stands for 'The Unorthodox Unprecedented Preacher'.

4. Both these stories are regularly published within anthologies of British folktales and are readily available. 'The Old Woman who Lived in a Vinegar Bottle' concerns an old woman who receives a series of wishes from a fairy. The first wish she uses to escape from her vinegar bottle by asking for a small cottage. However, she soon becomes dissatisfied and demands a larger house. There then follows a series of further demands as the woman asks for increasingly lavish accommodation. The story ends with the fairy losing her patience and returning the old woman to her vinegar bottle. 'The Old Woman and the Pig' is a cumulative tale which begins with a woman on her way home from market trying to encourage a reluctant pig to climb over a stile. She begins by asking a dog to bite the pig, thereby forcing him over the stile, but the dog refuses to act. One by one she asks a series of animals and inanimate objects to help and only succeeds when she bribes the cat into action with a saucer of milk. The story ends thus: 'So the cat drank the milk and then ... the cat began to kill the rat, the rat began to gnaw the rope, the rope began to hang the butcher, the butcher began to kill the ox, the ox began to drink the water, the water began to quench the fire, the fire began to burn the stick, the stick began to beat the dog, the dog began to bite the pig, and piggy jumped over the stile and that old woman got home that night!'

5. An example might be Duncan Williamson's story of 'The Devil's Salt Mill', which offers an explanation of why the sea is salty. This story could just as easily lead to discussions about the different life forms to be found in fresh-water and seawater environments, an investigation into the chemical properties of salt, or even industrial methods of extracting salt, from mining to desalination plants.

6. Perhaps my favourite example is the story of the three travelling salesmen who went to pay their hotel bill. The cost was £30 for all three of them, so they split it evenly and each paid £10. However, the landlord realized he had overcharged them by £5, so took 5 × £1 notes (this was a while ago) out of the till to refund the travelling salesmen. But he then realized that he had no change and could not split £5 three ways very easily, so he decided to give the travellers back £1 each and he quietly slipped the other £2 into his own pocket. This meant that each of the travelling salesmen had now paid £9 (i.e. £10 minus the £1 refund) and together they had paid, in total, £9 × 3 = £27. Plus there was the £2 in the landlord's pocket, making £29. So where is the missing pound? The solution, of course, lies in spotting the flaw in the mathematics. I'll say no more than that!

7. A separate curriculum was subsequently introduced into schools in Northern Ireland to take into account the very different demands upon the timetable made by religious education.

8. My emphasis.

9. An example would be the work of Dr Vayu Naidu from the University of Kent, who has worked with asylum seekers in the south-east of England. Further afield, Professor Evangelos Avdikos from the University of Thessaly has worked extensively with migrant Bulgarian communities in north-eastern Greece.

10. For example, see www.storysmith.co.uk, the website of UK-based storyteller Chris Smith or www.successstory.org.uk, the website of David Bash. Ohio-based Chris King's website at www.creativekeys.net is a US-based example. I'm not suggesting that these storytellers are the most prolific in the field of storytelling in business organizations, but their websites are typical of many.

11. According to David James, a storyteller and teacher based in Dorset, IBM, Nike and Coca-Cola all use storytelling as a training tool (www.leraconteur.scriptmania.com). Hewlett Packard's use of story-telling is the subject of Charlene Collison's article in *Storylines* (2001).

12. The World Social Forum, held in Brazil in January 2005, included an international gathering of storytellers, academics and those in related professions to discuss the very issue of the role of storytelling in the face of globalization.

Notes to Chapter 5: Theatre and Storytelling

1. For such a history, readers may wish to refer to Oscar Brockett's *History of the Theatre*, which presents two alternative theories concerning the origin of theatre. The first 'envisions theatre as emerging out of myth and ritual' (Brockett, 1998, p. 1): that is, a kind of sympathetic magic whereby primitive society attempts to explain the supernatural forces which, it assumes, control those elements of the environment outside of its power, such as the weather, by means of the creation of myth, and to influence those forces by means of the re-enactment of those myths. In favour of this theory are the clear parallels and shared performative elements between ritual and theatre, although Brockett rightly draws attention to the problematic nature of such a stance, as it is largely based on the precepts of Cultural Darwinism. The second theory that Brockett proposes is that theatre emerged from traditions of storytelling, where storytelling and story-listening are 'fundamental human pleasures' (Brockett, 1998, p. 5). In this sense Brockett is referring to the recounting of personal experiences and actual events, such as 'a hunt, battle or other feat' (Brockett, 1998, p. 5). What he fails to realize, however, is that such storytelling is not simply a fundamental pleasure, but a fundamental *need*, a way of understanding and acknowledging important experiences. Indeed the two theories that Brockett describes are two sides of the same theory – one that deals with *sacred* storytelling and another that deals with *secular*

storytelling. They both address the human need to make sense of the spiritual and actual world.

2. Instead we might now more readily view the work of those contemporary performance artists and experimental theatre companies since 1968 who have sought to challenge the narrative conventions of theatre, as being the essence of an anti-narrative position. It is arguable, though, whether these companies and individuals have completely rejected narrative or simply redefined its relationship with theatre. Narratives may be neither explicit nor linear, but that does not mean they are not there. It is difficult for humans to resist the narrative impulse, and even if a performer obscures, or even denies, a narrative, an audience will often seek to impose one, simply because narrative is such a powerful tool of interpretation. Arguably, seemingly anti-narrative, post-dramatic performance simply deals with narrative unconventionally by shifting the narrative responsibility from the performer to the audience.

3. For a full account of the making and touring of *The Cheviot*, see the essay 'The Year of *The Cheviot*', in McGrath, 2002, pp. 59–72.

4. Nikki Sved did, however, provide a well-attended workshop at the Society for Storytelling's Annual Gathering at the University of Exeter in 1995.

5. A reference to Duffy and Supple's *Beasts and Beauties*, which was running in Bristol at the same time.

6. Created in collaboration with a Jamaican-born jazz musician and composer, Orphy Robinson.

Primary Sources

It would be a task of gargantuan proportions to attempt to create a comprehensive list of books of folktales that the student might turn to in the search for appropriate source material. Therefore, what I have produced here is an indicative list, rather than an exhaustive one, of some of the books that I have personally found most useful in that respect. They have all been published (or re-issued) in the last thirty-five years and most more recently than that, so even those that are no longer in print should be readily available through the library system.

For the student in search of material, the most obvious place to begin looking is in the children's section of the library or bookshop. Although there are many excellent editions of folktales for children, I have not included any here for two reasons. First, because I don't think anybody would have any trouble finding children's folktale books, with or without my help, and secondly because many retellings of folktales for children have been purged of some of their most interesting details – the scatalogical, the sexual, the violent and, far too often, the socially and politically subversive. Of course, there are exceptions to this, but instead I have here concentrated on collections of stories that were published for an adult readership (the fact that many of these were published during the 1980s and 1990s is further testament to the general renaissance of interest in story at this time) and I will happily trust the individual storyteller to make appropriate editorial decisions according to their audience.

The Victorians were, of course, avid collectors of folktales and some of those collections, most notably those of **Andrew Lang** (*The Yellow Fairy Book*, *The Blue Fairy Book*, etc., written for children) and **Joseph Jacobs** (*Celtic Fairy Tales*, *More Celtic Fairy Tales*, *English Fairy Tales*), have never been out of print and are today available in a range of cheap editions. Whilst these can be an invaluable resource, one should be aware that they are shrouded in the romantic and lyrical language that was thought appropriate at the time, which will require stripping away in order to get to the raw essence of the story.

The collections made by the brothers Jacob and Wilhelm Grimm remain an essential resource for the storyteller in spite of their first being published almost two hundred years ago. Unless intending to access them in the original German, the English reader has a distinct advantage in that the stories are regularly re-translated, so that usable modern translations are easy to find. The stories can also be accessed on the internet (www.pitt.edu/~dash/grimm.html), but my favourite translations are those by Jack Zipes in *The Complete Fairy Tales of the Brothers Grimm* (New York: Bantam Press, 1992), which not only contains forty additional stories, never previously published in English, but also has a very useful introductory essay, detailing the collection in its socio-historical context.

In the late 1980s Penguin published a number of substantial collections of oral literature under the series title **The Penguin Folklore Library**. These tend to be ethnocentrically organized, but contain a wealth of varied and interesting material. They include **Henry Glassie's** *Irish Folktales* (1987), **Inea Bushnaq's** *Arab Folktales* (1987) and **Duncan and Linda Williamson's** *A Thorn in the King's Foot* (1987). Further volumes from Duncan Williamson's vast repertoire are published by Canongate and are particularly interesting, because, as the work of an oral storyteller, the stories retain a genuine and discernable flavour of the spoken tale. Penguin is also the publisher of **Italo Calvino's** classic collection *Italian Folktales* (1982).

Also of interest are those volumes published in the 1980s by Pantheon, including the collections by the renowned American folklorist **Roger D. Abrahams**, *African Folktales* (1983) and *Afro-American Folktales* (1985).

Of all the editions of traditional stories that were published at this time, however, perhaps the most interesting are *The Virago Book of Fairy Tales* (1990) and *The Second Virago Book of Fairy Tales* (1992), selected and edited by **Angela Carter**. These outstanding volumes are thematically arranged and contain a mixture of well-known and more obscure folktales, all featuring women as the central characters.

No list of this sort could possibly be complete without mention of **Katherine Briggs's** hefty masterpiece *A Dictionary of British Folktales*. Originally published simultaneously in Britain and the United States in four volumes by Indiana University Press and Routledge and Kegan Paul (1971 and 1972) and later republished in paperback form in the 1990s, this is invaluable as a work of reference, often listing a number of variants of the same story for comparison. It is, however, not one that everyone can afford to buy – the paperback version alone will cost you a couple of weeks' rent – but it's worth trying to locate a convenient library that holds a copy.

Finally, I would like to recommend two volumes that have only recently been published. They are *Beautiful Angiola* and *The Robber with the Witch's Head* (both Routledge, 2004). Both contain Sicilian folktales collected by **Laura Gonzenbach** at the end of the nineteenth century. They have only recently been rediscovered and appear here in English for the first time in modern translations by **Jack Zipes**. Gonzenbach originally collected the stories from Sicilian peasants (predominantly women) and then translated them into German for a bourgeois readership. However, Gonzenbach achieved something very rare in nineteenth-century collections. She exercised a relatively light editorial hand and, as a result, the stories retain all the raw details that would normally have been censored, as well as a flavour of the original oral language and the forceful expressions of the desire for social justice that are embedded within the texts.

Internet Resources

Simply typing 'storytelling' into your internet search engine will yield up to one and a half million results, so prolific is storytelling on the web. As with all internet research, it is wise to proceed with caution and not to attach the same degree of authority to web-based information as you would to writing that has been through some kind of editorial or peer review process, as is the case with books and articles in reputable journals. Having said that, there is a wealth of useful information available to the discerning surfer. The most useful place to start is probably the websites of the various national storytelling organizations. These invariably list information regarding their publications and conferences, as well as some kind of listing of forthcoming storytelling events. They also have a list of links to other storytelling-related websites. They usually operate on an open-access basis, allowing anybody to set up a link on their website, so the quality of the links cannot be guaranteed, but it's a less overwhelming way of looking for material than simply relying on your search engine. The main sites for English-speaking readers are as follows:

www.sfs.org.uk

This is the website of the Society for Storytelling (SfS), which primarily promotes storytelling in England and Wales. It has good listings and links sections and also posts information regarding forthcoming SfS events. The SfS publishes a range of research papers and information pamphlets, as well as the quarterly newsletter, *Storylines*.

www.storynet.org

This is the website of the National Storytelling Network (NSN) in the United States. Its coverage is similar to that of the SfS, but, of course, relating to storytelling in the US. This is the place for information on the huge (by British standards) National Storytelling Conference, held in July every year, and the National Storytelling Festival. The NSN publishes *Storytelling Magazine* on a bi-monthly basis.

www.scottishstorytellingcentre.org.uk/

This is the website of the Scottish Storytelling Centre, based at the Netherbow Arts Centre in Edinburgh. As might be expected, it contains listings of storytelling events in Scotland and other matters of interest, in particular the Scottish Storytelling Festival, which takes place annually in November.

www.australianstorytelling.org.au

This is the website of the Storytelling Guild of Australia. The Guild is organized regionally and the site will guide you to information on storytelling in those specific regions. Perhaps most usefully, the site contains a number of short articles and interviews with storytellers.

http://storytelling.org.nz/

The website of the New Zealand Guild of Storytelling. This is quite a modest site, but worth a visit to get an overview of the storytelling scene in New Zealand. The Guild publishes a journal, *Storylines*, not to be confused with the Society for Storytelling's newsletter of the same name.

www.sc-cc.com

This is the bilingual site of Storytellers of Canada/Conteurs du Canada and lists useful information regarding Canadian storytelling, which is often in danger of being swamped by the more developed scene of its neighbour. Storytellers of Canada produce a quarterly journal, *Appleseed*, and a newsletter, *Le Raconteur*.

www.verbalartscentre.co.uk

The Verbal Arts Centre in Derry, Northern Ireland, has been at the forefront of developing innovative storytelling practice in Britain and Ireland, and examples are documented on their website. The Centre also plays host to the Storytellers of Ireland.

I do not intend to list all other valuable storytelling websites here, but I would like to just add the following, which may be of interest to the student or researcher on the look-out for information on storytelling.

www.pjtss.net/ring/

This is the website of the Storytelling Ring, of which all the main storytelling organizations are members. It lists all storytelling-related websites of its members (in other words, those serious enough about storytelling to pay the subscription) and the surfer is able to organize the sites into those of individual storytellers, festivals, resource-based sites, etc. At the time of writing, it provides links to a comprehensive, but manageable, 177 sites.

www.factsandfiction.co.uk

Facts and Fiction is a storytelling journal independently produced by storyteller Pete Castle. It primarily contains features and interviews pertaining to the British and Irish storytelling movements, but does also have a modest international coverage.

http://courses.unt.edu/efiga/SSS/SSS_journal.htm

This is the website for *Storytelling, Self and Society*, a new academic, peer-reviewed journal. It emanates from the National Storytelling Network's Higher Education Special Interest Group and also hosts an annual academic conference.

(The Society for Storytelling also publishes an occasional series of internationally refereed research papers in the *Papyrus* series – details are available on the SfS website.)

www.pitt.edu/~dash/grimm.html

This is a very useful site. It is primarily dedicated to the work of the Brothers Grimm and includes English translations of *Grimms' Fairy Tales*, but it also contains much contextual information and extensive links to other story sites, most of which are of a good standard.

www.ils.unc.edu/~sturm/storytelling/resources.html

Brian Sturm from the University of North Carolina has compiled this useful list of resources for storytellers. Its main feature is a substantial booklist, although most are American publications and may be slightly harder to get hold of for the British or Irish reader.

www.timsheppard.co.uk/story/

Tim Sheppard is an English storyteller based in Bristol, who has invested a considerable amount of time and resources in building a storytelling resource website. It is certainly extensive and one of its best features is that it covers the storytelling scene on both sides of the Atlantic in equal measure. Not all of the material on the website is of the highest quality, but it does have an excellent booklist and links page, made particularly useful because many of the entries are annotated to give the readers an idea of what awaits them at each site.

Bibliography

Ardagh, Philip (2004) 'Angels, Ghosts and the Green Fairy', *Observer*, 11 July 2004.

Bakhtin, Mikhail (1984) *Rabelais and his World* (Bloomington: Indiana University Press).

Bauman, Richard (1977) *Verbal Art as Performance* (Prospect Heights, IL: Waveland Press).

Bauman, Richard (1986) *Story, Performance and Event: Contextual Studies of Oral Narrative* (Cambridge: Cambridge University Press).

Behan, Tom (2000) *Dario Fo: Revolutionary Theatre* (London: Pluto Press).

Benjamin, Walter (1973) *Illuminations* (London: Fontana/Collins).

Benjamin, Walter (1998) *Understanding Brecht*, translated by Anna Bostock (London and New York: Verso).

Berger, John (1977) 'Why Zoos Disappoint', *New Society*, 21 April 1977, pp. 12–13.

Bharucha, Rustom (1996) 'Disorientations in the Cultural Politics of our Times', in Patrice Pavis (ed.), *The Intercultural Performance Reader* (London: Routledge), pp. 196–212.

Birch, Carol L. (1996) 'Who Says? The Storyteller as Narrator', in Birch and Heckler, pp. 106–28.

Birch, Carol L. (2000) *The Whole Story Handbook* (Little Rock: August House).

Birch, Carol L. and Melissa A. Heckler (1996) *Who Says? Essays on Pivotal Issues in Contemporary Storytelling* (Little Rock: August House).

Brecht, Bertolt (1961) *Tales from the Calendar* (London: Methuen).

Brecht, Bertolt (1965) *The Messingkauf Dialogues*, translated by John Willett (London: Methuen).

Brecht, Bertolt (1966a) *Der Jasager und Der Neinsager: Vorlagen, Fassungen und Materialen* (Frankfurt am Main: Suhrkamp).

Brecht, Bertolt (1966b) *Parables for the Theatre*, translated by Eric Bentley (London: Penguin).

Brecht, Bertolt (1978) *Brecht on Theatre*, translated by John Willett (London: Eyre Methuen).

Brockett, Oscar (1998) *History of the Theatre* (New York: Prentice-Hall).

Brook, Peter (1988) *The Shifting Point: Forty Years of Theatrical Exploration, 1946–1987* (London: Methuen).

Brook, Peter (1998) *Threads of Time: A Memoir* (London: Methuen).

Bruner, Jerome (1990) *Acts of Meaning* (Cambridge, MA: Harvard University Press).

Campbell, Ken (1995) *The Bald Trilogy* (London: Methuen).

Campbell, Ken (1996) *Violin Time* (London: Methuen).

Carrière, Jean-Claude (1988) *The Mahabharata*, translated by Peter Brook (London: Methuen).

Chodzinski, Raymond T. (2004) *Bullying: A Crisis in our Schools and our Communities* (Welland, Ontario: Soleil).

Clarke, Gillian (2002) 'The Pen is Mightier than the Word', *A470*, no. 21

Collison, Charlene (2001) 'The Power of Stories in Organisations', *Storylines*, vol. 4, no. 17, p. 8.

Craig, Sandy (1980) *Dreams and Deconstructions: Alternative Theatre in Britain* (Ambergate: Amber Lane Press).

Crawford, Rhiannon, Brian Brown and Paul Crawford (2004) *Storytelling in Therapy* (Cheltenham: Nelson Thornes).

Crossley-Holland, Kevin (1998) *Different – But Oh How Like!* (London: Daylight Press/Society for Storytelling).

Croyden, Margaret (2003) *Conversations with Peter Brook, 1970–2000* (New York and London: Faber and Faber).

DiCenzo, Maria (1996) *The Politics of Alternative Theatre in Britain: The Case of 7:84 (Scotland)* (Cambridge: Cambridge University Press).

Eddershaw, Margaret (1994) 'Actors on Brecht', in Thomson and Sacks, pp. 254–72.

Evans, Debbie (2002) 'Debbie Evans responds to Gillian Clarke's article', *A470*, no. 22.

Florence, Peter (2002) 'Peter Florence responds to Gillian Clarke's article', *A470*, no. 22.

Fo, Dario (1988) *Mistero Buffo*, translated by Ed Emery (London: Methuen).

Fo, Dario (1991) *The Tricks of the Trade*, translated by Joe Farrell (London: Methuen).

Gersie, Alida (1992) *Earthtales: Storytelling in Times of Change* (London: Green Print).

Gray, Spalding (1988) *Swimming to Cambodia* (New York: Theatre Communications Group).

Haggarty, Ben (1996) *Seek Out the Voice of the Critic* (London: Daylight Press/Society for Storytelling).

Haggarty, Ben (2004) *Memories and Breath – Professional Storytelling in England and Wales: An Unofficial Report Conducted by E-mail Survey*, (www.sfs.org.uk).

Heywood, Simon (1998) *The New Storytelling* (London: Daylight Press/Society for Storytelling).

Heywood, Simon (2000) 'Storytelling Revivalism in England and Wales: History, Performance and Interpretation', unpublished PhD thesis, University of Sheffield.

Hilken, Peter (2002) 'Crick Crack Club Celebrates Twenty Years of the Storytelling Revival', *Storylines*, vol. 4, no. 19, p. 4.

Hirst, David L. (1989) *Dario Fo and Franca Rame* (Basingstoke: Macmillan).

Leith, Dick (1998) *Fairy Tales and Therapy* (London: Daylight Press/Society for Storytelling).

Leith, Dick (2003) *Storytellers' Keywords* (London: Daylight Press/Society for Storytelling).

Lupton, Hugh (2004) 'An Interview with Spiked Magazine' (www.spiked-magazine.co.uk/spiked8/lupton.htm).

Lyons, Robert (1999) 'In Search of Brecht: Notes from Rehearsals of "Leben des Galilei" at the Berliner Ensemble, 1997', *New Theatre Quarterly*, vol. 15, no. 59, pp. 256–79.

McGrath, John (1981a) *A Good Night Out: Popular Theatre: Audience, Class and Form* (London: Eyre Methuen).

McGrath, John (1981b) *The Cheviot, the Stag and the Black, Black Oil* (London: Methuen).

McGrath, John (2002) *Naked Thoughts that Roam About* (London: Nick Hern Books).

MacLennan, Elizabeth (1990) *The Moon Belongs to Everyone: Making Theatre with 7:84* (London: Methuen).

Martin, Rafe (1996) 'Between Teller and Listener: the Reciprocity of Storytelling', in Birch and Heckler, pp. 141–54.

Mitchell, Tony (1984) *Dario Fo: People's Court Jester* (London: Methuen).

Moffitt, Dale (ed.) (2000) *Between Two Silences: Talking with Peter Brook* (London: Methuen).

Morden, Daniel (2002) 'Daniel Morden responds to Gillian Clarke's article', *A470*, no. 22.

Needle, Jan and Peter Thomson (1981) *Brecht* (Oxford: Basil Blackwell).

Neuhauser, Peg C. (1993) *Corporate Legends and Lore: The Power of Storytelling as a Management Tool* (New York: McGraw-Hill Education).

Parkinson, Rob (1995) *The Elephant and the Four Counties: A Report on Storytelling in the South East* (South East Arts).

Rodari, Gianni (1996) *The Grammar of Fantasy: An Introduction to the Art of Inventing Stories*, translated by Jack Zipes (New York: Teachers and Writers Collaborative).

Rosen, Harold (1985) *Stories and Meanings* (Sheffield: National Association for the Teaching of English).

Rosen, Harold (1993) *Troublesome Boy* (London: English and Media Centre).

Ryan, Patrick (1995) *Storytelling in Ireland: A Re-Awakening* (Londonderry: Verbal Arts Centre).

Ryan, Patrick (1997) *Word in Action: A Report* (Londonderry: Verbal Arts Centre).

Ryan, Patrick (2001) *Shakespeare's Storybook* (Bristol: Barefoot Books).

Ryan, Patrick (2002) 'A Beautiful Game: Oral Narrative and Soccer', *Children's Literature in Education*, vol. 33, no. 2, pp. 149–63

Ryan, Patrick (2003) 'The Contemporary Storyteller in Context: A Study of Storytelling in Modern Society', unpublished PhD thesis, University of Glamorgan.

Schechter, Joel (1985) *Durov's Pig: Clowns, Politics and Theatre* (New York: Theatre Communications Group).

Smith, Donald (2001) *Storytelling Scotland: A Nation in Narrative* (Edinburgh: Polygon).

Sobol, Joseph D. (1999) *The Storytellers' Journey: An American Revival* (Urbana and Chicago: University of Illinois Press).

Stone, Kay (1986) 'Oral Narration in Contemporary America', in Bottigheimer, Ruth B. (ed.), *Fairy Tales and Society, Illusion, Allusion and Paradigm* (Philadelphia: University of Pennsylvania Press), pp. 13–31.

Taylor, Paul (2001) 'The Prisoners of Consciousness', *The Independent*, 28 November 2001, p. 11.

Thomson, Peter (2000) 'The Elizabethan Actor: a Matter of Temperament', *Studies in Theatre and Performance*, vol. 20, no. 1, pp. 4–13.

Thomson, Peter and Glendyr Sacks (eds) (1994) *The Cambridge Companion to Brecht* (Cambridge: Cambridge University Press).

Toelken, Barre (1996) 'The Icebergs of the Folktale', in Birch and Heckler, pp. 35–63.

Vallely, Paul (1989) 'The Longest Story Ever Told', *Sunday Correspondent*, 19 November 1989.

Westland, Ella (ed.) (1997) *Cornwall: The Cultural Construction of Place* (Penzance: Patten Press).

Wiles David (2000) *Greek Theatre Performance: An Introduction* (Cambridge: Cambridge University Press).

Williams, David (comp.) (1988) *Peter Brook: A Theatrical Casebook* (London: Methuen).

Williams, Gareth (1991) *George Ewart Evans*, 'Writers in Wales' Series (Cardiff: University of Wales Press).

Wilson, Michael (1997a) *Performance and Practice: Oral Narrative Traditions among Teenagers in Britain and Ireland* (Aldershot: Ashgate).

Wilson, Michael (1997b) 'Telling It As It Is: Storytelling in the China Clay Villages', in Westland, pp. 143–53 (published under the name 'Mike Dunstan').

Wilson, Michael (2002) 'Beyond the Border International Storytelling Festival', *New Welsh Review*, Summer 2002, pp. 97–9.

Wilson, Michael (2003) 'Revisiting Brecht: Preparing *Galileo* for Production', *Studies in Theatre and Performance*, vol. 22, no. 3, pp. 145–57.

Wilson, Michael (2004a) 'The Story was Sufficient: a Profile of Michael Harvey, Storyteller', *Cyfrwng*, no. 1, pp. 91–108 (published in Welsh as 'Roedd y Stori yn Ddigon ynddi'I Hun: Portread o Michael Harvey, Storïwr'; English version available at www.cyfrwng.com).

Wilson, Michael (2004b) 'Storytelling with Older Children: a Reflection on Practice', *Teaching and Learning*, Autumn 2004.

Zipes, Jack (1994) *Fairy Tale as Myth, Myth as Fairy Tale* (Lexington: University of Kentucky Press).

Zipes, Jack (1995) *Creative Storytelling: Building Communities, Changing Lives* (London and New York: Routledge).

Zipes, Jack (1996) *Revisiting 'The Storyteller'* (London: Daylight Press/ Society for Storytelling).

Zipes, Jack (1997) *Happily Ever After: Fairy Tales, Children and the Culture Industry* (London and New York: Routledge).

Zipes, Jack (2001) *Sticks and Stones: The Troublesome Success of Children's Literature from Slovenly Peter to Harry Potter* (London and New York: Routledge).

Zipes, Jack (2004) *Speaking Out: Storytelling and Creative Drama for Children* (London and New York: Routledge).

Index

References in bold refer to the storyteller interviews in this book.

219